ETHNOPOLITICS
IN THE NEW EUROPE

ETHNOPOLITICS
IN THE NEW EUROPE

John T. Ishiyama
Marijke Breuning

LYNNE
RIENNER
PUBLISHERS

BOULDER
LONDON

Published in the United States of America in 1998 by
Lynne Rienner Publishers, Inc.
1800 30th Street, Boulder, Colorado 80301

and in the United Kingdom by
Lynne Rienner Publishers, Inc.
3 Henrietta Street, Covent Garden, London WC2E 8LU

Library of Congress Cataloging-in-Publication Data
Ishiyama, John T., 1960–
    Ethnopolitics in the New Europe : John T. Ishiyama and Marijke
Breuning.
        p.   cm.
    Includes bibliographical references (p.   ) and index.
    ISBN 1-55587-610-2 (hardcover : alk. paper)
        1. Nationalism—Case studies. 2. Ethnic relations—Political
aspects—Case studies. 3. Ethnic groups—Political activity—Case
studies. I. Breuning, Marijke, 1957– . II. Title.
JC311.I76   1998
305.8'0096—dc21   97-48665
                                                                CIP

British Cataloguing in Publication Data
A Cataloguing in Publication record for this book
is available from the British Library.

Printed and bound in the United States of America

∞   The paper used in this publication meets the requirements
    of the American National Standard for Permanence of
    Paper for Printed Library Materials Z39.48-1984.

5 4 3 2 1

Contents

v

Tables

Preface

Political movements that appeal to voters on the basis of ethnic ties have captured the attention of policymakers and scholars alike in recent years. Much has been written about the topic. Quite often, reference is made to age-old conflicts; in many works, there appears to be a sense of helplessness in the face of the ferocity that ethnic conflict has displayed at times. We do not share this sense of helplessness, but hope to show in these pages how political leaders shape the course of ethnic politics within their societies. Of course, ethnic resentments must be present for leaders to successfully appeal to their constituents on the basis of ethnicity; but such resentments exist in far more numerous places than those where ethnic conflict is found. What makes ethnicity politically explosive in some places and not in others? We contend that political leaders and political parties are a crucially important variable in shaping the course of ethnic politics.

Political leaders and parties react to the incentives presented by the political institutions within which they function. If ethnic resentments are present, then the incentives or disincentives presented by these institutions shape whether or not leaders will choose to tap into these resentments for political gain. Political leadership is a crucial variable here: It can whip moderate resentments into strong political demands or allay strong resentments with reasonable and moderate political claims. Political leaders cannot manufacture resentments that are not present and cannot ignore severe inequities that face ethnic groups in a society. However, between these two extremes are endless possibilities for politicians and their parties. As we discuss cases from Western and Eastern Europe in the chapters that follow, it will become evident that in all these instances, irrespective of the degree to which resentments were present, political leaders and their parties shaped the course of ethnic politics in significant ways. The Turkish Movement for Rights and Freedoms in Bulgaria, the Hungarian parties in

Slovakia, the Russophone parties in Estonia and Latvia, the Flemish Volksunie and Vlaams Blok in Belgium, and the Scottish National Party and
Plaid Cymru in Britain have this in common: Their leaders calculated
whether to appeal to the sense of ethnic resentment among their constituents or to downplay it on the basis of the political possibilities presented by the political institutions of their society.

Hence, there is nothing natural or inevitable about ethnic conflict. Even
if these conflicts were "age-old," the sense of helplessness often conveyed
in the literature is premature. There is much to be learned from the choices
made by leaders to encourage or downplay the "ethnic card." In this volume,
we attempt to: (1) outline the shape and intensity of ethnic resentments that
are at the heart of each case; (2) explain how in each case political leaders
and parties choose to play into these resentments; and (3) straddle the traditional division between Western and Eastern Europe. As the Berlin Wall has
fallen, so have artificial disciplinary boundaries. Despite the real and significant differences in their recent histories, many of the states in both Western and Eastern Europe currently cope with political appeals based on ethnicity. A comparison of the political responses in this "new Europe" shows
that similar dynamics are at work in both the West and East.

This book is the product of close cooperation between both authors. The
design of the study, explained in Chapter 1, and the Conclusion were written
jointly. The chapters on the Turkish Movement for Rights and Freedoms in
Bulgaria, the Hungarian parties in Slovakia, and the Russophone parties in
Estonia and Latvia were first drafted by John Ishiyama; the chapters on the
Volksunie and Vlaams Blok in Belgium and the Scottish National Party and
Plaid Cymru in Britain were first drafted by Marijke Breuning. However, all
chapters were developed jointly so as to maintain consistency in the treatment of each case. The final product, then, is a work that is coauthored in the
true sense of the word.

This book would not have been possible without the consistent support and encouragement of our publisher, Lynne Rienner, and her staff.
Truman State University provided financial support to us at a crucial time
in the project, for which we are grateful. In the course of an endeavor such
as this, inevitably family and loved ones suffer the absence or absent-
mindedness of the authors absorbed in their subject. Rose and Toaru
Ishiyama and Eva and Max Breuning lived with each of us hunched over
laptops during those scarce visits. David Ishiyama had to forego some
summer fishing trips and other outings so that dad could finish his book.
Many others suffered our preoccupations with this endeavor and we thank
them all for their patience.

John T. Ishiyama
Marijke Breuning

1

Ethnopolitics and Ethnic Parties

Recent developments in Europe have sparked both a renewed interest in ethnic political conflict and a reassessment of the literature on political integration. Once-successful examples of politically integrated states such as Yugoslavia, Czechoslovakia, and the Union of Soviet Socialist Republics (USSR) have disintegrated. Plans for greater regional integration in Western Europe and the possible emergence of a United States of Europe remain on hold in the tangled aftermath of the Maastricht Treaty. Integration appears to be on the retreat; and disintegration, motivated by nationalist sentiment, seems the rule, rather than the exception, in the post–Cold War era.

While the earlier literature tended to be overly optimistic about the prospects for political integration,[1] the recent literature tends toward the pessimistic.[2] Some have concluded that ethnically plural societies are almost naturally and necessarily "defined by dissensus and pregnant with conflict."[3] In particular, the tragedy of Yugoslavia has compelled many to mark the Yugoslav example as a "cautionary tale for all post-communist countries."[4] As a result, the post–Cold War era has given rise to a new dogma, which holds that the "new world order" has unleashed primordial conflicts, thus making political integration and democracy nigh on impossible. From this perspective, "violence is assumed to follow ethnic tensions as night follows day."[5] Thus, the old system of states is labeled "unnatural," and the only real solution to this dilemma is to recognize these "natural" differences, divide up the real estate, and provide different peoples with their own homelands.[6] In a sense, this conjures up the "romantic notions of *Urvölker* whose unchanging nature asserts itself from time to time."[7]

Although there are truly formidable roadblocks to integration in states that are ethnically divided, it is misleading to assume that such states are predestined for disintegration and, worse yet, the miseries of civil war. To be sure, aspects of the environment make the emergence of powerful dis-integrative forces more likely. Economic, social, political, and historical factors can lead to the rise of extreme national sentiment and intense feel-ings of anger over current political arrangements.[8] However, this sense of anger does not inevitably translate into violent political action.[9] To assume that environmental conditions are sufficient to explain ethnic conflict de-tracts from the important role played by political leaders and the organi-zations they lead in aggravating, deepening, or dampening ethnic political conflict. Whether or not such feelings are translated directly into activi-ties that lead to disintegration depends upon the development of the orga-nizational expression of the national sentiment—the ethnopolitical party.[10]

The role played by ethnopolitical parties in fostering or retarding eth-nic political conflict has been noted by Donald Horowitz, Cynthia Enloe, Paul Brass, and Anthony Smith.[11] Although political parties may reflect the environment from which they arose, they also nurture and affect that environment.

> By appealing to electorates in ethnic terms, by making ethnic demands on government, and by bolstering the influence of ethnically chauvinistic el-ements within each group, parties that begin by merely mirroring ethnic divisions help to deepen and extend them. Hence the oft heard remark in such states that politicians have created ethnic conflict.[12]

Moreover, the appearance of an ethnically based party can set off a chain reaction in the party system such that the appearance of organized ethnic parties forces others to adopt similar political strategies.[13] In the end, this dynamic often produces a system of political parties that is not only conflict ridden, but antithetical to the basic characteristics of political democracy.[14]

Although the argument that the activities of political parties form an important set of intervening variables in explaining the incidence of con-flict in divided societies is not new, this book builds on the previous liter-ature in three ways. First, rather than focus on ethnic conflict and nation-alism in general, attention is concentrated on the level of the individual party as the unit of analysis. Certainly, as noted above, the actions of in-dividual parties can set off a chain reaction leading to an ethnic explosion; however, there are just as many instances where an ethnically based polit-ical movement does not lobby for an ethnically pure homeland or politi-cal separation, but seeks to behave according to constitutional norms and to accommodate the existing political structure. Thus, if conflict is explic-able in terms of the behavior of ethnic parties, then more explicit attention to the factors that explain individual ethnic party behavior is warranted.

Second, unlike most previous works on ethnic conflict that employ case studies to inductively build theoretical propositions, this book pro-poses to systematically subject existing theoretical propositions to the litmus test of empiricism in order to assess which of these provide a sufficiently general explanation to account for the behavior of ethnopolitical parties throughout the "new Europe."

Third, although most of the current and past literature on nationalism and ethnic politics in Europe focuses on differentiating between Eastern and Western or inclusive versus exclusive models of nationalism,[15] it is contended here that there are more shared commonalities among ethnopolitical parties in both Eastern and Western Europe than originally thought; thus, existing theoretical explanations can usefully be employed to shed light on the behavior of ethnopolitical parties in both Eastern and Western Europe.

To this end, the following sections of this chapter address conceptual issues, identify the behavioral patterns that can exist for ethnopolitical parties, and consider both the environmental (i.e., external) and internal factors that are often cited as affecting ethnopolitical party behavior. These comprise the basis for several theoretical expectations concerning ethnopolitical party behavior. Finally, the design of this book, justification for the selection of empirical cases, and an outline of the structure of each chapter are presented.

NATIONALISM, ETHNOPOLITICS, AND ETHNOPOLITICAL PARTIES

A commonly used concept in the study of politics in ethnically divided states is "nationalism." As a concept, nationalism is both complex and ambiguous, but at the heart of it is the notion of "the self-assertion of ethnic groups."[16] While such self-assertion might involve the strengthening of a group's identity, it can also be aggressive in relation to other groups. As Rasma Karklins notes, nationalism as a political doctrine has been linked not only to the emergence of modern democracy and anti-imperial struggles, but also to xenophobic dictatorship.[17] Nationalism has been at the root of the democratic value of national self-determination, but it has also been employed to justify the exclusion of cultural minorities and the destruction of the democratic state.[18]

The ambiguity of nationalism as a concept has caused some scholars in recent years to question its theoretical utility. Many, such as Joseph Rothschild and Karklins, have preferred to use the term "ethnopolitics" to broadly describe politics among ethnic entities.[19] Whereas nationalism is a "state of mind in which supreme loyalty of the individual is felt to be due the nation-state,"[20] and as such represents a "political doctrine to make culture and polity congruent,"[21] the more inclusive ethnopolitics encompasses aspirations short of the creation of a nation-state and the congruence of culture with polity. Further, the concept of ethnopolitics has the advantage of including politics that are not conflictual; although ethnopolitics can be conflictual, it can also be cooperative.

The organizational expression of ethnopolitics is the ethnopolitical party. Although in much of the literature on political parties, the party has been conceived as both an integrative and an electoral organization that represents the "buckle which binds one social force to another," leading to the creation of a national identity that transcends "more parochial groupings,"[22] other conceptions view the political party as a group of individuals who organize to achieve some specific purpose—winning competitive elections—as indicated by Leon Epstein's definition of "political party" as "any group of individuals, however loosely organized, whose avowed purpose is winning elections."[23] Similarly, Anthony Downs defines the political party as "a team seeking to control the governing apparatus by gaining office in a duly constituted election."[24] And Kenneth Janda defines the political party as "a set of organizations that pursue a goal of placing their avowed representatives in government positions."[25]

However, ethnopolitical parties do not fall easily into either of these two definitions. On the one hand, ethnopolitical parties do not begin as integrative organizations. They primarily represent the interest of an ethnic group, rather than primarily seek to broaden their appeal to other groups. On the other hand, ethnopolitical parties often do not begin as electoral organizations, but as pressure groups whose original purpose is the pursuit of goals such as cultural preservation or linguistic autonomy. Nonetheless, although ethnopolitical parties may begin as organizations that do not originally seek to place their avowed representatives in power, they inevitably attempt to do so over time. This is due to the shifting goal orientation of the ethnopolitical party, a shift that occurs because, although campaigning for election may not have been the original purpose of the organization, the temptation to pursue political power grows as it becomes more apparent that the most effective means to influence the power relations among ethnic groups is to hold office. This requires that the ethnopolitical party appeal beyond the limited confines of the group in order to obtain political power. However, the extent to which the party must expand its appeal beyond the group it purports to represent depends on other factors: the institutional rules of the game, the strength of the existing party system, and the structure of ethnic competition (the number of groups, the extent of ethnic fragmentation, etc.). For our purposes, then, an ethnopolitical party is defined as an organization that purports to represent a particular ethnic group and seeks political power to impinge on the "relative power or position of ethnic groups."[26] Ethnopolitical parties, from this perspective, are not naturally nationalist parties (which purport to make congruent culture and polity). However, they can become nationalist, particularly if means short of political separation prove ineffective.

DIMENSIONS IN CATEGORIZING TYPES OF
ETHNOPOLITICAL PARTY BEHAVIOR

What are the actions that an ethnopolitical party can adopt? There have been several attempts in the recent literature to conceptualize ethnopolitical party behavior and to classify different kinds of ethnopolitical parties.[27] One of the more interesting is that offered by Joseph Rudolph and Robert Thompson,[28] who have identified four types of "ethnoterritorial movements" in terms of the goals they pursue: (1) output-oriented parties, which are less concerned with achieving self-rule than with expanding their region's share of government outputs; (2) antiauthority parties, which are primarily concerned with affecting who makes decisions—that is, with the nature of existing political authority; (3) antiregime parties, which focus on changing the constitutional principles and political structures regulating the manner in which decisions are made (parties of this type often press for a federal-like system in which their region has autonomous control over those economic and cultural decisions affecting it); and (4) anticommunity parties, which challenge the fundamental legitimacy of the multinational political community in which they find themselves and champion independence.

In a more recent article, Raphael Zariski offers a different set of criteria by which to classify ethnopolitical party behavior. Rather than categorize parties by their attitudes concerning the political system, Zariski focuses on three behavioral characteristics: the willingness to use violence, ethnic exclusiveness, and separatism.[29] Ethnic exclusiveness refers to the "outright rejection of other ethnic groups, not only as models to be emulated . . . but even as allies to be courted for votes and political support or as recruits to be assimilated." Taken to its extreme, ethnic exclusiveness involves "racist contempt for lesser breeds."[30] Separatism is defined as a "movement that has a clearly articulated ultimate goal of independence and sovereignty."[31] Ethnic extremist parties, then, are those that rank high along these three dimensions. Presumably (although Zariski is not entirely clear on this point), nonextremist parties do not exhibit these characteristics.

A third approach has been offered by Janusz Bugajski,[32] who focuses on Eastern Europe. For Bugajski, the kinds of demands made are a function of the degree to which an ethnic group is territorially compact and whether an ethnic kin state exists upon which the ethnopolitical movement can draw external support. He identifies five major variants of ethnic politics: cultural revivalism, political autonomism, territorial self-determination, separatism, and irredentism. Cultural revivalism involves a focus on social, cultural, religious, and educational institutions and usually involves increasing participation by the ethnic group in regional or national politics, rather than a challenge to the existing state. Cultural revivalism is common among groups, such as the Romany (Gypsy) population in the Czech

Republic, that are spread throughout the country and have no kin state to provide external support. Political autonomism involves demands for control over political resources, particularly those dealing with minority culture and education. These demands often emerge when minorities have constituted majorities in previously existing states, when they possess a history of organized political involvement in a multiethnic country, and/or when their ethnic compatriots currently constitute a majority nationality in a neighboring kin state.

The difference between political autonomism and Bugajski's next two types of ethnopolitical behavior is a matter of degree. Territorial self-determinism is similar to political autonomism in every respect save for the focus on a formal territory that is identified with the ethnic group. Calls for territorial self-determination usually involve demands for restructuring the state into a federal or confederal structure in which specific regions are recognized as having "republican status." The emergence of the demand for territorial self-determination is most likely when the group is territorially compact. Separatism is a more extreme variety of territorial self-determination and usually involves a situation wherein the ethnic group is territorially compact and refuses to be included in the existing state, be it federal, confederal, or otherwise. Finally, irredentism, or the combination of separatism of the minority group joined with the imperial ambitions of a neighboring kin state, is most likely when the ethnic minority population is territorially compact and when ethnic compatriots currently constitute a majority nationality in a neighboring state.

What all of these schema have in common in categorizing different types of ethnic parties is the ultimate goal or end regarding the configuration of the political system and their community's role in that system. Thus, Zariski, Rudolph and Thompson, and Bugajski have distinguished between ethnic parties that seek a fundamental reorientation of the features of the existing system (separatism for Zariski and Bugajski, and anticommunity parties for Rudolph and Thompson). This distinction yields the primary component of ethnopolitical party behavior, which is here conceptualized as the activities of the ethnopolitical party regarding the arrangement of the state. Such activities can range from demands for more equitable treatment without altering the basic features of the state to outright demands for a separate state altogether. For the purposes of comparison, each party in this study will be coded using Rudolph and Thompson's criteria: zero (0) for output-oriented parties; one (1) for antiauthority parties; two (2) for antiregime parties; and three (3) for anticommunity parties. The demands made by ethnopolitical parties are considered more "extreme" if they tend toward desires for a fundamental restructuring of the state in the direction of separatism.

Yet beyond simple concomitant comparison across parties, we are also interested in comparisons over time. Many scholars have noted that ethnic parties evolve and that the operational objectives of these parties are consequently subject to change. A party may adopt an approach that initially intends accommodation but can later evolve into extremism. Conversely, a party that initially emerged as an extremist organization may be coaxed, however reluctantly, into pursuing less extreme strategies. What are the commonly cited factors that affect the evolution of ethnic parties?

Several factors have been cited in the literature that seeks to answer this question. These can generally be divided into three types of explanations: (1) those that focus on the effects of regime change; (2) those that emphasize the features of existing systems; and (3) those that concentrate on the internal characteristics of the parties.

REGIME CHANGE AND
ETHNOPOLITICAL PARTY BEHAVIOR

An important factor in activating ethnopolitical extremism is the effect of regime change, particularly a transition away from authoritarian rule (as in post-Franco Spain).[33] In ethnically divided societies, the introduction of democratic competition and expanded political participation has often led to disintegrative ethnic conflict.[34] This is especially true when an *abertura* (political opening) appears following a period of extensive repression of a community's aspirations, for pent-up frustrations often quickly flower into extremist ethnic politics. Thus, democratization in Eastern Europe has led to the greater appeal for all-encompassing nationalist slogans, especially in a world "accustomed to a monopoly of ideas and a permanent struggle with the enemy," making it far more difficult to "substitute the process of slow integration for the logic of destruction and war."[35]

Nevertheless, even when the opportunities presented by such regime change push the ethnopolitical party into making extreme demands, these demands may be tempered over time, especially if democratic transition is successful and there is a period of democratic consolidation. Indeed, as Colin Williams has observed, there is a strong incentive to moderate demands in the face of democratic competition, and this moderation is based on the ethnic parties' desire to expand their base of political support in order to gain access to political power. Although the "logical implication" of any desire for autonomy may be political independence, autonomists have generally "confined their demands to areas they perceive as being acceptable to the governing body." The latter, in turn, has usually been willing to negotiate, since it, too, appreciates that the cost of pushing a demand for autonomy to its logical conclusion would be extremely high. "But to reach the point where central leaders are willing to negotiate, ethnoterritorialisms must appear to speak for a large regional audience, which usually requires that the movements moderate their separatist nature."[36]

This would suggest the expectation that the pressure to make extreme political demands (meaning separatism or political autonomy) is higher in preexisting parties within societies undergoing democratic transition than in parties that emerged after the consolidation of political democracy.

ENVIRONMENTAL FACTORS AFFECTING PARTY BEHAVIOR

Economic Factors

Economic factors are most commonly cited as being associated with increased ethnic tensions. Studies of nationalism, for instance, have linked nationalism with economic development and modernization. Karl Deutsch contends that nationalism plays an important role in social communication, or the transmission of the culture of a people across territory and through history; this is particularly important in societies undergoing modernization that uproots traditional systems of social solidarity, requiring new concepts of community.[37] Ernst Gellner argues that nationalism is a modern phenomenon, resulting from the "distinctive structural requirements of industrial society."[38] Benedict Anderson, as well, contends that the rise of nationalism in the modern era is linked to the spread of a vernacular print culture that is linked to modernization and industrialization.[39]

Although modernization may generally be linked to nationalism, specific aspects of the modernization process affect whether political movements that aspire to represent a particular community adopt more or less extreme demands. Among these aspects is the differential economic performance among groups that may increase resentments in a segmented society. Moreover, not only can differential growth rates create the basis for resentments upon which ethnic parties can capitalize, but the timing of economic growth also impacts such resentments.[40] Further, "de-development," or periods of economic downturn, are especially related to the growth of resentments. Resource allocation issues are particularly divisive, especially as resources become increasingly scarce and there emerges a greater demand for the "equity" of such allocations.[41] Conflict, therefore, becomes more likely when the resource pie shrinks.[42]

Sociocultural Factors

A great many scholars have also noted that certain sociostructural features of a country exacerbate the degree of resentment produced by political and economic factors.[43] In particular, the existence of fewer groups tends to heighten resentments generated by developmental inequalities and the creation or lack of political opportunities. For instance, as R. S. Milne notes, the fewer and more equally sized the groups, the more likely that they will constitute opposite and impermeable poles. Resentments under such conditions are often quite strong, and the quality of politics is usually highly conflictual and conducive to extremist politics because there are no balancing or arbitrating groups to mitigate conflict.[44]

A second sociocultural factor that impacts the quality of resentments is what Horowitz has referred to as the "structure of group relations." On the one hand, there are "ranked systems" where social class and ethnic origins coincide. Under such conditions, ethnic groups are ordered in a hierarchy, with one superordinate and one subordinate. On the other hand, there are "unranked systems" where parallel "ethnic groups coexist, each internally stratified."[45] The latter is most common in bipolar societies where each ethnic group is territorially compact. The existence of ranked and unranked systems in turn affects the quality of resentments and the course of ethnic conflict. Often, resentments in ranked systems, when they emerge, are couched in terms of class conflict and demands for redistribution of resources, because the issues of ethnicity and class are intertwined. However, when unranked systems predominate, and unranked groups "constitute incipient whole societies," resentments usually revolve around issues of autonomy, not social transformation.[46]

International Factors

Extremist politics also results from changes in the international environment. Whether the political leadership of ethnic parties sees utility in pursuing accommodationist or separatist ends depends, to a large extent, on its perception of its community's role in the region within which the state is located. Two aspects of that regional environment within which a multiethnic state is located shape the structure of opportunities presented by that environment. One is the presence of cross-border ties among groups—for example, when a linguistic group transcends the confines of political boundaries. Second, the tendencies within the region toward political integration or its inverse, disintegration, will affect the opportunities facing political leaders.

Two different types of cross-border ties are particularly relevant in this regard. The first we refer to as an environment of "external threat," which is represented by the following hypothetical situation: Consider groups x and y in country A and adjacent country B; group y is culturally and linguistically related to the dominant portion of country B's population. In such an international environment, tensions between the two groups are often very high, first because one group (x) considers itself the titular and "rightful" owner of the country and often perceives the other group as interlopers and, worse yet, a "fifth column." Members of group y, on the other hand, may feel that they are the heir to a great civilization and that the presence of powerful potential support across the border may embolden their demands.[47]

Second, in addition to cross-border ethnic ties, tendencies within the region toward political integration or disintegration will affect both the perceptions and the actions of the leaders of ethnic segments within states. Indeed, greater regional integration might well promote the emergence of what Ernst Haas has referred to as extreme "micro-nationalisms."[48] The logic behind this expectation is that regional integration permits previously isolated ethnic groups to become more visible and, in certain cases, interact across national boundaries.[49]

The reverse situation creates a different set of incentives. Given the above logic, it may be the case that in a disintegrating regional environment, leaders of the various ethnic groups face greater incentives to arrive at political accommodation within the existing state. There is no other set of institutions, and the alternative to political accommodation is chaos and war. In other words, the greater uncertainties presented by a disintegrating environment are likely to make accommodation a more attractive proposition than it would be under other circumstances.

This does not necessarily mean, however, that a disintegrating international environment inexorably leads to domestic political accommodation. It may well be that some leaders perceive violence to give them their best chance to gain the settlement they desire; that is, they may expect that in a disintegrating environment, their chances to achieve their goals through violence are better than under other circumstances. To a large extent, this depends on whether leaders view such circumstances as opportunities or as risks. This in turn depends on the biases and prejudices leaders hold.

Political Factors

There has been a long-standing contention that political factors, and especially political structures, affect the opportunities ethnopolitical parties face. In the literature, there has been considerable debate over the effects of institutional factors on politics in ethnically divided societies, particularly the effects of representational mechanisms (such as the electoral law and federalism) and the structure of the constitutional order (or presidential versus parliamentary systems).[50]

Historically, there has been considerable debate over which representational mechanisms are most apt to promote political stability in ethnically divided new democracies. Two dimensions are involved in the debate over representational mechanisms. The first dimension deals with the *scope* of representation, or the extent to which representation is commensurate with political divisions in society. The second deals with the *quality* of representation, or the primary units to be represented.[51]

There has also been much debate in the literature on whether expanded representation is beneficial or detrimental in promoting ethnic peace in divided states. On the one hand, the "consociational" school contends that representing groups proportionally facilitates the integration of as many subcultures as possible into the political game, thus creating the conditions for interethnic cooperation.[52] Consociationalists therefore tend to favor political structures like proportional representation (PR) electoral systems and federalism, because they prevent the consistent denial of representation to important minorities.[53] Further, by securing representation for minority groups, PR serves to facilitate the integration of disaffected groups into the political system, which ultimately leads them to moderate their demands. On the other hand, "majoritarian" models of politics are inappropriate in ethnically divided societies because they "systematically exclude blocs," which is "likely to result in violence and democratic collapse."[54] Thus, by promoting "segmental political parties" and their representation "instead of creating conflict . . . . [they] now play a constructive role in conflict resolution."[55] Moreover, in the long run, there is the possibility that such inclusive mechanisms might also serve to activate the cleavages within ethnic blocs and hence weaken ethnic-based politics as a whole.[56]

However, critics have pointed out that the introduction of PR might lead to the representation of extremist or antisystem ethnic parties, intent on the destruction of an incipient political democracy, and there is no reason to believe that such parties will necessarily moderate their demands once they have attained access.[57] In addition, critics of federalism contend that when state borders coincide with those of the ethnic group, ethnic parties are availed representation that they often use as "springboards" for a bid at national power or, failing that, separation.[58]

Some suggest that the solution to ethnic political conflict does not lie with the scope of representation, but with its quality. For instance, Brass criticizes the consociational remedy as leading to the "freezing" of ethnic conflicts by promoting measures that reify ethnic groups.[59] He suggests a different means to deal with ethnic conflict: Give free play to individual competition that will ensure that the system does not discriminate on a group basis. Promoting individual competition and an individually based system of representation would diffuse ethnic conflict by undermining "the segmental cleavages of plural societies and permit inter-segmental alliances on other bases than inter-elite agreement."[60] The promotion of intraethnic divisions and crosscutting cleavages leaves open the possibility for integrating divided societies on a new basis other than ethnicity and promoting "individual rights and the future prospect of individual autonomy."[61]

Another point of contention concerns the impact of presidentialism versus parliamentary systems. Matthew Shugart and John Carey note that presidentialism tends to provide an incentive for politicians to broaden their appeal in the pursuit of office.[62] Thus, as Horowitz notes, the adoption of presidentialism coupled with election procedures designed to broaden support in, for example, Nigeria and Sri Lanka provide a moderating effect on ethnic politics.[63] Yet critics of presidential systems have linked more cases of political violence to these systems than to parliamentary systems. Juan Linz, for one, argues that in a presidential system, the political stakes of winning the presidency dwarf all other concerns, thus making it more likely that losers will not accept the outcome of an election.[64] Scott Mainwaring has also noted that political instability is likely to result from presidential systems because there is a greater likelihood for political deadlock when the different branches are dominated by polar opposites, which is often the case in ethnically divided societies.[65]

An additional political dimension that affects the appearance and behavior of ethnic parties is the structure of competition, or the features of the party system that affect the opportunities presented to ethnic parties and, hence, provide incentives to behave in certain ways. For Gordon Smith and Peter Mair, a key variable in explaining the behavior of "small parties" such as ethnic parties is the size of the dominant parties in the party system. From this perspective, for party systems that are dominated by large parties, there is no need for coalition building.[66] Thus, through exclusion, there is a strong incentive for ethnic parties to adopt increasingly extremist positions, especially if there are no mechanisms present to guarantee representation. On the other hand, positive political theorists working on spatial models of electoral competition have noted that the presence of a large number of small parties may also promote extremist political behavior. In a multiparty system, the presence of several parties may exert a "squeezing out" effect on political parties, compelling individual parties to "jump out" from the "pack."[67] This squeezing effect largely depends on the electoral law and the structures of the political system. When there are incentives present to broaden the party's appeal (such as under a plurality electoral rule), there is often a "crowding" effect that squeezes out smaller or weaker competitors, compelling them to adopt extremist positions in order to differentiate themselves from other competitors.[68]

Beyond the sheer number and size of the parties in a party system confronting the ethnic party, there is also the effect of the ideological features of the party system. In particular, the key variable is the strength of the parties that are in opposition to the ethnopolitical party. In other words, when nationalist parties that represent the politically dominant group are powerful, then the ethnopolitical party representing a political minority is more likely to adopt extremist political demands.

INTERNAL FACTORS AFFECTING PARTY BEHAVIOR

The discussion so far has focused primarily on the forces that shape the structure of opportunities facing political parties. Yet there are several scholars who contend that the internal characteristics of the party are the primary determinants in explaining party behavior. In particular, who leads the party is as important as the situation in which the party finds itself.

Some argue that who leads is a function of the stage of development a party has reached. For instance, Miroslav Hroch proposes that nationalist groups in the course of their development pass through distinct stages, defined in terms of the different social groups from which they draw their support. In the first, or the cultural, phase, some members of the middle and upper classes develop an interest in national history, language, and culture, and support organizations that endorse cultural demands. No clear political aims are articulated. The second phase involves the politicization of the movement. However, this is usually expressed in the form of pressure groups or civic action groups, rather than through a single party organization. The third stage sees the establishment of nationalist organizations as a mass movement, with the extreme nationalists satisfied with nothing less than total political independence.[69]

Although useful, Hroch's examination focuses primarily on historical cases. Indeed, in the modern era, the phases of development are less clearly separated. The instruments of mass communication have collapsed the first two stages such that cultural demands are now addressed to a mass audience and often take on immediate political significance. Further, Hroch's analysis is limited to explaining the evolution of ethnic parties prior to entering into electoral competition. As M. N. Pederson has noted, this is an important factor in that the behavior of the party is greatly affected by entrance into electoral competition.[70] For Pederson, the party's behavior is affected by four thresholds that differentiate the stages of party development: (1) the threshold of declaration, or the point at which a group of people declares it will participate in an election; (2) the threshold of authorization, or the legal regulations that have to be fulfilled by the party in order to participate in the election; (3) the threshold of representation, or when the party has gained enough support to gain representation in Parliament; and (4) the threshold of relevance, or when the party has entered as members in a coalition government. However, unlike Hroch, Pederson does not argue that the organization necessarily follows a linear process of development from one stage to the next. Rather, it is possible for a party to move back and forth along this dimension.

Yet, as James Kellas notes, the fact that behavior of the party may be different at different stages of its development is due less to some natural process of evolution and more to the fact that, at different times and under different conditions, different kinds of elites dominate the nationalist movement. For Kellas, there are three types of elites that comprise any nationalist movement: a political elite "comprising politicians, civil servants and military"; the cultural elite, "especially teachers, writers and clergy"; and the economic elite "comprising businessmen and trade union leaders. Each reacts differently towards nationalism and towards the central state."[71] The cultural elite is most likely to be inclined toward the extreme because, being so involved in education and the creative arts (especially writing and broadcasting), they have a "vested interest" in promoting an idealized national identity upon which their careers depend. Teaching, writing, and broadcasting a national language bring such people economic gains and a reason to favor more extreme (nationalist) political demands.[72] The economic elite is least likely to be nationalist since it is usually the case that it has links with wider markets and does not wish to have those market ties severed. The role of the political elite is crucial in the balance of power in the nationalist organization.[73] However, since those in the political elite are likely to be primarily motivated by the pursuit of political power, they often "blow" in the direction of the prevailing political winds.

Clearly, some characteristics of the political environment are apt to make more likely the emergence of certain types of leaders over others. As Angelo Panebianco contends, the perspective of leaders is affected by the environment in which they are situated. Although political parties often evolve from "systems of solidarity" (in which individuals who affiliate with the party are motivated by some sense of common ideals) to "systems of interests" (in which individuals develop a growing need for self-preservation, even at the expense of compromising ideals), evolutionary trajectories can be altered by environmental factors.[74] Generally speaking, the initial period of a party's evolution is characterized by an emphasis on dominating the party's environment (i.e., viewing other parties as enemies to be conquered) and the later periods by an emphasis on coming to terms with that environment (in order to promote political survival). However, certain environmental conditions will push the party toward the maintenance of ideals and the continued pursuit of strategies of domination. Other conditions will push the party toward adapting to its environment. Thus it follows that ethnic parties are likely to be more extreme when environmental conditions promote those who view politics as a "zero-sum" game versus those who view politics in shades of gray.

To rely solely on the characteristics of leaders to explain the behavior of the party, however, is to ignore other internal constraints on what leaders can do, particularly those imposed by the collective units they lead.

Indeed, it is one thing to have the existence of mass resentments; it is entirely another to mobilize and focus these into collective action.[75] Leaders do not lead completely homogeneous political organizations, nor are organizations merely a reflection of the aspirations of leaders. Rather, they are collective entities that often consist of individuals with widely variant views, opinions, and aspirations.[76] At times, especially when the organization is a heterogeneous entity, this constrains leaders since they must exert much energy on building internal consensus to maintain unity in the face of external challenges. Ceteris paribus, this often promotes a degree of moderation on the party of leadership, since they are required by the heterogeneity of the organization to act as consensus builders. In turn, this emphasis on consensus can spill over into the ways in which the party deals with others. In contrast, homogeneous organizations tend to lessen such constraints since leaders are less likely to expend political energy on building consensus within their organizations, which makes them less likely to seek consensus outside of the party.[77]

THEORETICAL EXPECTATIONS AND THE DESIGN OF THIS BOOK

The factors outlined above lead to six general expectations, which are the basic themes guiding our inquiry into the individual national cases.

Expectation 1. Because of pent-up frustrations harbored under a previous authoritarian regime, ethnopolitical parties in countries in transition are likely to make more extremist political demands regarding the arrangement of the state than are parties in consolidated democracies.

Expectation 2. (a) The greater the gap in economic performance among ethnic groups, the more likely it is that the ethnopolitical party representing the political minority group will make extremist demands; and (b) the greater the degree of economic downturn, the more likely it is that the ethnopolitical party will engage in extremist demands.

Expectation 3. The more regionally integrated the state, the less likely it is that the ethnopolitical party will make extremist demands.

Expectation 4. (a) The broader the scope of political representation, the less likely it is that the ethnopolitical party will make extremist demands; and (b) the more the quality of representation is based on individual competition and not on group competition, the less likely it is that the ethnopolitical party will make extremist demands.

Expectation 5. The more the current government is dominated by nationalists of another group, the more likely it is that the ethnopolitical party representing the political minority will make extremist demands.

Expectation 6. The more diverse the composition of the ethnopolitical party, the less likely it is that it will make extremist demands.

To assess these expectations, we studied Bulgaria, Slovakia, Estonia, Latvia, Belgium, and the United Kingdom (particularly developments in Scotland and Wales). All of these cases represent divided states where there are at least two large, geographically concentrated ethnic groups in competition with each other. Further, all of the national cases represent parliamentary systems (thus controlling for the effects of presidentialism), and all have ethnic kin states across their borders.

Although comparing West and East European cases runs the risk of comparing proverbial apples and oranges, we attempt to minimize this potential problem by dividing the comparative analysis into three sets of paired comparisons that generally represent the various types of ethnically bipolar countries in Europe. In the first set (Chapters 2 and 3), we compare the East European cases of Bulgaria and Slovakia. In both countries, the principal ethnic minority groups (Turks in Bulgaria and Hungarians in Slovakia) represent long-standing communities that suffered repression under Communist rule and that currently constitute territorially concentrated populations amounting to about 10 percent of the total population. In the second set (Chapter 4), we compare two Baltic states, Estonia and Latvia, both of which were part of the former Soviet Union. The Russophone populations of each are of only recent origin, but they comprise more than one-third of the population of each state. Finally, in Chapters 5 and 6, we compare the West European cases of Belgium and the United Kingdom. Both represent ethnopolitics in consolidated democracies, with long-standing ethnic communities that have developed relatively strong ethnopolitical parties.

In each chapter, we focus on the behavior of the ethnopolitical parties that represent the political minority population: the Movement for Rights and Freedoms in Bulgaria, the Hungarian parties in Slovakia, the Russophone parties of Estonia and Latvia, the Volksunie and the Vlaams Blok in Belgium (representing the Flemish population), and the Scottish National Party and Plaid Cymru in the United Kingdom. Specifically, we provide historical and socioeconomic backgrounds to the development of the ethnopolitical parties and discuss international dimensions, institutional features of the systems, the structure of competition, and the evolution of the ethnopolitical parties in recent years. At the end of each chapter, we assess our six expectations as they pertain to the individual national cases.

In the concluding chapter, we assess each expectation comparatively, highlighting those factors that appear to have the greatest general explanatory power in accounting for the development and behavior of the ethnopolitical parties.

NOTES

1. Haas, *Beyond the Nation-State*; Haas, *The Uniting of Europe*; Lindberg, *The Political Dynamics*. For a critique of this literature, see Jalali and Lipset, "Racial and Ethnic Conflicts," 585–587.

2. Druckman, "Nationalism, Patriotism, and Group Loyalty," 44–45; Jackson and James, "The Character of Independent Statehood"; A. Smith, *The Ethnic Revival*. Fred Parkinson's assertion that "constructing nations out of separate ethnic groups is not only a difficult but also an unnatural process" states this pessimistic view most explicitly ("Ethnicity and Independent Statehood," 339).

3. M. G. Smith, *The Plural Society*, xiii.

4. Michnik, "Dignity and Fear," 15.

5. Fearon and Laitin, "Explaining Interethnic Cooperation," 716.

6. See Rabie, *Conflict Resolution and Ethnicity*, 177–194.

7. Haas, "What Is Nationalism?" 725. See also Rustow, *A World of Nations*, and Deutsch, *Nationalism and Social Communication*.

8. Gellner, *Nations and Nationalism*, 11. See also Zariski, "Ethnic Extremism," 253–273.

9. Fearon and Laitin, "Explaining Interethnic Cooperation," 716.

10. Brass, *Ethnicity and Nationalism*.

11. This point is made by Giovanni Sartori when he notes that political parties both "pre-suppose" and "produce" political cleavages in society ("Political Development and Political Engineering," 261–298).

12. Horowitz, *Ethnic Groups in Conflict*, 291.

13. Sartori, "Political Development and Political Engineering," 293–298.

14. Horowitz, *Ethnic Groups in Conflict*, 298.

15. Kohn, *The Idea of Nationalism*, 576; Snyder, *The New Nationalism*.

16. Ra'anan, "The Nation-State Fallacy," 9.

17. Karklins, *Ethnopolitics*, 3.

18. A. Smith, *Theories of Nationalism*, 171.

19. Rothschild, *Ethnopolitics*, 84; Karklins, *Ethnopolitics*, 4.

20. Kohn, *Nationalism*, 9.

21. Gellner, *Nations and Nationalism*, 43.

22. Huntington, *Political Order in Changing Societies*, 405; Lipset and Rokkan, "Cleavage Structures, Party Systems and Voter Alignments," 4.

23. Epstein, *Political Parties*.

24. Downs, *An Economic Theory of Democracy*, 25.

25. Janda, *Political Parties*, 5.

26. Karklins, *Ethnopolitics*, 4.

27. See, for instance, Bugajski, *Ethnic Politics in Eastern Europe*.

28. Rudolph and Thompson, "Ethnoterritorial Movements and the Policy Process," 291–311.

29. Zariski, "Ethnic Extremism," 261.

30. Ibid.

31. Ibid., 256. See also A. Smith, "Nationalism, Ethnic Separatism, and the Intelligentsia," 17.

32. Bugajski, "The Fate of Minorities," 102–116.

33. Ibid.

34. See Deutsch, "Social Mobilization and Political Development," 493–514; Horowitz, "Three Dimensions of Ethnic Politics," 232–236; Enloe, *Ethnic Conflict and Political Development.*

35. Michnik, ed., "Dignity and Fear," 18

36. C. Williams, ed., *National Separatism,* 294.

37. Deutsch, *Nationalism and Social Communication,* 96–104.

38. Gellner, *Nations and Nationalism,* 35.

39. Anderson, *Imagined Communities,* 66–79.

40. Tiryakian and Rogowski, eds., *New Nationalisms of the Developed West,* 101; Frognier, Quevit, and Stenbock, "Regional Imbalances," 274.

41. Scott, "The Politics of New States," 29–30.

42. Landis and Boucher, "Themes and Models of Conflict," 21–22. See also Nordlinger, *Conflict Regulation in Divided Societies.*

43. Daalder, "The Consociational Democracy Theme," 604–621.

44. Milne, *Politics in Ethnically Bi-polar States*; Horowitz, *Ethnic Groups in Conflict,* 22–30.

45. Horowitz, *Ethnic Groups in Conflict,* 22–23.

46. Ibid., 30–31.

47. Milne, *Politics in Ethnically Bi-polar States*; Rothschild, *Ethnopolitics.*

48. Haas, "What Is Nationalism?"

49. Said and Simmons, eds., *Ethnicity in an International Context,* 18.

50. For a summary of this debate, see Lijphart, "Democracies," 1–4.

51. For a discussion of this debate, see Nordlinger, "Representation, Governmental Stability, and Decisional Effectiveness," 108–127; and Covell, "Ethnic Conflict, Representation, and the State in Belgium," 230–235.

52. Lijphart, *The Politics of Accommodation;* Lijphart, *Democracy in Plural Societies;* Nordlinger, *Conflict Regulation in Divided Societies;* McRae, *Consociational Democracy;* Daalder, "The Consociational Democracy Theme," 604–621; Lorwin, "Segmented Pluralism," 141–175.

53. Lijphart, *Power-Sharing in South Africa,* 106–107; Lijphart, "Proportionality by Non-PR Methods," 113–123; Lakeman, *How Democracies Vote.*

54. Lijphart, *Power-Sharing in South Africa,* 86; Duchacek, "Antagonistic Cooperation," 3–29.

55. Lijphart, *Power-Sharing in South Africa,* 106–107.

56. Horowitz, *Ethnic Groups in Conflict,* 649.

57. Barry, "Review Article," 57–67; Horowitz, *Ethnic Groups in Conflict,* 303–304.

58. Whitaker, *The Politics of Tradition*; D. Olson "Political Parties and the 1992 Election," 301–314. See also Wolchik, *Czechoslovakia in Transition,* and Wightman, "Czechoslovakia," 319–326.

59. Brass, *Ethnicity and Nationalism,* 339.

60. Ibid., 340.

61. Ibid., 346 n. 11.

62. Shugart and Carey, *Presidents and Assemblies,* chap. 10.

63. Horowitz, *Ethnic Groups in Conflict.*

64. Linz, "The Perils of Presidentialism," 51–69.

65. Mainwaring, "Presidentialism, Multi-partyism, and Democracy," 198–228; Stepan and Skach, "Constitutional Frameworks," 1–22.

66. G. Smith, "In Search of Small Parties," 23–40; Mair, "The Electoral Universe of Small Parties," 41–70.

67. Cox, "Electoral Equilibrium," 82–108.

68. Ibid.

69. Hroch, *Social Preconditions of National Revival in Europe.*

70. Pederson, "Towards a New Typology," 1–16.

71. Kellas, *The Politics of Nationalism and Ethnicity*, 81.

72. Tiryakian and Rogowski, *New Nationalisms of the Developed West.*

73. Kellas, *The Politics of Nationalism and Ethnicity*, 81.

74. Panebianco, *Political Parties*, 8–9.

75. M. Olson, *The Logic of Collective Action;* Frohlich and Oppenheimer, *Modern Political Economy.*

76. See Schlesinger, "On the Theory of Party Organization," 369–400. Horowitz holds that the actions of leaders are often constrained by general attitudes among the membership of the ethnic segment they lead (*Ethnic Groups in Conflict*, 564).

77. Panebianco, *Political Parties*, 14–15.

2

The Movement for Rights and Freedoms in Bulgaria

The ouster of Todor Zhivkov in November 1989 marked the end of not only the Communist era in Bulgaria, but also a period of the most virulent form of ethnic repression in Eastern Europe. During the Zhivkov era, the existence of minority groups was officially denied, and thousands of non-Bulgarians were subjected to a series of "Bulgarization" campaigns in the 1980s. Ethnic Turks in Bulgaria were especially targeted for persecution, with hundreds of thousands forced by the authorities to Bulgarize their names, cease the use of the Turkish language in publications, and suspend the practice of Islam. Thousands fled from Bulgaria to Turkey from 1985 to 1987 and again with the resumption of assimilationist policies in 1989. The assimilation drive ended with Zhivkov's ouster, but the political scars of this period left an indelible mark that has played an important role in shaping the politics of interethnic relations in post-Communist Bulgaria.

Despite the injuries committed against the Turkish minority in the period immediately prior to the collapse of Communist rule, injuries that might have been expected to heighten the grievances of the Turkish population, the primary post-Communist Turkish political organization in Bulgaria, the Movement for Rights and Freedoms (MRF), has not made extreme demands. Rather than agitating for political autonomy, the Turkish party has presented itself as an all-national party representing all Bulgarians and as a moderate political force in post-Communist Bulgarian politics. To be sure, the MRF has agitated for the protection of Turkish cultural rights, but the party's leadership has portrayed this effort as beneficial to the Bulgarian population at large.

Why has the MRF made only moderate political demands, despite the enormous resentments that exist among Bulgaria's Turkish population? To address this question, the following sections identify the historical, economic, demographic, and political pressures facing the MRF, as well as the political opportunities presented by the structural features of the post-Communist Bulgarian political system. The chapter concludes with a discussion of the internal fissures that have developed within the MRF, due largely to the moderate politics of the party's leadership.

HISTORICAL BACKGROUND

The Turks have long played an important role in Bulgarian history. Bulgaria became part of the Ottoman Empire in the late fourteenth century, and its history has been intimately connected with Turkey and Islam for more than 500 years. Bulgaria achieved independence from the Ottoman Empire in 1878, with Russian assistance, although its territories and full independence were curtailed by subsequent peace conferences. Bulgaria gained full independence from the Ottoman Empire only in 1908, after several popular uprisings led to the final expulsion of Turkish authority. From 1912 to 1913, Bulgaria engaged in two wars. In the first war, it combined with the other new Balkan states to drive the Turkish forces out of the region. In the second war, Bulgaria was defeated by the combined forces of Serbia and Greece and lost territories in Macedonia and Thrace. These territorial losses fueled Bulgarian irredentism, which led Bulgaria to align itself with the Central Powers during World War I. However, with the capitulation of Germany and Austria in 1918, Bulgaria was forced to accept a harsh peace and lost all access to the Aegean Sea. In World War II, Bulgaria again allied itself with Germany and temporarily regained territories in Macedonia and Thrace, although following the war, Sofia was forced to return these territories. Later, under the Communist regime, Bulgaria renounced its claims to Macedonia and Turkish and Greek Thrace.[1]

One of the most important legacies of the centuries of Ottoman rule was the large Turkish population left in Bulgaria. The Turks are by far the largest of Bulgaria's minority populations (amounting to about 10 percent of the population) that also includes Gypsies, Pomaks (Bulgarian Muslims), Jews, Armenians, and Macedonians (see Table 2.1). For the most part, ethnic Turks live in agrarian areas, primarily in the tobacco-growing Kardzhali region in south-central Bulgaria and Razgrad-Shumen in northeastern Bulgaria. Most of the Turkish population live in the provinces of Ruse, Varna, and Shumen in the north and Burgas and Haskovo in the south and form a majority in eight "subprovinces," four of which are in northern Bulgaria and four in the south. The four northern subprovinces are Omurtag, Kubrat, Isperih, and Dulovo, and the four southern subprovinces are Kardzhali, Momchilgrad, Krumovgrad, and Ardino.

Historically, the Turkish population in Bulgaria has been an object of animosity for xenophobic Bulgarian nationalists. Although the interwar

Table 2.1   Ethnic Composition of Bulgaria, 1920–1992

Ethnic Groups	1920 Population	%	1934 Population	%	1965 Population	%	1992 Population	%
Bulgarians and Macedonians	4,041,276	83.4	4,585,620	86.8	7,239,376	88.0	7,206,062	85.1
Turks	542,904	11.2	618,268	10.2	740,000[a]	9.7	822,253	9.7
Roma (Gypsies)	61,555	1.3	80,532	1.3	150,000[a]	1.8	287,732	3.4
Pomaks (Bulgarian Muslims)	—	—	—	—	—	—	65,546	0.8
Others	—	—	—	—	—	—	91,131	1.1
Total minorities	—	—	—	—	—	—	1,266,662	14.9

Sources: 1920, 1934, and 1965 figures from Rothschild, *East Central Europe Between the Two World Wars,* 328; 1992 figures from Bugajski, *Ethnic Politics in Eastern Europe,* 236.
Note: a. Estimated in 1965.

Bulgarian regime had been reasonably tolerant of its minority populations (extending collective and cultural rights to the Bulgarian Turks), these cultural and collective rights were abolished under the Communists and about 150,000 ethnic Turks were pressured to emigrate. Nonetheless, the 1947 constitution continued to recognize the existence of national minorities in Bulgaria, and there was at least a nominal commitment in the first decades of Communist rule to provide for "instruction in Turkish" in schools with "ten or more Turkish students."[2]

The adoption in 1971 of a new socialist constitution marked the beginning of a period of cultural intolerance and efforts at the forced assimilation of the Turks. Indeed, in the 1971 constitution, the mention of the existence of national minorities in Bulgaria simply disappeared, to be replaced by the term "non-Bulgarian." In part, this was in keeping with a very strict interpretation of Marxism-Leninism, especially the nonrecognition of nationalist deviations. However, it was also in keeping with the traditional Bulgarian nationalist argument that the Bulgarian Turks were actually Slavs who had been forced to convert under Ottoman rule. In the mid-1980s, these two principles were used to justify an assault on Turkish minority rights and the Bulgarization of non-Bulgarian minorities. From 1984 to 1989, ethnic Turks were subjected to a series of government-sponsored campaigns that included the forced Bulgarization of family names and limitations placed on the use of Turkish language, to the extent that children were directed to inform the authorities of the crime of using Turkish in public. In addition, it was reported that widespread violence was employed against communities that resisted the forced name-changing campaign. Estimates of the number of ethnic Turks who were killed in 1984–1985 resisting the campaign range between 800 and 2,500. As a result of this period of cultural repression, an estimated 350,000 Turks left the country.[3]

During the period of liberalization that followed the ouster of Zhivkov in November 1989, the government reversed itself. In December 1989, the ruling Bulgarian Communist Party renounced the policy of forcible cultural assimilation and allowed ethnic Turks to revert to their old names, practice Islam, and speak Turkish in public. Further, Turks were allowed to establish their own political, social, and cultural organizations.[4] Following the democratic changes in Bulgaria, an estimated 120,000 to 180,000 Turks returned to Bulgaria.

Despite these changes, anti-Turk sentiment has remained an important part of post-Communist politics. The Bulgarian Socialist Party (BSP), the successor to the Bulgarian Communist Party, has been particularly prone to capitalize on incipient anti-Turkish sentiment for electoral gain.[5] However, bouts of anti-Turkish rhetoric were not limited to the BSP. For instance, the leader of the Union of Democratic Forces (UDF) and prime minister in 1991, Dmitur Popov, remarked that Turks represented a threat to the Bulgarian nation, and in the regions of Bulgaria inhabited by ethnic Turks, Slavic Bulgarians were threatened with death. In particular, Popov warned against "Moslem aggression": "In some way it must be blocked so that it does not invade Europe."[6]

Nor is anti-Turkish sentiment limited to the political elite. Many Bulgarians still currently regard the ethnic Turkish minority as a potential Trojan horse and a Turkish "fifth column" on Bulgarian territory, a sentiment that is most powerful in the southeastern region of the country. In part, this is due to the proximity of Turkey, which has the most powerful military force in the region; with the dissolution of the Warsaw Pact, Bulgaria no longer has the means to defend itself against Turkey's superior armed forces. This fear has been reflected in public opinion polls. In a 1991 Gallup poll, 48 percent of the respondents regarded Turkey as a threat to Bulgarian national security.[7] Although the perception of the threat posed by Turkey has now declined somewhat, a similar poll conducted in December 1993 indicated that 34 percent of the respondents still considered Turkey a major threat to Bulgarian national security. In addition, the percentage of respondents declaring that ethnic groups and minorities in Bulgaria posed a serious threat to the nation's security stood at 46 percent in 1992.[8] Moreover, major barriers that divide Bulgarians and Turks continue to exist. Thus, in a nationwide survey conducted in 1994, respondents were asked whether they would be willing to accept a Turk or a Roma as a neighbor, a colleague at work, a close friend, or a member of their family by marriage. Fully 35 percent of the respondents said they would not accept Turks as neighbors (71 percent for Roma), 32 percent as colleagues at work (63 percent for Roma), 52 percent as a close friend (79 percent for Roma), and 77 percent as a relative by marriage (90.2 percent for Roma).[9]

Compounding this underlying distrust of the Turks, two additional issues continue to promote tensions between the Bulgarian and Turkish parts of the population. The first is the right to use the Turkish language. According to Article 3 of the 1991 constitution, Bulgarian was listed as the official language of the Bulgarian Republic, although Article 36 of the constitution guaranteed that "citizens whose mother tongue is not Bulgarian shall have the right to study and use their own language alongside the compulsory study of the Bulgarian language." In January 1991, a special council was created to investigate whether the teaching of Turkish as part of the secondary school curriculum was consistent with the constitution. The commission concluded that it was, but it failed to endorse the adoption of Turkish as part of the official educational program. As a result, several thousand Turkish students went on strike in southeastern Bulgaria.

A second area of controversy concerns the redress of property lost during the Turkish exodus of the Zhivkov period. A number of Bulgarians, particularly in the Razgrad-Shumen region of the northeast, profited immensely by purchasing property and goods at absurdly low prices and sold used cars and food for extortionate sums to Turks desperate to leave the country.[10]

The demands for the recognition of Turkish as an official language and for property redress have enraged xenophobic Bulgarian nationalists. In 1989, in Kardzhali—a city with a population of 60,000 where the ethnic Bulgarian and Turkish communities are roughly equal in size but situated in a rural area where Turks are estimated to outnumber Bulgarians by about four to one—local nationalists formed the Committee for the Defense of National Interests (CDNI) and campaigned against the government decision to restore minority language rights. In part, the reason for the backlash in Kardzhali derived from the fact that many of the ethnic Bulgarians in the area were descended from families driven out of Turkish and Greek Thrace in the Balkan Wars of 1912–1913. Hence there was a strong fear of Pan-Islamic resurgence in the area and traditional support for greater Bulgarian nationalism. Indeed, during the forced assimilation campaign of 1984–1985, at least 100 ethnic Turks were killed by local security forces in the region.[11]

THE MOVEMENT FOR RIGHTS AND FREEDOMS

The principal political organization that has emerged to champion the cause of Turkish political and cultural rights in the post-Communist era has been the MRF. The origins of the ethnic Turkish MRF lie with the official policies of repression practiced by the Communist regime in Bulgaria. It was during the period from 1984 to 1989 that organized opposition to the regime's efforts at Bulgarization began to appear, centered on the clandestine National Turkish Liberation Movement. This organization claimed to have been active in organizing the antigovernment protests in

May 1989, which ultimately signaled the beginning of the end for the Zhivkov regime. In particular, Ahmed Dogan (born 1954), an academic with a Ph.D. in philosophy, was active in establishing organized resistance to the assimilationist policies of the state.[12] He was arrested in June 1986 for "anti-state" activities and sentenced to ten years in prison.

While serving his term in prison, Dogan formulated the basis of a political program that, upon his release in 1989, became the centerpiece of the MRF's political program, which was formally founded in the city of Shumen on February 25, 1990.[13] A Constituent National Conference was held on March 26–27, 1990, in Sofia, which elected a Central Council of seven members, including Dogan as chairman and Osman Oktay, a close associate of Dogan, as general secretary. The early party program focused largely on demands for the freedom to use Turkic names and the Turkish language, the freedom to practice Islam openly, and the right to emigrate to Turkey.

However, the party later broadened its goals and emphasized that it was a party of all national minorities opposed to any "manifestation of national chauvinism, revenge, Islamic fundamentalism and religious fanaticism."[14] The party argued that its efforts were designed to contribute to "the unity of the Bulgarian people and to the full and unequivocal compliance with the rights of freedoms of mankind and of all ethnic, religious and cultural communities in Bulgaria."[15] Further, the party called for the promotion of measures designed to alleviate the economic problems facing minority populations in Bulgaria.[16]

By 1991, it was reported that the MRF had 140,000 members, up from the 100,000 members at its inception.[17] The MRF's organizational structure is comprised of three tiers: a Central Council at the top, district administrative bureaus in the country's thirty-three major regions, and local committees in cities and villages around the country. The movement's statutes stipulate that the Central Council convene at least once every two months; between meetings, a Central Administrative Bureau, composed of a seven-member executive committee and four regional coordinators, is responsible for the day-to-day administration of the party's affairs. The highest authority belongs to the national congress, which is required by the statutes to meet at least once every three years and is to be attended by one delegate for every 500 members. In all, there are between 800 and 900 branches and twenty-two regional offices throughout the country.

The MRF's attitude toward the major political forces in Bulgaria has generally been mixed. On the one hand, the BSP bore the responsibility for the "criminal assimilation policy" in the 1980s; Dogan himself in 1990 categorically "rejected any possibility of the MRF forming a coalition or conducting any other kind of cooperation with the BSP for either tactical considerations as well as for the consideration of principle."[18] On the other hand, the MRF's attitude toward the UDF was not entirely positive either. Indeed, many figures in the UDF had opposed the MRF's legalization as a party and had charged that the MRF was a militant "organization of the Turks in Bulgaria."[19]

STRUCTURE OF INCENTIVES

In addition to the legacy of intergroup animosity mentioned above, other features of post-Communist Bulgaria would seem to provide considerable incentive for the emergence of extremist demands made on the part of the ethnic Turks and the principal party that represents them. The growing social and economic gap that separates the ethnic Turkish population from other Bulgarians would suggest that there is considerable pressure for the MRF to move in the direction of more extremist and particularistic demands. Yet these pressures have been mitigated somewhat by other factors, most notably, the impact of political structures and the related structure of political competition.

Social and Economic Pressures

The economic transition in Bulgaria has been fraught with much difficulty. Many of the current problems are the result of the legacy bequeathed by the ill-conceived economic policies of the previous Communist regime. In the early years after the Communist takeover in 1944, Bulgaria—more so than other Eastern European countries—followed a growth strategy that was closely modeled after the Soviet experience. Indeed, the first of a series of five-year plans witnessed the emphasis on investment in heavy industry and a growing reliance on raw materials imported from the Soviet Union. By the 1960s, heavy industry accounted for 48 percent of the net material product, as opposed to only 23 percent in 1948. As a result, as with all Soviet-style planned economies, after an initial expansion in industry and agriculture, production had stagnated by the late 1960s, and the need for economic reforms became increasingly clear to the Bulgarian Communist leadership.[20]

Two of the most important legacies left by the past Communist regime were the great degree of integration of the Bulgarian economy with the Council of Mutual Economic Assistance (CMEA), with its accompanying dependence on Eastern European markets and raw materials, and the amassing of one of the most crushing foreign debt burdens among the Communist states. Much of this debt, which was estimated to have reached $9.2 billion in 1989, had been incurred in order to purchase consumer goods and raw materials from Organization for Economic Cooperation and

Development (OECD) countries, rather than capital equipment. In sum, the regime attempted to maintain levels of consumption, leading to less investment in production.

The economic dislocation caused by the collapse of the CMEA had a direct impact on the economic condition of the Turkish population in Bulgaria. As Table 2.2 indicates, as late as 1990, CMEA countries accounted for 75.9 percent of Bulgaria's imports and purchased over 80 percent of the country's exports (with the USSR alone accounting for 56.5 percent of imports and 64.4 percent of exports). Bulgaria was particularly reliant on the import of iron ore and timber from the USSR, which was priced below world market prices, and the Communist bloc was the primary market for Bulgarian industrial and agricultural products, particularly tobacco. With the collapse of the CMEA, and with the shift to international prices in 1991, the effects on Bulgaria were disastrous. The OECD estimated that the shift to international prices in 1991 led to a 27 percent loss in terms of trade, a 67 percent decline in exports to the former Soviet Union, and a 60 percent decline in import volumes, which produced a fall in real gross domestic product (GDP) of about one-third between 1989 and 1991.[21] Coupled with the effects of adopting an International Monetary Fund–approved macroeconomic stabilization plan, the economy performed far worse than expected in 1991–1992.

Of the various affected sectors, agricultural production was particularly hard hit. Although the decline in industrial production had begun to taper off by 1993–1994, agriculture continued to languish, with the largest single decline occurring in 1993 when gross agricultural production fell by 16.3 percent. To a large extent, this was due to the loss of important markets for Bulgarian products, particularly tobacco and wine. Moreover, the former product appears to have little opportunity to recover, particularly as Eastern European and Russian markets—the traditional consumers of Bulgarian tobacco—have become saturated with Western brands.

The effects of economic adjustment have been particularly injurious to the situation of the ethnic Turks. Most Turks worked in the tobacco industry, yet with the introduction of Western brands in Eastern Europe, the economic condition of the Turks declined dramatically. Many villages in the tobacco-producing regions of the southeast have been entirely abandoned, the residents leaving the fields unharvested. Many have left for Turkey, but emigration to Turkey has become difficult, particularly since Turkey has imposed unofficial visa restrictions to try to stem the flow.[22]

Given the continuing economic difficulties facing the Turkish portion of the Bulgarian population, despite the overall recovery of the economy, one might expect greater pressures for more radical solutions to the Turkish problem as the economic gap grows between the Turks and other Bulgarians.

Table 2.2   Macroeconomic Indicators and Degree of Regional Integration, Bulgaria, 1990–1994

	1990	1991	1992	1993	1994
Change in real GDP	–9.1	–11.7	–5.7	–4.2	–2.0
Gross industrial production	–12.5	–18.6	–11.2	–3.9	–4.0
Gross agricultural production	–3.7	7.7	–13.8	–16.3	n.a.
Unemployment	1.6	10.8	15.5	16.0	n.a.
Inflation	72.5	338.9	79.6	64.0	59.5
Real industrial wages (1990 = 100)	100	100	60	51	61
Exports (% of total)					
To EC/EU[a]	5.0	15.7	29.4	28.1	31.5
To Russia and Eastern Europe	80.2	57.7	39.2	35.4	34.5
Imports (% of total)					
From EC/EU[a]	9.6	20.7	31.1	30.2	40.3
From Russia and Eastern Europe	75.9	48.5	36.3	42.9	28.2

Source: Hardt and Kaufman, eds., *East Central European Economies in Transition.*
Note: a. EC = European Community; EU = European Union.

In fact, Dogan has admitted that there have been widening internal cleavages within the MRF, particularly over such issues as the growing socioeconomic gap and the problem of unemployment within the Turkish population.[23] Furthermore, the emigration to Turkey has been largely made up of those Turks who could afford to emigrate, particularly the most educated and talented portion of the population, which in turn has siphoned off the political base of the MRF. Thus, since 1989, over 9,000 Turkish intellectuals have left Bulgaria for Turkey, which, according to Dogan, has seriously weakened the "intellectual potential" of local organizational cadres. Such emigration has consequently contributed to the radicalization of local party organizations and a growing gap between the party's center and local organizations.[24]

Political Incentives

Political Structures. Two features of the post-Communist Bulgarian political system have had a great influence on the development and behavior of the MRF. The first has been the provision contained within the Bulgarian constitution that specifically bans parties based on race, religion, or ethnic origin from participating in the electoral process. Despite this ban, the MRF contended that it was a movement open to all Bulgarians, even though most of the party's membership was Turkish. The Central Election Commission accepted this contention, and the MRF was allowed to participate in the 1990 election campaign for the constituent Grand National Assembly.

With the adoption of the new constitution in 1991, the question again arose as to whether the MRF should be allowed to participate in the October 1991 parliamentary elections. Anticipating such a confrontation in August 1991, fifty-five Bulgarian members of the MRF organized the Party for Rights and Freedoms (PRF) and elected Dogan, the chairman of the MRF, as its chair. The lower courts ruled, however, that the party could not register, and this decision was upheld by the Supreme Court on September 12, 1991. Nevertheless, the MRF maintained that it need not reregister because it had been placed on the official party registry in 1990. The Central Election Commission accepted this argument and on September 11, registered the MRF.[25]

The decision to ban the PRF but not the MRF was to set an important precedent for the future development of the MRF. By refusing to register the PRF on the grounds that it represented an ethnic party but allowing the MRF to remain a registered political movement, the courts and the Central Election Commission effectively anointed the MRF as the only political organization that could legally represent the ethnic Turkish population in Bulgaria. Thus, any other potential Turkish contenders who aspired to participate in the electoral process and who were dissatisfied with the MRF were effectively closed off from competing.

In addition to enjoying a quasi-official monopoly on the representation of the Turkish population, the political structures of the current post-Communist political system, primarily electoral law, have also provided opportunities for the MRF. Initially, the June 1990 election law pertaining to the unicameral constituent Grand National Assembly (named in remembrance of the first Grand National Assembly created by the Turnovo constitution in 1875) allowed for 400 members, with 200 seats filled by competition in single-member electoral districts of relatively equal population; it was agreed that district size could vary up to 20 percent from the average. The law also provided for twenty-eight multimember districts for the purposes of electing 200 deputies by the proportional representation formula. The election of the 200 deputies by a single-member mandate with a majority-vote requirement was to provide an opportunity to produce a governing majority. The election of another 200 by PR was to ensure that the voices of smaller parties would be heard. A 4 percent threshold on the national list vote was required for a political party to share in the proportional representation formula. This threshold was employed to eliminate destructive "splinter" parties.

However, following the 1990 elections, several political organizations, especially certain factions of the UDF and the independent trade union Podkrepa, charged that the election law had been manipulated to ensure a BSP majority, particularly because the BSP had benefited from the single-member constituencies in the rural areas where the Socialists enjoyed an organizational advantage over their rivals. To counter this bias, the UDF and Podkrepa proposed the adoption of an exclusively proportional representation with parties campaigning on party programs. The BSP, in contrast, wanted to maintain the mixed system used in the 1990 elections. Ultimately, the democratic opposition won out, and the 1991 election was conducted on a purely PR basis with a 4 percent threshold for parties to receive representation; the d'Hondt method was adopted to allocate seats at the national level. Once seats were allocated to the parties nationally, party strength in the thirty-one electoral regions determined precisely how many individuals on a given party's regional list would be elected to Parliament.

The net result of the electoral law was to promote a large proportion of "wasted" votes in the elections of 1991 and the overrepresentation of the major parties. As indicated in Table 2.3, overrepresentation was most pronounced in the 1991 parliamentary election, where only three parties passed the 4 percent threshold to win seats in Parliament. Thus, the BSP won only 33.14 percent of the popular vote yet received 44.17 percent of the seats in Parliament. Similarly, the UDF, the party that won the most seats in Parliament (110) that year, won only 34.36 percent of the vote. Perhaps most noteworthy was the performance of the MRF, which won 7.55 percent of the vote but received 10 percent of the seats, making it the third major party in Bulgaria. More important, since neither the UDF nor the BSP had been able to win a majority of seats (unlike in 1990), the MRF became the central actor in coalition politics, giving it far more influence on the course of Bulgarian politics than it had enjoyed the year before.

The Structure of Competition. An additional factor that has impacted the evolution and behavior of the MRF is the competition it has faced. In particular, the weakness of the MRF's most vehement opponents provided opportunities for the political moderates to dominate the MRF and steer the party away from extremist demands.

Generally speaking, extreme Bulgarian nationalists targeted the Turkish population for many of Bulgaria's past woes and insisted that the assimilationist policies of the past should be maintained. Essentially, ideologists for Bulgarian nationalist parties like the Fatherland Party of Labor (FPL) and the Bulgarian National Radical Party see Bulgaria as the primary

Table 2.3 Parliamentary Election Results, Bulgaria, 1990–1997[a]

Party	1990 Parliamentary Election		1991 Parliamentary Election		1994 Parliamentary Election		1995 Municipal Election	1997 Parliamentary Elections	
	% Vote[b]	% Seats (No.)	% Vote	% Seats (No.)	% Vote	% Seats (No.)	% Vote	% Vote	% Seats (No.)
BSP	47.15	52.75 (211)	33.14	44.17 (106)	43.50	50.28 (125)	41.0	22.0	24.2 (58)
UDF	37.84	36.00 (144)	34.36	45.83 (110)	24.23	28.75 (69)	24.7	52.2	57.1 (137)
MRF[c]	6.5	5.75 (23)	7.55	10.00 (24)	5.40	5.42 (13)	8.2	7.6	7.9 (19)
BAPU[d]	8.03	(16)	—	—	—		—	—	—
PU[e] (BAPU and Democratic Party)[f]					6.25	7.5 (18)	12.3	—	—
Bulgarian Business Bloc	—		—		4.76	5.41 (13)	5.0	4.9	5.0 (12)
Euroleft Coalition (Social Democratic defectors from BSP)	—		—		—		—	5.6	5.8 (14)

Sources: The October 13, 1991, Legislative and Municipal Elections in Bulgaria; Krause, "Elections Reveal Blue Cities amid Red Provinces."
Figures in parentheses are raw numbers of seats held.

Notes: a. Includes only parties that passed the 4 percent threshold.
b. Percentage of votes won according to party list vote.
c. Ran in coalition with Monarchists in 1997.
d. BAPU = Bulgarian Agrarian Peoples' Union.
e. PU = Peoples Union.
f. Ran in coalition with UDF in 1997.

battleground in the defense of "Europe against Islam."[26] Another group, the CDNI, has targeted the Turkish MRF as representing the primary threat to the integrity of the Bulgarian state, arguing that the MRF was a tool of Turkey in its desire to "Turkify" Bulgaria.

Although the public appeal of the nationalist parties remains relatively small, these parties have been quite vocal in organizing anti-Turkish spectacles. For instance, from April to June 1990, the CDNI was active in organizing strikes to protest the introduction of redress measures for Bulgarian Turks who had lost their property during the last assimilation campaign in 1989. In June 1990, the CDNI staged protests against the decision to allow the MRF to compete in the elections to the Grand Assembly; and in November 1990, it participated in the formation of the Association of Free Bulgarian Cities in the south of the country along with other nationalist groups that subsequently refused to recognize Sofia's authority and elected its own alternative parliament.

Despite such spectacles, Bulgarian nationalists have had only a marginal impact on the political process because the major political parties have attempted to distance themselves from the extreme nationalist and assimilationist policies of the past Zhivkov regime and have avoided putting too strong an emphasis on patriotic sentiments. Indeed, during the formative period of the opposition parties, "breaking with the expression of extreme nationalism became part of the political identity of the opposition parties and even the slowly reforming communist party. Subsequently, all major parties officially adhered to the idea of ethnic pluralism and supported the view that rights of minorities must be safeguarded by law."[27]

Since many Bulgarians are disoriented about the old ideological approaches to nationality issues, attitudes about nationalism are susceptible to the influence of Western perceptions. It is widely understood that Western political and economic support is likely to depend on Bulgarian policies toward minority groups. As a result, the major political parties are quite cognizant of the fact that any overt anti-Turkish statements will be interpreted as an attack on national minority rights, and no party wants to be responsible for the interruption of potential political and economic support from the West.

Yet the apparent political weakness of the overtly nationalist parties in Bulgaria belies a more ominous connection between nationalism and the opportunistic post-Communist Bulgarian Socialist Party. By tapping into the underlying suspicions concerning the ethnic Turks and by capitalizing on Article 44 of the 1991 constitution that explicitly forbids organizations purporting an ethnic agenda, the BSP initially attacked the MRF in an attempt, as one nationalist leader put it, to gain "a monopoly on the national cause."[28] Throughout 1991, the BSP daily newspaper

Duma ran articles that attacked the MRF as an organization having affiliations with terrorist groups and seeking to create a "political monopoly" in areas inhabited by Turks. In particular, in the fall of 1991, the BSP stepped up its attacks on the MRF, opposing the participation of the latter in the elections of 1991 on the grounds that it would violate "the norms of the new constitution" and that the "neglect of constitutional principles and the national interest of the Bulgarian people . . . could have serious repercussions for the transition to Democracy."[29] Andrey Lukanov, former prime minister and at that time a member of the BSP's Supreme Council, summarized the BSP's objections to the MRF participation as follows:

> Today we see that this is an organization established along ethnic and religious lines—this I no longer call into question. Second we see that in those regions where the MRF dominates, there are no other parties—no democracy exists. People have no freedom of choice there. Third we see that the MRF is defended from abroad.[30]

Having been unsuccessful in opposing the participation of the MRF in the October 1991 parliamentary election, the BSP concentrated its attacks on the MRF instead of the UDF opposition, particularly in areas where there was a mixed Bulgarian-Turkish population. This strategy seemingly had two effects. First, by placing the MRF under constant fire, the BSP succeeded in attracting nationalist voters to its banners. Second, by focusing attention on the "threat" posed by the MRF, the BSP inadvertently compelled Turkish voters to rally around the MRF's banner, boosting its electoral support. The MRF increased its share of seats from 5.75 percent in 1990 to 10.0 percent in 1991, despite a Parliament whose size was much decreased—from 400 in 1990 to 240 in 1991.

Although the BSP was the principal antagonist facing the MRF from 1990 to 1991, the erstwhile democratic UDF was not overly eager to embrace the MRF either. Despite the poor showing of the UDF in ethnically mixed regions of the country (see Table 2.4), the UDF was able to emerge from the election of 1991 as the single largest party in the Bulgarian Parliament, having received 34.36 percent of the vote and 110 of the 240 seats. Although coalition logic dictated that the UDF form a partnership with the MRF, which was not positively disposed toward the BSP anyway, the UDF leadership decided on October 28, 1991, to set up a minority government, excluding the MRF. To a large extent, this decision was seen as a move to placate nationalists both outside of the UDF and within the party.[31] Indeed, several leading figures in the UDF had been quite outspoken in their opposition to the MRF. Some UDF members had even supported the BSP-sponsored effort to ban the MRF's participation in the 1991 elections.

Table 2.4 **Percentage of National Vote in Select Regions, Bulgaria, 1991 and 1994**

	1991			1994		
Region	BSP	MRF	UDF	BSP	MRF	UDF
Kardzhali	16.9	65.8	5.6	25.0	50.5	6.4
Razgrad	24.3	43.9	6.5	36.5	34.3	6.8
Targosvishte	34.6	27.1	10.7	46.7	20.6	10.0
Shumen	22.8	24.3	15.2	43.7	18.1	11.7
Silistra	33.8	27.5	13.7	45.4	18.2	10.6
Nationwide	33.1	7.6	34.4	43.5	5.4	24.23

Sources: Engelbrekt, "Nationalism Reviving," 4; *The October 13, 1991, Legislative and Municipal Elections in Bulgaria;* Krause, "Elections Reveal Blue Cities amid Red Provinces"; *Durzhaven Vestnik,* December 10, 1994, 9–13, in FBIS-EEU, March 22, 1995, 7–16.

THE EVOLUTION OF THE MRF

From the above review of post-Communist Bulgarian politics, it is clear that there have been pressures that should have compelled the MRF to adopt more extreme political demands. Specifically, that it represented a population whose economic status had deteriorated significantly, that lingering anti-Turkish popular sentiments persisted, and that it was confronted by politically hostile forces are all reasons that would have warranted the MRF to seek more radical political solutions. Yet the MRF has thus far remained committed to making only relatively moderate political demands without calling for the restructuring of the post-Communist Bulgarian polity. What accounts for the persistence of moderate demands made by the MRF? To a great extent, the evolution of the party in the early years after the collapse of Communist rule conditioned the party's continued commitment to moderation.

The MRF had initially emerged in 1990 as a broad-based movement the primary goal of which was to rectify as quickly as possible the injuries committed by the previous regime on the ethnic Turks. However, as noted earlier, the MRF categorically denied that it was an ethnic party, claiming that its goals were designed to protect "rights of all ethnic groups in Bulgaria, not simply of Turks,"[32] and Dogan consistently refuted the charge that the MRF harbored "separatist or autonomist ambitions."[33] Moreover, the MRF has stated that it stands for peaceful coexistence, and that "the movement is doing its utmost to avoid extremism, irrespective of who the instigators might be."[34] Other leaders, such as Yunal Lyufti, the MRF's parliamentary caucus chair, also have condemned any "manifestation of Turkish nationalism," as well as Bulgarian nationalist chauvinism.[35]

Yet despite the claims that the party is committed to the general protection of all minority groups, over 90 percent of the party's membership remains Turkish,[36] and the bulk of the MRF statutes in 1991 were focused on the specific problems facing the Bulgarian Turks: (1) the return of property seized from Turks who fled Bulgaria in 1989; (2) the restoration of mosques, the lifting of the ban on publishing Islamic literature, including the Quran, and the lifting of the ban on religious rites; and (3) the reform of the educational system, particularly via the introduction of optional teaching of Turkish to ethnic Turkish students and the optional teaching of Islamic theology in Bulgarian schools to ethnic Turk pupils.

Even with opposition from both ends of the Bulgarian political spectrum, the MRF secured a solid third-place finish in the 1991 election and became the primary balancing force between the BSP and the UDF, winning twenty-four parliamentary seats with 7.55 percent of the popular vote. Moreover, the party fared well in the local elections, winning over 1,000 local council seats and 650 village and twenty-five district mayoralties.

The MRF's ability to influence the course of Bulgarian politics was evidenced in the aftermath of the October 1991 elections. Although the MRF had declared prior to the election that it did not aim for ministerial posts and that it agreed with the UDF (which had won the 1991 election) on most basic issues,[37] the UDF minority government of Fillip Dimitrov governed with only the tacit support of the MRF. The UDF-MRF informal coalition remained quite fragile, and as time passed, the relations between the two parties grew increasingly worse, particularly over measures concerning the reform of the agricultural sector and state support for the tobacco industry. On July 24, 1992, a vote of no-confidence, initiated by the opposition BSP, was defeated in a vote of 130 to 104. Most of the MRF deputies had voted with the government, except MRF chairman Ahmed Dogan, who had voted for the measure. Dogan contended that he had supported the vote of no-confidence because of the "government's unscrupulous anti–trade union policy" and its failure to accelerate market reform, particularly the decentralization of the tobacco industry. His vote was also a "signal . . . to save the government and warn it that it must begin a dialogue" with the MRF.[38] Other members of the MRF parliamentary group, such as deputy Mehmed Hodzha, who had voted for the Dimitrov government, stated that the party's support was conditional and motivated not as much by support for the government's policies as by the fact that the MRF would never join a coalition with the BSP.[39]

By the fall of 1992, however, the MRF had become fully disenchanted with the Dimitrov government. Many of the party's leaders complained that the UDF had "forgotten" the informal UDF-MRF coalition and had consistently ignored MRF-sponsored proposals, especially those regarding reforms in the agricultural sector.[40] Further, the MRF wanted a greater and more prominent role in the government, particularly by acquiring cabinet portfolios.[41] On September 23, the MRF itself introduced a no-confidence vote, but last-minute negotiations between the UDF and the MRF postponed the vote.[42] Finally, on October 28, the MRF sponsored a vote of no-confidence, a measure supported by the BSP, that brought down the Dimitrov government by a vote of 120 to 111.

Following the vote of no-confidence, the MRF continued to negotiate with the UDF to form a new and "genuine" coalition government that would include the MRF receiving several cabinet portfolios.[43] In the meantime, the MRF had established contacts with the BSP and began moves to sponsor an alternative BSP-nominated candidate. On November 30, the MRF leadership announced support for the head of the National Statistical Institute, economics professor Zahari Karamfilov, as prime minister. Karamfilov declined the nomination on the grounds that he would be unable to marshal enough support from the UDF to form a "government of national accord."[44] Following the rejection of another BSP nominee, President Zhelev asked the MRF itself to try to form a government, which then proceeded to nominate Lyuben Berov, a nonparty candidate and former adviser to President Zhelev. The MRF was able to recruit enough support from the BSP and the UDF breakaway factions to confirm Berov as prime minister on December 30.

Thus the opportunity to act as the political kingpin had proven to be too great a temptation for the MRF leadership. As one observer noted, the MRF leadership not only played the "balancing role in the parliament, but also fully mastered this role."[45] However, the MRF's newfound political influence was not without costs. Having turned on the UDF, the latter began a campaign directed against the MRF, charging in early 1993 that the party was engaged in the forced Turkification of the Bulgarian Muhammadans (Pomaks).[46] Moreover, the relationship with the BSP was tenuous at best; some members of the BSP leadership continued to publicly claim that the Turks were arming themselves and that the MRF had secret plans to promote a secessionist movement in Bulgaria similar to the "Bosnia scenario." Within less than a year, the MRF had also become dissatisfied with the Berov cabinet and especially with its Socialist partners, who had effectively excluded the MRF from important decisions and continued "to govern in a dictatorial fashion."[47] Support for the Berov government had also not reaped any benefits for the Turkish minority population, particularly regarding the tobacco industry and unemployment, issues crucial for the ethnic Turkish population.[48]

Perhaps the greatest negative consequence of the MRF's political flip-flop was the rise of dissent within the MRF itself. Such dissent had been brewing for some time, particularly over Chairman Dogan's propensity to rule the MRF in an authoritarian fashion and to surround himself with political cronies. Just prior to the October 1991 election, an ethnic Bulgarian deputy, Miroslav Durmov, openly criticized Dogan and the MRF leadership for abandoning the party's original multiethnic principles and accused Dogan of moving the party toward "ethnic isolation."[49] Durmov, along with another Turkish parliamentarian, Husayn Yumer, further accused Dogan of being a prima donna and his close associates Yunal Lyutviev and Member of Parliament (MP) Ibrahim Tartarlu as being corrupt.[50] Durmov later broke with the MRF and formed his own political organization, the Constitutional Rights and Freedoms political club, on August 29, 1991, which ran in the October 1991 election as a partner of the Bulgarian Socialists.[51]

A more serious challenge to the leadership of the MRF emerged after the MRF's decision to collaborate with the BSP in late 1992. At the root of the movement's troubles lay the credibility crisis caused when the party switched sides in Parliament and joined the BSP in forming a coalition government, abandoning its informal alliance with the UDF. Since the 1984–1989 forced assimilation campaign, most Turks had regarded the BSP as the chief antagonist on minority rights issues, and many were upset with the new alliance. Dogan himself had earlier affixed the principal responsibility for the assimilation campaign squarely on the Bulgarian Socialists.[52] However, the MRF was now openly cooperating with "the devil" to the extent that Dogan publicly lunched with the retired architect of assimilation, Todor Zhivkov.

Protest to this volte-face came in the form of the establishment of an alternative ethnic Turkish party, the so-called Turkish Democratic Party (TDP), at the end of November 1992 by former MRF parliamentary deputy Adem Kenan.[53] The party's opening congress on December 12, 1992, held in Razgrad, included eighty delegates who proceeded to formulate a program that advocated national self-determination and demanded the "recognition of a Turkish national minority and [the establishment of] cultural administrative communities."[54] The TDP also accused Dogan of being a traitor who "played the games of the communists" and had been in league with the former state security agency during the Zhivkov years.[55]

In response to this challenge, Dogan and the MRF leadership denounced the formation of the TDP as detracting from the Turkish cause and categorically refused to cooperate with what they depicted as an overtly ethnic separatist party.[56] The MRF leadership moved quickly to distance itself from the TDP and to reaffirm its proclaimed identity as a nonethnic party. Thus Ivan Palchev, an ethnic Bulgarian spokesperson for the MRF, accused the TDP of contributing to the penetration of "certain Islamic states" that, according to him, established contacts with the TDP in order to foment "Islamic expansionism."[57]

At the same time, however, the MRF reaffirmed its self-proclaimed role as the primary champion of minority rights. Indeed, the existence of the TDP had been of some help to the MRF, which was now able to portray itself as a force of moderation and reason, as opposed to the separatist TDP. In an interview with *Trud* in January 1993, Dogan proclaimed that although the MRF was an ethnic party, it was in the best position to serve the national interest. Defending the interests of a particular group was "not paradoxical" because "a party which started out from the ethnic issue and assumed the task of defending the rights of citizens of a given ethnic group against a policy of ethnic-cultural genocide and state terrorism . . . should adopt the defense of *human* communities. These principles lead logically to the realization and implementation of a policy which should be exclusively of overriding nationwide interest."[58] Further, Dogan and the MRF leadership denounced charges made by some members of their coalition partner, the Bulgarian Socialist Party, that the MRF was in actuality a conduit for Turkish influence; at the same time, they defended the party leadership's decision to form a governing coalition with the BSP. In fact, Dogan contended that the best way to serve the national interest was for both Bulgarians and Turks to support the MRF since the continued stability of the MRF was "the only way to exclude the possibility of any pro-Turkish or other partisan policy being imposed that runs counter to the national interest."[59]

In the end, the TDP was prohibited from registering as a political party in early 1993 because of its overtly ethnic program, and the crisis was averted. To a large extent, this was due to the successful polemic waged by the MRF against the TDP. Although the challenge to the MRF leadership had been quite serious, Dogan himself dismissed the actions of the previous year as merely reflective of the growing pangs of any political party, and he claimed that such differences of opinion were "natural." Certainly, since the "bulk of the main issues of [the party's] election program," such as "language study, the names and equality of all Bulgarian citizens," had been fulfilled, it was only natural that differences should emerge over practical issues, such as the economy and the rate of unemployment. He defended the party's record, even the collaboration with the BSP, as being necessary to promote "human and community rights" and to avoid "bloodshed of the Bosnian type in Bulgaria."[60]

Nonetheless, despite Dogan's skillful leadership, which temporarily postponed the crisis for more than a year, by late 1993, discontent over the BSP-MRF alliance was again burgeoning in the party ranks. At the second national conference of the MRF held in Sofia on November 27–28, 1993, Dogan's leadership was strongly criticized by the MRF deputy from Kardzhali, Mehmed Hodzha, who said that the decision made in 1992 to back the BSP government and thereby join an informal alliance with the BSP had been a major tactical error. After alleging that several top MRF members were former state security agents, Hodzha and the other Kardzhali delegates staged a walkout.[61] At the MRF party conference of February

1994, two MRF parliamentary deputies, Hodzha and Redzheb Chinar, also from Kardzhali, accused Dogan, Osman Oktay, and parliamentary caucus leader Yunal Lyufti of corruption and announced that they, along with two other deputies, were leaving the party. Although ostensibly these deputies left because of Dogan's alleged "totalitarian" methods and the overt corruption of other members of the MRF leadership,[62] the primary reason was the MRF's cooperation with the much-despised BSP.[63] Later, Hodzha, Ismail Ismail, and a former leader of the defunct TDP, Sabir Hussein, joined together to form an alternative party in May 1994, the Party for Democratic Changes, which declared itself to be "non-nationalist" and "on the right" of the political spectrum. The new party declared that it would seek an alliance with all noncommunist forces and rejected any cooperation with the BSP. Although the new party categorically dissociated itself "from the manifestations of nationalism and separatism," Yunal Lyufti of the MRF described it as an exclusively ethnic party and an "outside-inspired" attempt to split the MRF.[64] He predicted that it would suffer the same fate as did the defunct and illegal TDP.

In response to the renewed challenges within the MRF, the Dogan leadership pushed for measures to promote greater "coordination" and internal party discipline. The party conference officially denounced the defection of MPs Hodzha and Ismail and adopted a number of measures that were designed to promote the "synchrony" between the MRF Central Council and the MRF parliamentary group.[65] Dogan continued to defend the MRF's participation in the BSP-led government as the best way to defend the interests and cultural rights of the Turkish population, and he denounced as "absurd" the idea that "nationalism and chauvinism of any individual ethnic group" should become the dominant factor in the MRF.[66]

By early 1994, the previous year's defections had seriously reduced the MRF's influence; more alarming, opinion polls suggested that the previous year's flip-flops had seriously undermined the MRF's appeal among voters, with some suggesting that the MRF would even fail to surpass the 4 percent threshold in the scheduled December 1994 election.[67] To repair the damage, the party's leadership proceeded along two lines. First, Dogan began to make concerted overtures to the MRF's former coalition partner, the UDF. In a letter to the UDF parliamentary caucus on February 22, 1994, Dogan proposed a resurrection of the previous alliance between the parties, citing his concern over the progress of economic and political reforms and the "recommunization" of Bulgarian society. However, the UDF was lukewarm in its response, and its chairman, Fillip Dimitrov, initially rebuffed these efforts and ruled out any form of dialogue until after the December election.[68] Second, the MRF leadership began to sharpen its demands for Turkish language rights, particularly in the military. In July, Dogan called for the use of Turkish in Bulgarian military units in which ethnic Turks served. More ominously, he was reported as stating that ethnic Turks should disobey orders in the event that Bulgarian was made the exclusive and compulsory language of the military.[69]

Despite these attempts to recoup the losses of the previous year, the parliamentary elections of December 1994 were an unqualified disaster for the MRF. Voter dissatisfaction with the MRF's reversals was evident when the party received only 5.4 percent of the vote, down from 7.5 percent three years earlier, and only thirteen seats, eleven fewer than in 1991.[70] More important, the MRF lost its crucial position as the balancer in the Bulgarian Parliament. The BSP won an absolute majority of seats in the National Assembly and was now free to govern alone. The MRF also lost its strategic position as the third-largest party in the Bulgarian Parliament to the electoral alliance the Peoples Union (PU; a coalition that included the Bulgarian Agrarian Peoples' Union [BAPU] and the Democratic Party, both of which had been shut out in the 1991 election). Notably, as Table 2.4 indicates, the MRF lost considerable support in regions where there was a large concentration of ethnic Turkish voters. The largest single decline was in the strategic Kardzhali region, where the MRF had won 65.8 percent of the vote in 1991 but barely mustered half the vote in 1994 (50.5 percent).

Following the Socialist victory, the new government of Zhan Videnov made several ministerial appointments that were considered by several within the MRF as evidence of a renewed effort at assimilating the Bulgarian Turks. In particular, the appointment of Ilcho Dimitrov as educational minister in January 1995 was considered a direct affront to the MRF. Dimitrov, a historian, had been the head of the so-called Coordinating Council of the Bulgarian Academy of Sciences, which had been directly involved in the assimilation campaigns under Zhivkov. Moreover, he had never denounced the assimilation campaign. Although Dimitrov claimed that he had not taken an active part in the forceful Bulgarization campaigns, he had previously attacked the MRF as unconstitutional and harmful to the national interest. The appointment, from the perspective of the MRF leadership, was indicative of the BSP's continuing hostility toward the ethnic minorities and an attempt to further restrict Turkish language and cultural rights.[71]

The losses of 1994 and the inability to prevent the appointment of anti-Turkish ministers in the BSP government led to ever-growing dissatisfaction with the MRF leadership and particularly with Chairman Dogan himself. The leadership of the MRF met on July 22, 1995, to discuss holding an extraordinary party conference; some local leaders wanted to remove MRF Deputy Chairman Osman Oktay and Yunal Lyufti and demanded structural changes that would give localities greater voice in candidate selection. Sixteen of the twenty-two regional council chairmen urged that the conference take place in order to discuss such changes, but Dogan refused. Instead, he submitted the resignation of the entire leadership, including himself, arguing that since they had been elected collectively at the party's second conference in 1993, they could only resign collectively. The internal opposition had to back down because if the entire leadership resigned, the MRF would have to reregister as a party, and in all likelihood (given the BSP's control of the registration process), the party would be unable to take part in the fall local elections if registration were delayed for any reason.[72]

Having skillfully survived the crisis, Dogan set out to rebuild the political stature of the MRF. First, the party approached the other opposition parties. Initially, the UDF had been somewhat reluctant to cooperate with the MRF since it had already come to an agreement with the PU to jointly nominate candidates for county and city mayoralties and to coordinate their national campaigns. Finally, the UDF, the PU, and the MRF agreed to sign a memorandum on joint action in the fall 1995 local elections. The agreement allowed local opposition organizations to jointly nominate candidates for mayoral elections, although the UDF leadership said it would not sign an agreement with the MRF for cooperation at the national level.[73] However, following the first round of voting on October 29, 1995, talks began among the leaders of the UDF, the PU, and the MRF to discuss a nationwide agreement concerning cooperation in the second round of voting. In Sofia the PU withdrew its candidates in favor of the UDF candidates. In the ethnically mixed regions of the northeast and the southeast, the UDF supported MRF candidates.[74]

The results of the local elections showed some improvement in the fortunes of the MRF when compared to the December 1994 parliamentary election. The percentage of the popular vote the MRF received increased from about 5.4 percent in 1994 to 8.2 percent of the vote in the municipal legislative elections of October 1995. Moreover, the MRF actually increased the number of county mayoral seats it won, from twenty-five to twenty-six (see Table 2.5). Thus the strategy of cooperation with the other opposition parties had benefited the MRF. However, the electoral campaign illustrated the increased pressures on the MRF to move vigorously to defend itself and the Turkish community from the BSP onslaught. This, in turn, caused the MRF to adopt harsher and more ethnocentric rhetoric, a far cry from its earlier denials that it was an ethnic party. This was demonstrated quite clearly in the mayoral election campaign in the city of Kardzhali.

Kardzhali is the center of one of the two areas with a compact ethnic Turkish population in Bulgaria, although the town itself is almost equally populated by ethnic Bulgarians and ethnic Turks. In 1991, the MRF candidate from the region had won the mayoral election. Keeping the seat was

Table 2.5   Mayoralties of County Seats, Bulgaria, 1991 and 1995

Party	1991 % (No.)	1995 % (No.)
BSP	47.24 (120)	76.47 (195)
UDF	37.0 (94)	6.27[a] (16)
MRF	9.84 (25)	10.20 (26)
Others[b]	5.91 (15)	7.06 (18)

Sources: The October 13, 1991, Legislative and Municipal Elections in Bulgaria; Krause, "Elections Reveal Blue Cities amid Red Provinces."

Notes: a. The UDF and the PU combined forces to sponsor several joint candidates. Figure combines UDF and PU candidates.

b. Other parties in the 1991 local elections included the Bulgarian Agrarian Peoples' Union–Ekoglasnost or BAPU-E (10 seats), the Bulgarian Agrarian Peoples' Union–Nikolai Petkov or BAPU-NP (4), and the UDF Center (1).

considered vitally important for MRF chair Dogan, who considered the Kardzhali seat a key to the MRF's reconstruction after the 1994 debacle. The BSP, for its part, wanted to take the town for itself.

The campaign was marked by a great degree of controversy. The MRF continually accused the local security authorities, who answered directly to the BSP-appointed ultranationalist Bulgarian governor of the Haskoy region, Angel Nayedonov, of systematically threatening local Turkish voters, warning them not to be "too active" in the local campaign.[75] On the other side, the BSP charged that the MRF had bought off Turkish voters, and local nationalist parties, including the FPL, called on all Bulgarian voters in the city to vote to prevent the election of an ethnic Turkish mayor.

Two figures emerged from the first round of the election as the leading candidates; the MRF's Rasim Musa (46.1 percent) and the BSP's Georgi Georgiev (33.2 percent). In the November 12 runoff, the smaller Bulgarian nationalist parties threw their support behind Georgiev, and the UDF decided to support Musa. Musa won the second round of the election by a scant 658 votes. On November 17, the BSP petitioned the Kardzhali city court to invalidate the election on the grounds that 731 people had been imported from constituencies outside of Kardzhali and had illegally voted for Musa.[76] Although the municipal electoral commission declared the elections valid and the regional court in Kardzhali rejected the BSP petition, Nayedonov refused to confirm Musa's election or to convene a meeting of the city council.[77] At the end of January 1996, the BSP-led government declared the election in Kardzhali annulled, which led to several demonstrations in protest of the action.[78]

The election in Kardzhali served to sharpen the MRF's campaign rhetoric. Dogan, for instance, had threatened that he would turn the MRF into a purely ethnic Turkish party (in direct challenge to the constitution) if the Bulgarian parties united against the MRF candidate in Kardzhali. Following the election, the MRF again made several thinly veiled threats. An MRF statement accused the BSP of trying to create tension in the ethnically mixed region and argued that "any attempt to invalidate the election results in Kardzhali in a Balkan manner will return like a boomerang on Bulgaria and its people."[79]

Following the annulment of the election results, the situation grew worse. At a press conference on December 5, Dogan said the Kardzhali crisis demonstrated that the BSP was "prepared to play the nationalist card" and was exploiting nationalist fears to achieve political ends. However, despite the heightening of tensions that resulted from the Kardzhali crisis, Dogan was quite careful to not paint the situation solely in interethnic terms, preferring to depict the crisis as injurious to the whole of Bulgaria. Thus, at a rally of 6,000 ethnic Turks on February 17 in Kardzhali protesting the annulment of the local election of the city council and mayor after the elections, Dogan warned, "If this house catches fire, everything will burn down."[80]

Eventually, the Kardzhali crisis passed, as the ability of the MRF to sustain protests waned. However, events provided new opportunities for the MRF. Bolstered by electoral victory of the UDF presidential candidate Petar Stoyanov in the fall of 1996, mass demonstrations were mounted by the opposition in the winter of 1996–1997 to protest the disastrous economic policies of the Videnov government. Ultimately, the government was forced to grant early elections in April 1997. To prepare for the campaign, Dogan and the new leader of the UDF, Ivan Kostov, agreed on March 10 to cooperate following the elections, and Dogan insisted on running separate electoral lists for the 1997 elections. Although willing to cooperate with the UDF in opposition to the Bulgarian Socialists, Dogan still sought to steer the MRF between the BSP and UDF camps. Indeed, Dogan argued that one of the reasons for not running a joint list with the UDF was his desire to not see the UDF win an absolute majority in the new Parliament lest it become intoxicated with its success and suffer the same fate as the Socialists.[81] Moreover, Dogan suggested that both the BSP and the UDF were behind police raids in Kardzhali conducted against ethnic Turkish businesspeople. So throughout the campaign, Dogan adopted the strategy used in earlier campaigns, trying to chart a middle course between the BSP and the UDF while distancing the MRF from both.[82] In the end, the MRF formed an unlikely union with a group of Monarchists called the Union for National Salvation, which supported Tsar Simeon as the heir to the Bulgarian throne.

Dogan's reluctance to cooperate with the UDF against the despised BSP again sparked internal protest within the ranks of the MRF. In March, MRF chapters in the northern parts of Bulgaria met in Razgrad and voted to support a move sponsored by parliamentarian Giuner Tahir to independently form a Turkish organization that would fall under the UDF umbrella. This group, the Initiative Committee for Renewal, condemned Dogan's refusal to merge with the UDF.[83] Yet again, despite challenges to his leadership, Dogan survived, and the MRF did remarkably well in the April election, winning 7.6 percent of the vote, as well as nineteen seats.

Thus, despite considerable pressures built up against it, the MRF has survived four national parliamentary elections and has recovered from its losses in 1994. Moreover, Ahmed Dogan's position (at the time of this writing) appears to be relatively secure. To a large extent, the MRF has become a permanent part of the Bulgarian party system and will likely remain an important political force in Bulgarian politics for the foreseeable future.

DISCUSSION AND CONCLUSION

The evolution of the MRF in Bulgaria since the collapse of the Communist regime represents a case of an ethnopolitical party that largely follows an accommodationist course, making every effort to present itself as a non-ethnic party designed to serve all national ethnic groups, even though the overwhelming majority of its leadership and membership is made up of a specific ethnicity. Moreover, the MRF has thus far been primarily concerned with expanding the Bulgarian Turkish community's share of government outputs (as with any output-oriented party), rather than with replacing the existing authorities or reconfiguring the political system. Indeed, the MRF has made great efforts to cooperate with whoever is in power, even to the extent of cooperating with the political descendants of the much-hated Zhivkov regime. However, although the MRF leadership has publicly renounced violence and constantly points to Bosnia as an example of what can happen when arms are taken up in defense of minorities, the party has become increasingly willing to stage mass demonstrations to protest the actions of the current Socialist government, rather than to rely wholly on parliamentary means to advance its cause.

Nonetheless, as stated above, the MRF represents a classic case of an accommodationist ethnopolitical party. And this is so despite the fact that there was a considerable amount of pent-up frustration over the previous Zhivkov regime on the part of the Bulgarian Turkish population (contrary to Expectation 1 in Chapter 1) and despite the economic hardship encountered in the post-Communist era by the largely agrarian Bulgarian Turkish population, which was most affected by the severance of Bulgaria's economic ties with the CMEA (contrary to Expectations 2a and 2b). Moreover, despite the fact that Bulgaria has suffered more than any other East European state as a result of the termination of the CMEA, this has not led to the rise of extremist behavior on the part of the MRF (contrary to Expectation 3).

Yet the above review of the Bulgarian case does suggest that the scope of representation (Expectation 4a) and the structure of competition (Expectation 5) affected the behavior of the MRF. In particular, the fact that the MRF not only was able to gain a significant amount of representation in Parliament, but that it also played the pivotal role as the major balancing force between the BSP and the UDF afforded the leadership of the MRF much greater influence on policy than had been expected. This influence was also strengthened by the MRF facing little competition for the allegiance of the Turkish population (largely due to the law that forbade the participation of ethnic parties, which the MRF cleverly circumvented) and by the weak (albeit quite vocal) representation in government of the anti-Turkish Bulgarian nationalists. Taken together, these conditions allowed the MRF leadership to pursue a moderate and accommodationist approach to the BSP and the UDF (both of which needed the MRF in order to govern); from 1990 to 1994 the party had little to fear from either anti-Turkish parties or potential competitors for Turkish votes.

Another explanation for the relatively moderate strategy adopted by the MRF is that it remains one of the more internally diverse ethnopolitical parties in Eastern Europe. Although the party is heavily Turkish, represented within the MRF leadership are not only ethnic Turks, but Pomaks and Bulgarians as well. Further, especially until 1994, the MRF represented a broad coalition of Bulgarian Turkish politicians, ranging from those who favored some form of national-cultural autonomy to those who wished to maintain the commitment to "multiethnic" principles, a heterogeneity that in part was due to the fact that the MRF was the only party representing ethnic Turks that could legally exist. To placate the various groups within the MRF, the leadership under Dogan has skillfully charted a middle course, making relatively more forceful demands on the cultural front (particularly over language issues) while categorically rejecting any demands for cultural or political autonomy and distancing itself from more "radical" politicians.

Yet despite the relatively moderate course initially charted by the MRF leadership, since the parliamentary election of 1994, the party under Dogan has moved toward a more confrontational position vis-à-vis the BSP-led government. In particular, the loss of the role as balancer between the UDF and the BSP reduced the influence of the MRF on the course of Bulgarian politics. Moreover, the outright victory of the BSP in 1994 meant that the MRF could no longer dictate the course of governmental policy regarding minority populations, nor could it prevent a renewed assault on the Turkish community and Turkish language rights that was expected under the BSP-led government. Indeed, the appointment of key officials in the Videnov cabinet who had been associated with the Zhivkov policies of the past, coupled with the Kardzhali incident in 1996 following the local elections, signaled the weakness of the position of the MRF. It also signaled the beginning of a new effort to redefine the organization as the primary party defending the rights of the Turkish community in Bulgaria.

NOTES

1. Crampton, *A Short History of Modern Bulgaria*; McIntyre, *Bulgaria*; Bell, *The Bulgarian Communist Party*; Simsir, *The Turks*.
2. Simsir, *The Turks*, 208.
3. Ibid.
4. Ashley, "Ethnic Unrest," 4–11.
5. Engelbrekt, "The Movement for Rights and Freedoms," 5.
6. Quoted in Perry, "The New Prime Minister," 9–10.
7. Bulgarian Telegraphic Agency (hereafter referred to as BTA), September 23, 1991.
8. Rose and Haerpfer, *Adapting to Transformation in Eastern Europe*, question 28; Rose and Haerpfer, *New Democracies Barometer III*, question 69.
9. Gradev, "Bulgaria," 56–67.
10. Ashley, "Ethnic Unrest," 8; Nikolaev, "Property of Bulgarian Turks."
11. Ashley, "Ethnic Unrest," 7.
12. *Koi Kak've*, 74–75.
13. Engelbrekt, "The Movement for Rights and Freedoms," 5.
14. *Koi Kak've*, 75.
15. Engelbrekt, "The Movement for Rights and Freedoms," 5–6.
16. "Turkish Party 'Balancing Centrist Factor,'" BTA in Foreign Broadcast Information Service–Eastern Europe (hereafter referred to as FBIS-EEU), June 6, 1990.
17. In April 1991, in an interview with Oktay, Kjell Engelbrekt reports that Oktay claimed that the MRF's registered membership was about 120,000 (Engelbrekt, "The Movement for Rights and Freedoms," 6).
18. Ibid.
19. Ibid.
20. Wyzan, "Bulgaria," 532–533; Lampe, *The Bulgarian Economy*, 139–155.
21. OECD, *Bulgaria*, 99–101.
22. Phillipa Fletcher, "Bulgarian Party Rallies Ethnic Turkish Electorate," Reuters News Service, December 15, 1995; Kjell Engelbrekt, "Bulgarian Turks Leave," *RFE/RL Daily Report*, July 23, 1992.
23. Interview with Dogan reported in *Prava I Svobodi*, no. 41 (October 14, 1993): 1–2.
24. "Dogan: Civil War If BSP Assumes Power," 1993, 2, in FBIS-EEU, March 24, 1993, 4–5.

25. Engelbrekt, "Movement for Rights and Freedoms to Compete in Elections," 1–5.

26. Interview with FPL chair Popov in *Duma*, May 20, 1992, 2; see also interview with Bulgarian National Radical Party chair Georgiev, "We Are Struggling for Christian Values Against the Offensives of Islam," *Ostchestven Vestnik*, February 4, 1993, in FBIS-EEU, February 10, 1993, 10.

27. Engelbrekt, "Nationalism Reviving," 2.

28. BTA, October 24, 1991.

29. Quoted in Engelbrekt, "Movement for Rights and Freedoms to Compete in Elections," 2.

30. Ibid., 5.

31. Engelbrekt, "Nationalism Reviving," 6.

32. BTA in FBIS-EEU, October 20, 1990.

33. "Turkish Party 'Balancing Centrist Factor,'" in FBIS-EEU, June 7, 1990, 6–7; "Dogan Advocates Peaceful Ethnic Coexistence," BTA, November 5, 1990, in FBIS-EEU, November 6, 1990, 6.

34. BTA, November 5, 1990, in FBIS-EEU, November 6, 1990, 6.

35. "Ethnic Turk Movement States Position in Assembly," in FBIS-EEU, October 1, 1990, 22.

36. Bugajski, *Ethnic Politics in Eastern Europe*, 250.

37. Nikolaev, "The New Noncommunist Government," 2.

38. "MRF Leader Explains Anti-Government Vote," in *Trud*, July 25, 1992, 1–2, in FBIS-EEU, July 31, 1992, 31.

39. Kjell Engelbrekt "Bulgarian Cabinet Fends Off No-Confidence Vote," *RFE/RL Daily Report*, July 27, 1992.

40. Duncan Perry, "Bulgarian Parliamentary Troubles," *RFE/RL Daily Report*, September 24, 1992.

41. Kjell Engelbrekt, "Pressure Increasing on Bulgarian Government," *RFE/RL Daily Report*, October 4, 1992.

42. BTA, September 21, 1992.

43. Kjell Engelbrekt, "Bulgarian Turks Suggest Coalition Cabinet," *RFE/RL Daily Report*, November 12, 1992; Kjell Engelbrekt, "MRF Demands Posts in New Bulgarian Cabinet," *RFE/RL Daily Report*, November 16, 1992.

44. Kjell Engelbrekt, "BSP Candidate Declines Offer to Form Cabinet," *RFE/RL Daily Report*, December 2, 1992.

45. Konstantinov, "Gift for Mr. Dogan," 6.

46. *Demokratsiya*, March 20, 1993, 1; *Demokratsiya*, March 22, 1993, 1.

47. Kjell Engelbrekt, "Minority Leader Critical of Bulgarian Socialist Party," *RFE/RL Daily Report*, September 10, 1993.

48. Kjell Engelbrekt, "Bulgaria's MRF Party Dissatisfied with Cabinet," *RFE/RL Daily Report*, February 16, 1994.

49. "Ethnic Isolation Tendencies in MRF Assessed," in *Faks*, June 24, 1991, 1–2, in FBIS-EEU, June 28, 1991, 4.

50. Ibid., 4–5.

51. "Official Register of Political Parties Detailed," in FBIS-EEU, July 31, 1992, 3–6.

52. "Turkish Minority to Back Opposition in Elections," in FBIS-EEU, June 7, 1990, 7.

53. *Duma*, November 23, 1992, 1.

54. "Establishment of Turkish Democratic Party Detailed," *24 Chasa*, December 14, 1992, 2.

55. "New Turkish Party Seen Helping MRF Image," in *Kontinent*, December 14, 1992, 6, in FBIS-EEU, December 16, 1992, 11.

56. "Ethnic Turkish Parties Reportedly Proliferate," BTA, January 12, 1993, in FBIS-EEU, January 13, 1993, 18–19.

57. "MRF Spokesman Warns of Islamic Expansion," BTA, February 24, 1993, in FBIS-EEU, February 24, 1993, 3

58. "Ahmed Dogan Discusses MRF Priorities," in *Trud*, January 5, 1993, 1–3, in FBIS-EEU, January 12, 1993, 14–16.

59. Interview with Dogan in *Trud*, in FBIS-EEU, January 13, 1993, 17–18.

60. Interview with Dogan by Radio Free Europe, in *Prava I Svobodi*, no. 41 (October 14, 1993): 1–2.

61. Kjell Engelbrekt, "Dogan Reaffirmed as MRF Leader," *RFE/RL Daily Report*, November 29, 1993; Kjell Engelbrekt, "Former Bulgarian Intelligence Official Says Dogan Ex-Agent," *RFE/RL Daily Report*, November 5, 1992.

62. In particular, parliamentary spokesperson Sherife Mustafa and Deputy Chairman Osman Oktay were both accused of accepting bribes. Dogan, as well, was accused of receiving moneys from the Kameya company, which had provided transport for criminals who had committed acts of "barbarism" during the Bulgarization campaign of the 1980s.

63. "Mehmed Hodzha Discusses MRF Leadership," in *Kontinent*, August 15, 1994, in FBIS-EEU, August 17, 1994, 3; Kjell Engelbrekt, "Bulgaria's MRF Party Dissatisfied with Cabinet," *RFE/RL Daily Report*, February 16, 1994.

64. "Former MRF Deputies Form New Party," in *Kontinent*, March 30, 1994, 1, in FBIS-EEU, April 2, 1994, 4–5.

65. "MRF Council to Continue Support of Cabinet," in FBIS-EEU, February 13, 1994, 7–8.

66. "MRF Official Explains Party Views," *Standart News*, October 24, 1994, 23.

67. Konstantin Subev, "Each to His Own People," in *Kontinent*, August 15, 1994, 4, in FBIS-EEU, August 17, 1994, 3.

68. Kjell Engelbrekt, "Bulgaria: UDF 'Postpones' Dialogue with Ethnic Turkish Party," *RFE/RL Daily Report,* March 2, 1994.

69. BTA, July 5, 1994.

70. Englebrekt, "Political Turmoil," 19–22.

71. Stephen Krause, "Bulgarian Education Minister Still Under Fire," *OMRI Daily Digest*, January 31, 1995.

72. Stephen Krause, "Leaders of Bulgarian Ethnic Turkish Party Meet," *OMRI Daily Digest*, July 24, 1995.

73. Stephen Krause, "Bulgarian Opposition Agrees to Sign Election Memorandum," *OMRI Daily Digest*, June 16, 1995.

74. Stephen Krause, "Bulgarian Opposition Prepares for Cooperation in Local Elections," *OMRI Daily Digest*, November 1, 1995.

75. Stephen Krause, "Ethnic Turkish Party in Bulgaria Claims Police Threatened Its Voters," *OMRI Daily Digest*, November 8, 1995.

76. Stephen Krause, "Bulgarian Socialists Want to Invalidate Mayoral Election," *OMRI Daily Digest*, November 20, 1995.

77. Stephen Krause, "Bulgarian Ethnic Turkish Party Asks President for Help," *OMRI Daily Digest*, November 29, 1995.

78. Stephen Krause, "Bulgarian Ethnic Turks Protest Annulment of Kardzhali Elections," *OMRI Daily Digest*, February 19, 1996.

79. Krause, "Bulgarian Socialists Want to Invalidate Mayoral Election"; Krause, "Bulgarian Ethnic Turkish Party Asks President for Help."

80. Quoted in Krause "Bulgarian Ethnic Turks Protest Annulment of Kardzhali Elections."

81. "Separate Electoral Lists for Bulgarian Parties," *OMRI Daily Digest,* March 15, 1997.

82. "Bulgarian Election Update," RFE/RL Newsline, April 15, 1997.

83. "Bulgarian Election News," RFE/RL Newsline, April 8, 1997.

3

The Hungarian Parties in Slovakia

The collapse of the Czechoslovak Communist regime after the Velvet Revolution of December 1989 marked not only the end of one of the most Stalinist systems in Eastern Europe, but also the revival of the political activism and aspirations of the Hungarian minority population in Slovakia. Since the dissolution of the Czechoslovak federation in 1992, Slovakia's Hungarian minority, with an active and very vocal political leadership, has succeeded in drawing international attention to the plight of ethnic Hungarians in the country.

Unlike in Bulgaria, where the incorporation of ethnic Turkish representation in the political process led to the moderation of the MRF's political demands (but ultimately also to the emergence of political fissures within the movement), in Slovakia, the ethnic Hungarians were originally divided into several groups and three major political parties—Coexistence (Együttélés), the Hungarian Christian Democratic Movement (HCDM), and the Hungarian Civic Party (HCP). At first, the Hungarian parties cooperated easily with the anti-Communist Slovak parties. For instance, in the June 1990 parliamentary elections, the HCP (at that time called the Hungarian Independent Initiative) ran on the ticket of the umbrella anti-Communist alliance the Public Against Violence (PAV). After the electoral victory of the PAV, the party was awarded a ministerial portfolio in the Slovak cabinet. The other major parties, Coexistence and HCDM, formed a coalition in 1990 and received 8.64 percent of the vote and fourteen seats in the Slovak Parliament. Unlike the HCP and the HCDM, Coexistence (as was the case with the MRF in Bulgaria) presented itself not as a Hungarian ethnic party, but as a party that would represent all minorities in Czechoslovakia, including Poles and Germans.

So while a single organization emerged to represent the ethnic Turks in Bulgaria, several parties have emerged in Slovakia that claim to represent the Slovak Hungarian minority. Although later, in 1994, the Hungarian parties overcame their differences and formed a common electoral front, this front did not moderate its demands, but increased its call for a number of legislative changes that would grant political autonomy for Hungarians in Slovakia, along with greater cultural, educational, and language rights. These demands sparked a negative reaction by many Slovaks who argued that the legal rights of ethnic Hungarians in Slovakia were already far above those granted to minority populations in the West. This has resulted in the emergence of growing mistrust and political tension between the ethnic Slovak and Hungarian communities.

Why has it been the case that the evolution of the Hungarian Slovak parties has differed so greatly from that of the MRF in Bulgaria? For, as we shall demonstrate shortly, the historical, economic, demographic, and political pressures on the Hungarian population in Slovakia were similar to those experienced by the Turkish population in Bulgaria. But this alone cannot explain the growing radicalization of the demands made by the Hungarian political parties. What, then, are the primary factors that account for these demands in Slovakia?

To address this question the following sections will first identify the various pressures affecting the Hungarian parties in Slovakia. Second, we will identify the political opportunities presented by the structural features of the post-Communist Czechoslovak and the postindependence Slovakian political systems, as well as the structure of competition the Hungarian parties faced. It is the contention of this chapter that the political opportunities presented by the Czechoslovak and then the Slovakian political systems, along with the structure of competition, have provided the incentive for the radicalization of the demands of the Hungarian ethnopolitical parties.

HISTORICAL BACKGROUND

Hungary ruled over what is now Slovakia for more than 1,000 years until the new state of Czechoslovakia was created following World War I. For the first 800 years, Slovaks and Magyars coexisted in relative harmony. The histories of both people were interlocked. After the Turkish occupation of the Hungarian plain following the battle of Mohacs in 1526 and the transfer of the core of the Hungarian kingdom to Slovakia, the political class of the Hungarian kingdom remained Magyar. However, the Hungarian kingdom now ruled over a population that was Slovak speaking. Although much of the Magyar nobility learned to speak Slovak and identified with Slovak culture, there was really no linguistic or national equality.[1] For Slovaks, individual social advancement meant learning Magyar and ultimately assimilating the traditions and practices of the Magyar nobility.

In the nineteenth century, with the rise of Hungarian nationalism and the struggle for political independence from the Hapsburg Empire, Hungarian rule in Slovakia was marked by the adoption of an official policy for the Magyarization of the Slovak population. Magyarization not only became a requirement for membership in the Hungarian state, but also for participation in its political life. In the revolutionary years of 1848–1849, the Slovak leadership sided with the Hapsburg authorities in suppressing the Hungarian rebellion; thereafter, Slovakian cultural and political aspirations became identified as diametrically opposed to Hungarian nationalism. Thus, after the infamous Austro-Hungarian compromise, Ausgliech, which created the Austro-Hungarian Empire, the Magyarization of the Slovak population was pursued with special ferocity. In particular, as C. A. Macartney notes, the focus was on the Magyarization of the educational system, the intent of which was to ensure that "all members of society at the peasant-worker level should at least speak and understand Magyar."[2] Magyarization, therefore, largely severed the linkages between Slovak nationalist elites and the Slovak-speaking masses. In turn, this stunted the development of the Slovak nationalist movement. As Joseph Kalvoda notes:

> While the Czechs had a full range of well-organized political parties reflecting class and ideological divisions in the nation, the Slovak National Party was a loose political organization of leaders without a mass following. The party's representation in the Budapest parliament consisted of three deputies before World War I, and it shrunk to just one after the declaration of war. . . . Although the policy of Magyarization affected all the national minorities living in Hungary, the nationally and politically conscious Slovaks were on the verge of extinction when the war began.[3]

Thus, with the collapse of the Central Powers in the fall of 1918, the Slovak nationalists were in no position to operate independently. The Slovak National Party readily agreed in October to cooperate with Czech nationalists in the Czech National Committee, and together they proclaimed Czechoslovak independence on October 28, 1918. However, during the years of the interwar republic, coexistence between the Slovak and the Czech nationalists became increasingly less satisfactory for Slovak nationalists. "Czechoslovakism," the official ideology of the Czech-dominated interwar republic, held that Czech and Slovak were in reality two branches of one nation and two dialects of one language. In reaction, Slovak nationalists became increasingly extreme in the 1920s and 1930s, giving rise to a protofascist movement led by former priest Andrej Hlinka, which later became the core of the Nazi collaborationist regime in Slovakia after 1939. This program of Czechoslovakization, however, was also directed at the 634,000 Hungarians (21.5 percent of the population of

Slovakia in 1920; see Table 3.1) left by the territorial revisions made by the Treaty of Trianon, most of whom were concentrated in western Slovakia.

With the Communist coup in 1948 and the establishment of a central-ized economic and political system, the new authorities, who staunchly op-posed any effort at regional autonomy for minorities, continued the policy of Czechoslovakizing the Hungarian minority. Although "official Hungar-ians" and other minority populations (particularly, Ruthenians and Ukrainians) were granted the legal right to operate their own schools, newspapers, and cultural associations in the 1960s, these activities were strictly supervised by the Communist Party of Czechoslovakia (CPCS). With the coming of the Prague Spring in 1968, restrictions on the opera-tion of cultural and educational facilities were loosened, and there was even some discussion of granting a measure of Hungarian autonomy within a loosened Czech and Slovak federation. However, following the suppression of the reforms with the Soviet intervention in 1968, the au-thorities under the Soviet-installed general secretary of the CPCS, Gustav Husak, reversed these policies and renewed the drive toward the creation of a purely Czech and Slovak state, an effort that continued throughout the 1970s and 1980s.

Following the collapse of the Communist regime in 1989, pressures emerged very rapidly—pressures that drove the Czech and Slovak Re-publics apart. Once the common enemy had been vanquished, several par-ties whose existence had been defined in terms of opposition to the Com-munist regime were left to search for a new raison d'être. Some parties, such as the Slovak National Party, had already adopted a proseparatist po-litical platform and had fared well in the parliamentary election of 1990 after using ultranationalist (and often anti-Hungarian) rhetoric.[4] Through-out 1990, several other Slovak political parties began to take up the banner of self-determination and accused the Czechoslovak federal government of ignoring the painful effects economic reform was having on Slovakia. The

Table 3.1 Ethnic Composition of Slovakia, 1920–1991

Ethnic Groups	1920 Population	%	1930 Population	%	1961 Population	%	1991 Population	%
Slovak	1,941,942	65.7	2,224,983	68.4	3,560,216	85.3	4,511,679	85.6
Hungarian	634,827	21.5	571,988	17.6	518,782	12.4	566,741	10.8
Czech	71,733	2.4	120,926	3.7	45,721	1.1	53,422	1.0
German	139,880	4.8	147,501	4.5	6,259	0.2	5,629	0.1
Ruthenian	85,628	2.9	91,079	2.8	35,435	0.8	16,937	0.3
Others	81,988	2.8	97,712	3.0	110,822	2.7	114,527	2.2
Total minorities	1,014,056	34.3	1,029,206	31.6	717,019	17.2	757,256	14.4

Slovak Christian Democratic Movement (CDM) embraced a more nationalist line shortly after the general elections of June 1990 and had clearly benefited from this stance; the CDM defeated the ruling PAV in the local governmental elections in the fall of 1990 and was ranked as the strongest political force in the country in opinion polls at the beginning of 1991. This prompted growing centrifugal trends in the heretofore profederalist PAV, culminating in the secession of Vladimir Meciar and the creation of the overtly Slovak nationalist Movement for a Democratic Slovakia (MDS) in March 1991.

The parliamentary election of 1992 further exacerbated the growing divide between the Czech and Slovak parts of the federation. Although opinion polls indicated that the majority of Slovaks favored the maintenance of the federation, proindependence forces had scored well in the second post-Communist parliamentary elections. By the summer of 1992, for all intents and purposes, two distinct and separate party systems had emerged in the Czech and Slovak Republics.[5] With little to bind them together, the Slovak and Czech parties went their separate ways, and by the fall of 1992, the Czech government of Vaclav Klaus agreed to a formal division of the country. On January 1, 1993, the newly independent states of the Czech Republic and Slovakia were declared.

Caught in the middle of this disintegrative process were the Hungarian parties in Slovakia. The principal Hungarian party, Coexistence, had gained representation at both the federal level and in the Slovak National Council, and it had pressed since 1990 for the expansion of Hungarian educational and cultural rights, as well as for some degree of autonomy within a loosened Czechoslovak federation. The Hungarian parties viewed with suspicion the Slovak drive for independence, fearful that the rising tide of Slovak nationalism would lead to future restrictions and discrimination against the Hungarian minority should Slovakia become independent. These parties were also uniformly alarmed by the success of the more extreme Slovak nationalist parties, particularly the Slovak National Party itself, and the latter's growing ties with the MDS. Although the MDS had toned down its anti-Hungarian rhetoric in 1992 after the replacement of Vitazoslav Moric in 1991 with the more moderate Josef Prokes, the Slovak National Party continued to contend that the Hungarian parties were in league with Budapest and that together they harbored secret aspirations to reunify Hungarian-inhabited areas of Slovakia in a "Greater Hungary."[6]

THE HUNGARIAN PARTIES

Three entities comprise the major Hungarian parties in Slovakia: Coexistence, the Hungarian Civic Party, and the Hungarian Christian Democratic

Movement; accompanying them are two other minor Hungarian parties. Coexistence, the largest of the parties, had been formerly known as the Forum of Hungarians in Czechoslovakia and was founded in February 1990 by the prominent dissident and Hungarian national rights activist Miklós Duray. In 1978, Duray, a geologist, had founded the Independent Committee for the Protection of Hungarian Minority Rights in Czechoslovakia. The committee had been organized initially to resist the Czechoslovak Communist government's decision to close down the Hungarian schools and to introduce an almost exclusively Slovak curriculum in the 1970s. Duray had been arrested twice, first in 1978 and again in 1983, for "agitating national minorities."[7] In his first trial, which gained a considerable amount of international attention, Duray engaged in a spirited self-defense, and he was freed from imprisonment. However, following the publication of his book *Kutyaszorito* (Cornered) in New York, he was arrested again in 1983 for antistate activities.

Coexistence was one of five Hungarian parties that emerged following the Velvet Revolution of 1990. The others were the above-mentioned HCDM and HCP, as well as two smaller entities, the Hungarian Peoples Party (HPP) and the Social and Democratic Union of Hungarians in Slovakia (Socialny a Demokraticky Zvaz Mad'arov na Slovensku [SZDMS]); this latter was the successor to the sole Hungarian organization approved by the Communist regime, the Cultural Association of Hungarian Working People in Czechoslovakia (Csemadok). Initially, each of the Hungarian parties differed from the others in three important ways: (1) in the constituencies they purported to represent; (2) in their respective attitudes concerning the relationship between political and economic reform and minority rights; and (3) in their positions regarding the effects of Slovakian independence on the Hungarian population.

For its part, Coexistence originally purported to represent the interests of all minorities in Czechoslovakia, including Poles, Germans, Ukrainians, and Ruthenians, although this changed very rapidly after the declaration of Slovak independence. The party contended that the protection of minority rights took precedence over the broader process of democratization and reform, which made it the special target of the Slovak nationalists as a radical separatist Hungarian party. In terms of the party's attitude toward Slovak independence, Coexistence's leadership maintained that an independent Slovakia would be detrimental to the rights of Slovakia's minority populations, and the party strongly supported the maintenance of the Czechoslovak federation.[8] Once independence became inevitable, however, the leadership of Coexistence argued for a new administrative framework to be established in independent Slovakia, one that would recognize the cultural and administrative autonomy of Hungarian majority regions.[9] Moreover, Coexistence was quite vocal about noting the importance of Hungary in maintaining the rights of the Hungarian population in Slovakia.[10]

The second major force, the HCDM, which was founded in March 1990, grew out of the Hungarian Christian Democratic Clubs in Slovakia. The HCDM formed an electoral coalition with Coexistence for the first competitive parliamentary election in June 1990. Shortly following the election, the HCDM experienced internal conflicts over whether the party should strengthen its ties with Coexistence. Ultimately, the pro-Coexistence forces within the party were able to pressure the chairman, Béla Bugár, to pursue closer ties with Coexistence. To further unity in 1992, the political program of the HCDM was adjusted to include demands that also appeared in the Coexistence program, particularly the demands for cultural autonomy, opposition to the dissolution of the Czechoslovak federation, and the importance of Hungary in protecting the Hungarian minority in Slovakia.[11] After Slovak independence, differences emerged between the two parties, especially over the issue of Hungarian political autonomy.

The third major player, the HCP, emerged from the Hungarian Independent Initiative, which had been established in November 1989 by long-time dissidents Laszlo Nagy, Lajos Grendel, Kálmán Balla, and Károly Tóth. Originally, the party had existed under the PAV umbrella; but in the 1990 elections, the party ran as part of the PAV list and won a total of six seats in the Slovak National Council. Like Coexistence, HCP traces its origins to Duray's Independent Committee for the Protection of Hungarian Minority Rights in Czechoslovakia. However, unlike Coexistence and the HCDM, the leadership of HCP argued that democratization must precede the drive to fully gain Hungarian group rights and generally opposed the demand for territorial-political autonomy for the Hungarian community in Slovakia. Relations between Coexistence and the HCP prior to Slovak independence were strained at best. The leaders of the Coexistence and HCDM coalition (particularly Duray) viewed the HCP as essentially a collaborationist party. For its part, the HCP considered the radical demands of Coexistence as an invitation for the dangerous reaction of antidemocratic forces in the Slovak community.[12] Despite the HCP being the most moderate of the Hungarian parties in Slovakia, Slovak parties have been reluctant to cooperate with it for fear that such behavior may cost them politically. In 1992, for instance, the PAV refused to extend coalition partnership to the HCP because the PAV leadership reckoned that allowing its predecessor (the Hungarian Independent Initiative) a place on the movement's list had cost the PAV 20,000 votes.[13]

Two other noteworthy Hungarian organizations emerged during 1990–1992; the first was the HPP, founded in December 1991 by historian and former member of Coexistence Gyula Popély. The HPP was the only party to argue that Slovak independence would have a positive effect on the

Hungarian minority; an independent Slovakia, it claimed, was the lesser of two evils when compared to the antidemocratic Czechoslovakia.[14] The HPP, however, remained small and ineffectual. In the 1992 elections, the party could not muster the 10,000 signatures required under the electoral law to place its label on the ballot, although it was able to include its candidates on the Coexistence and HCDM lists.[15] The second organization was the SZDMS, the descendant of the "official" Hungarian organization during the Communist period. Although its leader, Gyozo Bauer, publicly stated that the movement does "not want to interfere in politics," its avid defense of Hungarian language and educational rights has aligned the movement with Coexistence.[16]

ECONOMIC FACTORS

The economic challenges the Slovak Republic has faced as a newly independent state are largely the result of the economic policies of the previous Communist regime. Under Communist rule, industrial investment expanded rapidly in Slovakia, somewhat mitigating the gap that had traditionally existed between the Slovak and Czech economies. However, the development of Slovak industry was pursued by constructing large heavy-industrial enterprises, particularly in metalworking and machine building, as well as the construction of numerous large armaments factories. By the late 1980s, defense-sector plants accounted for 6 percent of Slovak industrial output, and more than 80 percent of this output was earmarked for export.

The collapse of the Communist regime in 1989 was followed by the adoption of a series of economic reforms by the Czechoslovak federal government, which were implemented in 1991. These included price liberalization and the introduction of the now well-known voucher method of large-scale privatization. The shift to price liberalization and to world market prices was particularly injurious to the Slovak economy. The collapse of the CMEA forced the Slovak Republic to pay higher prices for Soviet oil and natural gas imports from 1991 onward, which damaged the heavy-industrial base of the Slovak economy. Further, with the dissolution of the Warsaw Pact and the ban imposed by the Czechoslovak federal government on weapons exports to the developing world, the Slovak armaments industry suffered badly.[17] Although it was hoped that privatization would make available investment funds for retooling Slovak industry, Slovak investors were more interested in investing in Czech firms, and Czechs showed very little interest in purchasing shares in Slovak firms.[18]

The net result, as in other Eastern European economies in transition (such as Bulgaria), was widespread unemployment and the contraction of

Table 3.2   Macroeconomic Indicators and Degree of Regional Integration, Slovakia, 1990–1995

	1990	1991	1992	1993	1994	1995
Change in real GDP	−2.5	−11.2	−7.0	−6.5	4.8	7.0
Gross industrial production	−4.0	−25.4	−13.7	−13.5	6.7	n.a.
Gross agricultural production	−7.2	−7.4	−13.9	−15.9	n.a.	n.a.
Unemployment	1.5	11.8	10.4	14.2	14.5	n.a.
Inflation	10.4	61.2	10.0	25.1	14.0	9.9
Real industrial wages (1990 = 100)	100	72	68	65	85	n.a.
Exports (% of total)						
To EC/EU	n.a.	n.a.	17.2	n.a.	n.a.	n.a.
To Russia and Eastern Europe	n.a.	71.4	63.8	42.5	n.a.	n.a.
Imports (% of total)						
From EC/EU	n.a.	n.a.	16.7	n.a.	n.a.	n.a.
From Russia and Eastern Europe	n.a.	77.3	71.4	n.a.	n.a.	n.a.

Source: Hardt and Kaufman, eds., *East Central European Economies.*

the economy. Unemployment rates in Slovakia were similar to those reported in Bulgaria (see Table 2.2), with the highest unemployment occurring in areas that were most dependent on the armaments trade: Rimskava Sobota (21.6 percent), Michalovce (20.4), Roznova (19.9), Orlova (20.0), and Velky Krtis (20.0). The lowest rates were reported in Bratislava (4.3), Trncin (7.7), Mikulas (8.1), and Kosice (8.4). The transition had a particularly damaging effect on the Slovak Hungarian population. As indicated in Table 3.3, unemployment rates in districts with a large ethnic Hungarian population have been generally higher than in other districts.

POLITICAL INCENTIVES

Two features of the post-Communist Czechoslovakian system and the post-independence Slovakian political system had a great influence on the development and evolution of the Hungarian parties in Slovakia. The first was the federal nature of the Czechoslovak state. Indeed, of all the countries of Eastern Europe, Czechoslovakia was nearest to the structural arrangements characteristic of the consociational solution. Federalism had been an innovation introduced during the reforms of the Dubcek era that had survived the post-1968 repression. The election law was based on the list proportional representation system used during the interwar republic, albeit with modification. In part, this was due to the perceived necessity of

Table 3.3   Unemployment Rates and Hungarian Population in Selected Districts, Slovakia, 1992–1994

| | % Unemployment | | | % Population |
District	1992	1993	1994	Hungarian
Bratislava-vidiek	9.6	13.3	11.3	7.7
Dunajska Streda	16.3	20.4	20.9	89.0
Galanta	14.9	19.9	21.1	46.6
Komarno	12.7	21.7	20.6	72.4
Levice	11.8	16.6	18.2	35.7
Nitra	12.6	14.7	16.9	8.6
Novy Zamoy	11.3	17.8	19.0	42.2
Lucenec	14.3	20.3	22.5	24.1
Rimskava Sobota	16.6	26.4	29.4	48.4
Velky Krtis	13.8	21.7	20.0	35.1
Kosice-vidiek	16.5	22.6	25.4	13.7
Roznava	17.0	28.0	24.7	13.6
Trebisov	19.3	19.6	16.6	40.9
Average for Hungarian and mixed districts	13.3	20.2	19.0	n.a.
Average for all other districts	10.5	14.9	15.6	n.a.

Sources: Szlovakiai jelentes, *A magyar kisebbseg allapotarol, 74; Statisticka Rocenka Slovenskej republiky, 1994,* 460–462, 478; *Statisticka Rocenka Slovenskej republiky, 1995,* 529.

quickly implementing a rapid transition to democratic government, as well as establishing a measure of continuity with the first Czechoslovak Republic.[19]

While the scope of representation was tempered to some extent by the use of a 5 percent threshold, the threshold was established for each republic separately, rather than for the federation as a whole. This meant that the effective barrier a party had to pass was lower than if a federation-wide 5 percent barrier had existed. Further, the threshold for election to the republican Slovak National Council was only 3 percent, as compared to the 5 percent threshold established for the Czech National Council. As indicated in Table 3.4 this arrangement made it possible for ethnic parties to gain representation by concentrating on only individual republics. This was evidenced by election results for the Slovak National Party and Coexistence, which ran only in the Slovak Republic. Although the former received only 3.5 percent of the total federation vote for the House of the People and 3.88 percent for the House of the Nations, it received sufficient concentrated support in the Slovak Republic to surpass the 5 percent barrier within that republic and hence gain a voice at the federal level.

The quality of representation, based as it was on the use of party lists and ethnically homogeneous federal states, promoted group competition over individual competition. Thus, the quality of representation led to the emergence of politicians who pursued an ethnically based political agenda

Table 3.4   Slovak National Council Election Results, 1990–1994

Party	1990		1992		1994		
	% Vote	% Seats (No.)	% Vote	% Seats (No.)	% Seats in Sept. 1994 (No.)	% Vote	% Seats (No.)
PAV	29.3	32.0 (48)	—	—	—	—	—
MDS	—	—	37.2	49.3 (74)	35.3 (53)	35.0	40.7 (61)
CDM	19.2	20.7 (31)	8.9	12.0 (18)	12.0 (18)	10.1	11.3 (17)
CPCS	13.3	14.7 (22)	—	—	—	—	—
PDL/CC[a]	—	—	14.7	19.3 (29)	18.7 (28)	10.4	12.0 (18)
Slovik National Party	13.9	14.7 (22)	7.9	10.0 (15)	6.0 (9)	5.4	6.0 (9)
Coexistence	8.6	9.3 (14)	7.4	9.3 (14)	8.0 (12)	—	—
HC[b] (Együtélés, HCDM, HCP)	—	—	—	—	—	10.2	11.3 (17)
Democratic Party	4.4	4.7 (7)	<5	—	—	—	—
DU[c]	—	—	—	—	12.7 (19)	8.6	10.0 (15)
Greens	3.5	4.0 (6)	<5	—	—	<5	—
SWA[d]	—	—	—	—	0.6 (1)	7.3	8.7 (13)

Sources: Statisticka Rocenka Slovenskej republiky, 1994, 460–462, 478; *Statisticka Rocenka Slovenskej republiky,* 1995.
Notes: a. PDL/CC = Party of the Democratic Left/Common Choice.
b. HC = Hungarian Coalition.
c. DU = Democratic Union.
d. SWA = Slovak Workers Association.

because emphasizing group differences proved to be an effective way of winning seats. This was especially true in the Slovak Republic, particularly as the adverse effects of market reforms on the Slovak economy became increasingly apparent from 1990 to 1991. Although the Czechoslovak election of 1992 established additional thresholds of 7 percent for coalitions consisting of two to three parties and 10 percent for coalitions of four or more parties, the initial establishment of ethnic party representation placed Hungarian-Slovak relations clearly on the political agenda. Moreover, as David Olson notes, federalism and the electoral law essentially converted the initial "country-wide elections into Republic-centric contests," which provided a strong incentive for politically affiliated parties to run as separate organizations in the two republics.[20] In sum, the incentives generated by the representational mechanisms in turn created the incentives that affected the development of the transitional parties, which itself paved the way for the centrifugation of Czechoslovak politics.

An additional environmental factor that has impacted the evolution and behavior of the Hungarian parties is the structure of competition they have faced. Indeed, the character of the structure of competition created a sufficient degree of threat to compel the various Hungarian parties to forge an alliance. In particular, the growing strength of anti-Hungarian sentiment provided opportunities for more politically radical elements to take the lead in the Hungarian Coalition (HC; Madyardska Koalicio) and steer the coalition in the direction of more direct political demands.

Two developments contributed to this trend: the radicalization of the Slovak National Party in 1994 and the growing nationalism of the overall Slovak party system. In January 1994, the National Party voted to oust its moderate chairman, Ludovit Cernek, and replace him with ultranationalist Jan Slota. More ominously, the party voted to politically rehabilitate its virulently nationalist first chairman, Vitazoslav Moric.[21] Upon his ascendance as chairman, Slota proclaimed that the Slovak National Party had been "purified" and declared his party's wholehearted support for the government of Vladimir Meciar.[22] Slota then called for Pan-Slavic cooperation and generally questioned the need for Slovakia to join the North Atlantic Treaty Organization (NATO).[23]

The first Slovak parliamentary election following independence was held in October 1994. As with the previous 1990 and 1992 elections, the 1994 election was governed by a list proportional representation system based on a 5 percent threshold in four large-mandate electoral districts: Bratislava, West Slovakia, Central Slovakia, and East Slovakia. In comparing the results of the 1994 election with the results from 1992, several observations concerning the structure of competition can be made. First, the Slovak nationalist coalition of Meciar's MDS and the Slovak National Party did much better than expected. The MDS captured sixty-one seats in the election—down from the seventy-four it had won in 1992, but up eight seats from the number the party controlled just prior to the 1994 election (see Table 3.5). Further, its major coalition partner, the Slovak National Party, maintained the same number of seats (nine). Following the election, the two formed a governing coalition with the ultraleft-populist Slovak Workers Association (SWA). The biggest losers in the election were the Communist-successor Party of the Democratic Left (PDL) and the Democratic Union (DU), both of which had been the most in favor of a "multiethnic" Slovakia and most opposed to the efforts by the Meciar government to revise the language law. Thus, following the 1994 election, the government was firmly in the hands of the parties that

Table 3.5 Slovak National Council Election Results by Region, 1994

Party/Coalition	% Vote All Regions	Total No. of Seats Allocated	% Vote Bratislava	No. of Seats Allocated	% Vote West Slovakia	No. of Seats Allocated	% Vote Central Slovakia	No. of Seats Allocated	% Vote East Slovakia	No. of Seats Allocated
MDS/AP Coalition	34.96	61 (40.67%)	25.44	4	33.56	19	44.35	24	28.71	14
MDS		58		4		18		23		13
AP[a]		3		0		1		1		1
CC	10.41	18 (12.0%)	13.88	2	9.39	7	8.66	3	12.62	6
PDL		13		2		7		3		3
SSDP[b]		2		0		5		0		1
Greens		2		0		1		0		1
Movement of Peasants Party		1				1				
HC	10.18	17 (11.33%)	3.41	0	20.71	12	4.51	2	5.99	3
Coexistence		9		0		5		2		3
HCDM		7				6		2		2
HCP		1				1		0		1
CDM	10.08	17 (11.33%)	12.42	1	8.14	4	8.18	4	13.91	0
DU	8.57	15 (10.0%)	18.40	2	6.45	3	7.86	5	9.02	8
SWA	7.34	13 (8.67%)	3.99	0	5.48	4	7.74	4	10.14	5
Slovak National Party	5.40	9 (6.0%)	9.11	2	5.53	3	6.57	3	2.79	5
Others	12.95	0	13.26	0	10.74	0	12.13	0	16.82	1
Total	100	150	100	11	100	52	100	45	100	42

Sources: Narodna Obroda, October 6, 1994, 2, in FBIS-EEU, October 4, 1994, 14–15; Abraham, "Early Elections in Slovakia."
Notes: a. AP = Agrarian Party.
b. SSDP = Slovak Social Democratic Party.

represented the greatest threat to the political aspirations of the Slovak Hungarian parties.

THE EVOLUTION OF THE HUNGARIAN PARTIES

Unlike the Turkish political movement in Bulgaria, the Hungarian movement in Slovakia did not begin organizationally unified. In the case of the MRF, Ahmed Dogan retained his position as the single most recognizable and vocal Turkish politician in Bulgaria; but in Slovakia, there were several identifiable leaders of the Hungarian movement, each of which had his own political base. Further, each of the major parties represented different political constituencies in the Hungarian community: The HCP tended to consist of intellectuals; Coexistence had a more working-class constituency; and the HCDM was rooted in the Hungarian Catholic community, having grown out of the Hungarian Christian Democratic Clubs that had emerged just prior to the collapse of Communist rule. In sum, unlike the Bulgarian Turkish movement, the various political strands in the Hungarian community were more clearly articulated. Considering this disunity, coupled with numerous personality conflicts, it was little wonder that the Hungarian movement was fraught with internal disputes and a marked degree of fragmentation throughout 1990–1992.

Slovak independence changed all of this. Initially, the establishment of an independent Slovak state was met by the Hungarian parties with varying degrees of trepidation. Bugár, of the HCDM, remarked that independence brought with it a sense of anxiety within the Hungarian community in Slovakia—an anxiety that was justified "in part because many recall the Slovak state during the war, and in part because independent Slovakia has the same government that showed little understanding for people of other nationalities during the past six months."[24] Nagy, head of the HCP, saw the potential for increased tension yet also the possibility of accommodation in the new regime.[25] Duray, of Coexistence, was most optimistic. Although he did not view the new Slovak government in favorable terms, he saw the coming of Slovak independence as presenting "a huge opportunity" to reorder the existing political framework along the lines of "a compromise that could not be reached either in the framework of the Austro-Hungarian monarchy or in Czechoslovakia."[26]

Throughout 1993, however, the situation facing the Hungarian parties grew progressively worse. Several top officials in the ruling MDS accused the Hungarian parties of threatening violence against ethnic Slovaks in such Hungarian majority regions as Dunjaská Streda. Prime Minister Meciar began to direct rather harsh rhetoric against Coexistence, the HCDM, and the HCP, accusing them of being "purely nationalistic" and completely heedless to Slovakia's needs.[27] For their part, the Hungarian parties in unison complained of the pervasiveness of anti-Hungarian discrimination under the Meciar government in Slovak political life, noting the virtual absence of Hungarian representation in the national ministries of the new Slovak state. They accused Meciar of promoting policies that were even more exclusionary than those "in the period of socialism."[28]

As a result, the Hungarian parties moved to more closely coordinate their actions. To combat what they viewed as the growing nationalist, and hence anti-Hungarian, orientation of the Meciar government, they appealed collectively to the international community to intervene on their behalf. Thus, when Slovakia applied for admission to the Council of Europe along with the Czech Republic in June 1993 (Czechoslovakia had been a member), Coexistence, the HCDM, the HCP, and the HPP sent a joint memorandum to the Council requesting that Slovakia's admission be delayed until Bratislava ratified the European Charter on Regional and Minority Languages and complied with the Council's Recommendation 1201. The latter provision called for the establishment of autonomous authorities where a national minority was in the local majority, but this was not issued as a condition for membership in the Council.[29] In particular, they requested that the Slovak Republic be required to revise the 1990 Slovak language law, which, although permitting use of the minority language in official dealings in communities where the minority comprised at least 20 percent of the population, did not provide for the use of bilingual town and village signs in those regions. Further, they demanded that the Hungarians in Slovakia be allowed to register birth names in Magyar (a 1950 Czechoslovak law had forbidden this) and called for the abolition of Czechoslovakia's infamous 1945 decrees, issued by President Eduard Benes, which had assigned collective guilt for war crimes to the country's Hungarian and German minorities.

At this time, the right-wing government of Jozef Antall, the Hungarian prime minister, emerged as the champion of the Hungarian community in Slovakia. Hungary, which was already a member of the Council of Europe, threatened to veto Slovakia's membership if Bratislava did not draft legislation that would grant the demands made by the Slovak Hungarian parties. Slovak-Hungarian relations had already been strained by the controversial Gabricikovo Dam project and by remarks made by Antall himself when he declared in 1990 that he was prime minister "in spirit" of all fifteen million Hungarians, including those outside of Hungary. Although Budapest was convinced by other Council members to abstain on the vote to admit the Czech Republic and Slovakia, this came only after assurances that Bratislava would comply with the Council recommendations. However, the legislation to provide for Hungarian language signs was vetoed by President Michal Kovac under pressure from Prime Minister Meciar. In response, Hungary refused to sign a bilateral treaty with Slovakia that would guarantee existing borders until the Slovak government guaranteed the "basic rights" of ethnic Hungarians in Slovakia. Hungarian Foreign Minister Geza Jeszensky went so far as to suggest that Slovakia be reorganized administratively into "ethnic cantons."[30]

Tensions within Slovakia also intensified from 1993 to 1994. Some worried that the government policy was creating a "Nagorno-Karabakh in Slovakia" and pointed to polls indicating that Hungarians in southern Slovakia were increasingly advocating political autonomy. Whereas in 1990, only 7 percent of Hungarians in Slovakia had favored political autonomy, by September 1993, 45 percent supported a fundamental political reorganization of the country. Emboldened by these figures on December 7, the HCDM-Coexistence coalition and other local Hungarian groups held a "historic meeting" in the border town of Komarno for the purpose of establishing a "self-administering" Hungarian province with a "special legal status" within Slovakia. Further, the meeting moved to elect a 100-member alternative assembly and called for united opposition to the current Meciar government, which "was leading the minorities to ruin."[31] In particular, the assembly condemned the government proposal made in early January 1993 to reorganize the country's principal political arrangement into eight new regions, drawing the borders such that Hungarians would be a less than 20 percent minority in each region, thus de facto nullifying the 1990 language law. On January 8, 1994, about 3,000 protesters in Komarno called for "self-government."[32]

Following the meeting in Komarno, a storm of criticism was directed against the meeting organizers, which included opposition Slovak parties that had cooperated with the Hungarian parties in Parliament, as well as leaders of other Hungarian organizations. In particular, the leadership of the HCP declared that the Komarno meeting did not reflect the opinion of most Hungarians in Slovakia and that minority problems could be solved only within the existing Parliament, not in "extra-parliamentary forums."[33] This storm of criticism caused HCDM leader Bugár to disassociate his party from the call for territorial autonomy, claiming that the statements issued at Komarno reflected the opinion of Coexistence leader Duray only and not of the HCDM-Coexistence coalition.[34] Moreover, Bugár categorically denied that the demand for territorial autonomy meant the establishment of "ethnic borders" and distanced himself from the originator of the call for self-government, the mayor of Komarno, Stepan Pasztor.[35] Pal Csaky, the parliamentary fraction chair of the HCDM, also went to great lengths to condemn the call for political autonomy, labeling the demands "ill-conceived."[36]

Despite these disagreements, the Hungarian parties began to move in the direction of unifying their respective organizations into a single Hungarian political movement. The leadership of the HCP issued a call in February

1994 for the formation of a three-party coalition among itself, Coexistence, and the HCDM, a proposal to which Duray responded favorably. To a large extent, the move toward greater cooperation among the three main Hungarian parties was motivated not only by a common antipathy toward the Meciar government, but also by the opportunity to oust that government brought on by the defection of several dissident MDS and Slovak National Party factions from the governing coalition. In March 1994, the Hungarian parties together supported a vote of no-confidence lodged against the minority government, and Meciar was ousted as prime minister.

The new left-of-center coalition government that took over from Meciar's was led by the chairman of the DU, Jozef Moravcik. The DU was made up of three breakaway factions from the MDS and the Slovak National Party. Together with members from the CDM and the PDL, then, the government that succeeded Meciar's was basically a five-party coalition; it functioned with the tacit support of the fourteen deputies of the two Hungarian parties in Parliament. Under Moravcik, interethnic tensions declined, particularly after the passage of two laws granting rights that had been supported by the Hungarian parties: the recognition of Hungarian names on official birth registries and the provision of bilingual signs.[37] In addition, political changes in Hungary contributed to the reduction of tensions. In May 1994, the Hungarian Democratic Forum lost the general election to the Hungarian Socialist Party, and Gyula Horn, an ex-Communist, became the new prime minister. Upon his election, the new Hungarian government immediately sought to normalize relations with its neighbors and hastened to complete the bilateral treaty with Slovakia.[38]

Despite these developments, the attitude of the Hungarian parties vis-à-vis the Moravcik government remained ambivalent. The HCDM, and Bugár in particular, was generally hesitant to pressure the Moravcik government for greater concessions out of fear that this might provide the MDS and the Slovak National Party, now in opposition, with political fodder for the future. The HCP was also positively disposed toward the government.[39] However, Coexistence began to lobby for ministerial posts in the new government and warned that the "vote of no-confidence against Meciar was not connected with support" for Moravcik.[40] Moreover, Duray complained openly that the government was not doing enough to help minorities in Slovakia and contended that support for the Moravcik government was only temporary.[41]

Although the next parliamentary elections were not scheduled until June 1996, one of the governmental coalition partners, the ex-Communist PDL, insisted on holding new elections as quickly as possible. This demand was motivated by the desire to establish a popular mandate for the coalition, as well as by the PDL's expectation that it would improve its political position (and hence its position in the coalition) if earlier elections were held.[42] New elections were scheduled for October 1, 1994.

As the election approached, a certain degree of anxiety began to emerge among the Hungarian parties. Bugár fully expected that the Slovak National Party and the MDS would attempt "to exploit the issue of ethnic minorities in their election campaign. They will be taking advantage of every step of the government in order to demonstrate who is 'the savior of the nation' and who 'protects the Slovak nation against the Hungarians.'"[43] Duray expected the "political tranquility we have in Slovakia right now to end with the start of the election campaign."[44] Nagy also expected that the MDS and the Slovak National Party would seek to "intensify Slovak-Hungarian tension."[45] Further, the Hungarian parties could not count on the other parties to consistently support them, even the PDL, which was attempting to woo Hungarian voters by including ethnic Hungarians on its electoral list. Indeed, as HPP chair Popély noted, "Every Slovak party would lose popularity in the eyes of Slovak voters if they cooperated with us."[46]

As the election approached, the idea of forming a single Hungarian electoral coalition gained increasing momentum. In April 1994, the Coexistence leadership proposed a "union" of all Hungarian parties, calling for a commitment by the HCDM and the HCP to form a joint deputies' group in Parliament, to put forward a joint candidate list in the parliamentary election in October, and to create joint local government and foreign affairs councils.[47] The HCP reacted positively to this call in May 1994, stressing that the party wanted to avoid the fate it had suffered in the 1992 election when it had been shut out of the Slovak National Council. HCP spokesperson Kalman Petocz called for the formation of a political union that "would be the sole legal entity within which the present parties could operate only as . . . factions."[48] But the HCDM, which had cooperated with Coexistence in running joint candidate lists in 1990 and 1992, was rather lukewarm in its response to the proposal for a single unified Hungarian party, arguing that it was simply "not feasible before the elections." As Béla Bugár noted, "The Hungarian parties had a chance to prove that they are able to cooperate. They have been unable to accomplish this in four years."[49] Furthermore, Bugár was less than enthusiastic about the proposal to form even a common parliamentary faction, arguing that it was "far more advantageous to have two clubs than just one." He was suspicious of Coexistence's intentions and asserted that if unification came about, it would be dominated by the Coexistence agenda and would serve only "narrow party interests."[50]

Nevertheless, after several negotiating sessions, the HCDM and Coexistence agreed on July 24, 1994, to move in the direction of merging their two organizations after the parliamentary election in October. This agreement was necessary, according to Bugár, in order to fend off the Slovak nationalists' attempts to "break it up."[51] However, negotiations with the HCP were bogged down by Nagy's insistence that 25 percent of the electoral list presented by the coalition be reserved for candidates selected by the HCP. Both the HCDM and Coexistence rejected this claim as "ridiculous." Although both agreed that the HCP should be included on the coalition's electoral lists, the Coexistence National Council insisted that both its members and those of HCDM councils approve HCP candidates before their inclusion.[52] On July 21, the HCP relented on its demand for guaranteed slots on the list and finally signed the agreement to join Coexistence and the HCDM in forming the Hungarian Coalition. In subsequent weeks, the HCDM and Coexistence began to screen HCP candidates who had been proposed, forcing the HCP to remove two Central Slovakia candidates because they were considered politically unreliable and less than fully committed to the Hungarian movement.[53] To preserve harmony within the coalition, the HCP reluctantly acquiesced to the demand.[54]

The campaign itself was marked by mudslinging and a good deal of populist and antiminority rhetoric. Shortly before the election, polls indicated that Meciar's MDS would win the most votes but that the parties supporting the Moravcik government would win enough seats to fend off yet another Meciar-led government. Meciar conducted an extremely energetic campaign, however, attacking Parliament, President Kovac, and the "anti-Slovak" media, promising virtually everything to everyone. As a result of these efforts, the MDS won an impressive 35 percent of the vote, which was only about 2 percent less than what the party had received in 1992; and it won a total of sixty-one seats, three of which were assigned to its tiny electoral coalition partner, the Agrarian Party (AP)—an increase of eight over what the party had controlled in September. Thus the MDS recouped the losses it had suffered following the defection of MDS factions in the spring of 1994. Moreover, the party's past coalition partner, the Slovak National Party, held its own with 5.4 percent of the vote and nine seats, maintaining the number it had held just prior to the election. Another winner was the far-left SWA, a party whose leader, Ján Lupák, had broken with the PDL and preached a gospel of opposition to chaotic transition and the corruption of the "capitalist class."[55] Despite internal bickering, the HC fared well with 10.18 percent of the vote and seventeen seats in the new Parliament. The biggest losers in the election were the parties that had comprised the core of the Moravcik government: the DU; the CDM; and the Common Choice (CC) coalition of the PDL, the Slovak Social Democratic Party (SSDP), the Greens, and the Movement of Peasants. Indeed, the CC coalition barely passed the 10 percent threshold for four-party coalitions, as required by the Slovak election law.

In terms of the regional breakdown of the vote, the HC did well in western Slovakia, as expected, where the largest number of Hungarians were concentrated (see Table 3.5 above). Within the HC, Coexistence was the single largest Hungarian party with nine seats, followed by the HCDM (seven seats) and the HCP (one seat). However, in the critical western Slovakia region, the HCDM received more mandates (six) than did Coexistence, whose mandates were more thinly spread throughout the country. The HCP received only one seat, awarded to the party's chairman, Laszlo Nagy.

Following the election, the new government engaged in a number of measures that were viewed by the Hungarian parties as fundamentally anti-Hungarian. Although the government program announced in January 1995 guaranteed minority rights on an individual basis, these rights were limited to only activities that did not threaten Slovakia's "territorial integrity." In addition, the government proclaimed that religious services in ethnically mixed areas of the country must be held in Slovak. The appointment of radical Slovak National Party deputies as the defense and education ministers further angered the Hungarian parties. Most alarming was the adoption in April by Parliament of a new law on educational administration, which allowed the Ministry of Education to remove directors of schools who were deemed incapable, providing enormous power to the Slovak National Party to direct educational policy. Education Minister Eva Slavkovska had declared that such "incapability" included lack of fluency in Slovak and announced her intent of promoting the use of the Slovak language in all public affairs. In particular, Slavkovska advocated the intensive training of Hungarian children in Slovak and that Slovak language, literature, history, geography, and civics "be taught only by ethnic Slovak teachers."[56] Additionally, state subsidies to Hungarian cultural organizations were cut, while the budgets of such rabidly nationalist Slovak cultural organizations as Matica Slovenska grew after 1994. Further, the government revived the 1993 draft law on rearranging Slovakia's regions so that the proportion of Hungarians in each district would be reduced to under 20 percent. This meant that the 1990 language law that provided for the use of minority languages in official contacts in areas where a minority makes up at least one-fifth of the population would be effectively nullified, making the use of Hungarian practically absent in public affairs.[57] Finally, as noted earlier, the ruling parties generally viewed the Hungarian parties as a potential fifth column in Slovakia, demanding in May 1996 that the Hungarian parties swear their loyalty to the Slovak constitution before any further negotiations over the rights of ethnic minorities be discussed.[58]

The Hungarian parties' reactions to the actions of the third Meciar government have been uniformly negative. Duray described the education and language laws as "atrocities"[59] and called its program "reminiscent of the plans of the German government in the 1930s."[60] Laszlo Gyurovszky, deputy chairman of the HCP, labeled the regime as "Fascistoid."[61] Laszlo Nagy called the Meciar government a "parliamentary dictatorship" and stated that the regime pursued policies that would prove disastrous for the Hungarian minority.[62] And Béla Bugár referred to the government's program as "the worst since 1948" for the national minorities in Slovakia.[63]

Despite their unanimity in opposing yet another Meciar government, the Hungarian parties appeared to be incapable of forming a common stance. In fact, shortly after the election, the HCDM reneged on the agreement to form a joint Hungarian deputies' faction in Parliament, claiming that the Hungarian population would be better served by two factions rather than one. Coexistence chair Duray called this move a "major breach" in the agreement and warned of dire consequences if the agreement were not upheld. Moreover, contrary to the preelection agreement, Coexistence, the HCDM, and the HCP ran separate slates for the mayoral and town council elections in November 1994, often in direct competition with one another. Although Coexistence finished with the most mayoralties and members of town councils of any single Hungarian party (4.66 percent and 6.3 percent, respectively), the combined HCDM and HCP totals rivaled that of Coexistence: Taken together, the more moderate Hungarian parties garnished 4.2 percent of the mayoralties and 6.2 percent of the town council seats (see Table 3.6).

In mid-March 1995, the signing of the long-awaited bilateral treaty with Hungary revealed different attitudes held by the Hungarian parties. Although all three of the parties in the Hungarian Coalition reacted favorably to the treaty, Duray was not as unconditionally supportive as were the HCDM and HCP. He openly expressed his doubts as to the sincerity of the Slovak side in implementing the treaty's provisions concerning national minorities in Slovakia.[64] Although he did not reject the treaty, he criticized the document for being ambiguous in key areas and for being "sewn very carelessly."[65] Earlier, at the Fifth Congress of Coexistence in Dunajská Streda, Duray had warned that if the Council of Europe's recommendation for self-administration was not upheld as part of the treaty, then Coexistence would call for "territorial autonomy."[66] He added that the current

Table 3.6 **Hungarian Mayoralties and Town Council Seats by Party, Slovakia, November 1994**

Party	Mayors		Members of Town Councils	
	Number	% Share	Number	% Share
Coexistence	131	4.66	2,215	6.30
HCDM	56	1.99	1,367	3.89
HCP	62	2.21	812	2.31
HPP	—	—	3	0.01

Source: Statisticka Rocenka Slovenskej republiky, 1995, 511.

Slovak Republic was not democratic and that only through territorial autonomy would it be possible to create a democratic self-adminstrative system: "If we cannot do it for all of Slovakia then let us do it at least for a part of it."[67] For its part, the HCDM, although critical of the government's actions, generally limited its demands to cultural and educational rights, carefully denying that the Hungarian movement as a whole sought territorial or political autonomy.[68]

The differences among the Hungarian parties became even more evident as 1995 progressed. For instance, upon returning from a visit to the United States in July 1995 where they met with U.S. government officials, Duray, Bugár, and Nagy jointly proclaimed that the United States was prepared to act to protect the Hungarian minority in Slovakia. Duray in particular claimed that the United States was willing to consider removing Slovakia from NATO's Partnership for Peace program if the country did not continue with the democratization process, a claim the United States later emphatically denied.[69] Shortly thereafter, Duray linked the future of the Slovakian Hungarians with the fate of a Greater Hungary and warned of an international coalition involving Slovakia, Romania, and Serbia uniting "against the Hungarian people." At a meeting of the World Union of Hungarians at Debrecen, Hungary, he proclaimed that the draft language law in Slovakia was akin to "cultural Fascism"[70] and likened the conditions of Hungarians in Slovakia to those of Nazi death camps.[71] In November, Duray compared the Slovak cabinet to the assassins who took the life of Israeli Prime Minister Yitzhak Rabin.[72] Duray's rhetoric became increasingly shrill toward the end of 1995, which smacked of a degree of paranoia; he stated repeatedly that he was being secretly investigated by the Slovak security service, a claim that his colleagues viewed with much skepticism.[73]

Indeed, Duray's behavior in his relations with his ostensible Hungarian Coalition colleagues has also been quite erratic. After being highly criticized for comments following his visit to the United States, for instance, he surprised everyone by apologizing on behalf of the Hungarian movement to both the United States and the Slovak cabinet for these comments without consulting either Bugár or Nagy. Some observers suggested that Duray was maneuvering to curry the favor of moderate Slovaks and appear as the most reasonable of the three Hungarian leaders; others, including Nagy, wondered whether Duray had come to some secret agreement with Meciar. Whatever the case, Bugár and Nagy jointly condemned Duray's actions and noted that "the fact that Miklós Duray took a specific initiative upon himself is neither normal nor correct."[74] Yet shortly after this episode, Duray renewed his call for territorial autonomy and "self-administration," an approach that the HCDM chair publicly labeled as "unconstructive." Although, in Bugár's opinion, cultural and educational autonomy "clearly belong in the hands of the minorities" and comprise a realizable goal, "the demand for territorial autonomy does not solve our problems, even though some Hungarian politicians [i.e., Duray] keep voicing it more frequently."[75]

Bugár and Nagy have both become increasingly critical of their supposed coalition partner Duray: The former deemed Duray's dramatic comments "ill-considered " and "deplorable," remarking that such statements would only "make things more difficult"; and the latter added that such rhetoric would only provide ammunition for the Slovak nationalists to use "for a campaign not just against the Coexistence chairman but against the entire Hungarian coalition and against Hungarians in Slovakia." Despite this criticism, Duray refused to apologize to his compatriots for his comments and questioned the ultimate intentions and loyalties of his coalition partners.[76]

At the beginning of 1996, then, the Hungarian parties remained as divided as ever. Although increasingly isolated both domestically and abroad, the HC failed to provide a united front in the face of an increasingly aggressive Slovak government. The major impediments to unity included the lack of coordination and the clash of personalities. Yet the potential for the greater radicalization of the Hungarian movement remains a very real possibility for the future. As Sharon Fisher has noted, "some fear that if the Slovak government continues to disregard the demands of minorities events like the Debrecen meeting will become more commonplace, and Hungarian politicians will grow more radical. If that should happen, the demands made on Slovakia may grow to the point that the government can no longer handle them." Indeed, over time, the "Hungarian minority issue promises to remain a point of contention . . . at least until Slovaks grow more secure in their identity and are comfortable with their new-found statehood."[77]

DISCUSSION AND CONCLUSION

The evolution of the Hungarian parties in Slovakia since the Velvet Revolution stands in stark contrast to that of the MRF in Bulgaria. Rather than one party, there have been at least three that have played a major role in the Hungarian political movement in Slovakia. Attempts at forming a unified ethnopolitical party have largely failed, even in the face of increasing Slovak nationalist influence in government. Much of the responsibility for this lack of unity can be attributed to the fact that all of the three major parties—Coexistence, the HCDM, and the HCP—have largely followed very different programs, with Coexistence the most assertive in demanding political autonomy, and the HCDM and the HCP much less so. Indeed, Coexistence, more than any other Hungarian party, has exhibited characteristics that correspond to the profile of an antiregime party, or one that focuses on changing the political and constitutional principles and structures regulating the manner in which decisions are made. In particular, the leader of Coexistence, Miklós Duray, has consistently pressed for territorial political autonomy for Hungarian majority regions in Slovakia. At times, Duray has even questioned the legitimacy of the post-Communist political regime, especially after the victory of the Slovak nationalists in the election of 1994. In contrast, the HCDM and the HCP, both of which fared well in the local elections of November 1994, have generally limited their efforts to criticizing the existing political authorities, rather than calling for a reorientation of the political system. Thus their behavior corresponds to that of antiauthority parties.

Why has it been the case that despite a similar proportional share of the population (around 10 percent of the total) and similar patterns of past repression and current economic decline, the Bulgarian and Slovakian cases represent very different patterns in the development of ethnopolitical parties? More specifically, why has it been the case that the Slovak Hungarian parties appear incapable of forming a coherent Hungarian political organization? And why do the Hungarian parties in Slovakia appear on the whole to be more radical than the MRF in Bulgaria? The answer to these questions lies with the development of the Hungarian parties prior to the democratic transition, the structure of competition, and the posttransition scope of representation.

First, unlike the MRF in Bulgaria, which had basically been the only unified organization representing ethnic Turks prior to the transition, there were three major Hungarian parties already organizationally in place at the time of the transition. These organizations represented very different constituencies, with Coexistence appealing to working-class Hungarians, the HCP to intellectuals and former anti-Communist dissidents, and the HCDM to members of the Hungarian Christian Democratic Clubs, which had operated independently of Duray's committee. In addition, unlike in Bulgaria, where the single personality of Ahmed Dogan has dominated the MRF, there are several Hungarian leaders in Slovakia with relatively equal dissident and anti-Communist credentials. In other words, in Slovakia, no single leader has dominated the Hungarian political movement as Dogan has dominated that of Bulgaria.

Second, the fact that the constitution specifically forbidding the formation of an ethnic political party in Bulgaria was adopted *after* the formation of the MRF meant that *despite* the existence of a proportional representation election law that provided incentives for the entrance of competitors, the MRF has no competitors of which to speak. Thus, the MRF has had a virtual monopoly on representing ethnic Turks in Bulgaria.

In Slovakia, on the other hand, no such prohibition exists, and the use of PR means that there is always a strong incentive for the various Hungarian parties to remain organizationally independent. Hence, there are many parties in Slovakia purporting to represent the Hungarian population and standing in competition with one another.

In general, however, all of the Hungarian parties in Slovakia have made demands that are relatively more radical than those made by the MRF. There are several reasons for this difference. First, in the initial elections, the MRF was able to not only gain a significant amount of representation in Parliament, but it also played a pivotal role as the major balancing force between the BSP and the UDF. This afforded the leadership of the MRF much greater influence on policy than had been expected. In Slovakia, conversely, the Hungarian parties that have gained representation in the Slovak National Council (i.e., Coexistence and the HCDM) have played only a marginal role in policy and have not had the parliamentary strength to block important legislation such as the language law and the proposal for regional restructuring. Indeed, quite unlike Bulgaria's MRF that has actively been courted as a coalition partner, the Hungarian parties in Slovakia represent pariahs with which even the most moderate of the Slovak parties have been reluctant to cooperate.[78] Moreover, in Bulgaria, overtly Bulgarian nationalist and anti-Turkish parties have been only weakly represented in government; but in Slovakia, Slovak nationalists dominate the political process. Coupled with the current Hungarian Socialist government's seeming disinterest in promoting the interests of Hungarians outside of Hungary, the Slovak Hungarian parties are isolated and marginalized and face the threat of renewed intolerant Slovak nationalism alone. Thus, it is little wonder that the Slovak Hungarian parties, even the most moderate ones, have pressed their demands for some form of regional autonomy.

On the issue of the scope of representation, Bulgaria and Slovakia likewise differ. In Bulgaria, the MRF remains one of the more internally diverse ethnopolitical parties in Eastern Europe; in Slovakia, the Hungarian parties are exclusively Hungarian (despite Coexistence's claim to be otherwise). This is due, to a large extent, to the preference of other minority groups—particularly the Roma—to form their own political organizations, rather than affiliate with parties that purport to represent minority populations in general. But the opportunities created by the proportional representation electoral system and the lack of any restriction on the formation of ethnic parties have made the appeal for an all-minority party in Slovakia a hollow one. Whereas internal heterogeneity has limited the MRF in terms of making demands that will appeal to many minorities (which excludes the demand for territorial autonomy) lest certain groups defect from it, the Slovakian Hungarian parties are not so limited. Hence, the more radical demand for territorial autonomy has become part of the agenda for Hungarian political parties.

NOTES

1. Kirschbaum, *A History of Slovakia.*

2. Macartney, *Hungary,* 183–187; Seton-Watson, *History of Czechs and Slovaks.*

3. Kalvoda, "National Minorities in Czechoslovakia," 110.

4. D. Olson, "Political Parties and the 1992 Election," 311; Pehe, "Political Conflict in Slovakia," 1–6.

5. D. Olson, "Political Parties and the 1992 Election," 312.

6. Ishiyama, "Representational Mechanisms."

7. Kostya, *Northern Hungary,* 175–177.

8. Fisher, "Ethnic Hungarians Back Themselves into a Corner," 58–63; Oltay, "Hungarians in Slovakia."

9. See comments by Miklós Duray in *Uj Szo,* January 4, 1993, 4, in FBIS-EEU, January 7, 1993, 25–26.

10. Bencikova, "The Internal 'Enemies' of National Independence," 299.

11. Oltay, "Hungarian Minority in Slovakia."

12. *Narodna Obroda,* January 5, 1994, in FBIS-EEU, January 10, 1994, 16.

13. Bugajski, *Ethnic Politics in Eastern Europe*, 346.

14. *Uj Szo,* January 4, 1993, 4, in FBIS-EEU, February 3, 1994, 25.

15. Reisch, "Hungarian Parties Prepare."

16. See Czech Television Network (CTK), in FBIS-EEU, April 5, 1993, 27; *Republika,* April 5, 1993, 4, in FBIS-EEU, April 7, 1993, 22.

17. Blejer and Calro, eds., *Eastern Europe in Transition;* Szayna, "Defense Conversion in East Europe," 133–140.

18. Brada, "The Slovak Economy," 522.

19. A draft of this law appears in the March 7, 1990, edition of *Rude Pravo.* In 1990, Czechoslovakia was divided into twelve electoral regions (eight in the Czech Republic and four in the Slovak Republic). The Federal Assembly was comprised of 300 seats, divided into two chambers: the House of the People (with 150 members, 101 from Czech lands and 49 from Slovakia) and the House of the Nations (with 150 members, 75 from each republic). In each of the republics, there were unicameral legislatures, the Czech (200 members) and Slovak (150 members) National Councils, which were also elected on June 8–9. For both the Federal Assembly and the National Councils, all seats were elected from party lists, and additional seats were allocated according to a standard d'Hondt formula.

20. D. Olson, "Political Parties and the 1992 Election," 313.

21. Slovak Television (hereafter cited as STV), January 15, 1994, in FBIS-EEU, January 19, 1994, 17.

22. STV, February 19, 1994, in FBIS-EEU, February 22, 1994, 15.

23. *Slovenska Republika,* February 18, 1995, 1.

24. Quoted in *Uj Szo,* January 4, 1993, 4, in FBIS-EEU, February 3, 1993, 25–26.

25. Ibid.

26. Ibid.

27. Czech Television Network (CTK), March 27, 1993, in FBIS-EEU, March 31, 1993, 16.

28. See comments by Laszlo Dobos, the Coexistence deputy in the Slovak National Council, in *Narodna Obroda,* December 7, 1993, 9, in FBIS-EEU, December 17, 1993, 23.

29. Reisch, "Slovakia's Minority Policy."

30. Fisher, "Treaty Fails to End Squabbles," 3.

31. Czech Television Network (CTK), December 14, 1993, in FBIS-EEU, December 17, 1993, 24.

32. Fisher, "Treaty Fails to End Squabbles," 4. See also FBIS-EEU, December 20, 1993, 23, and STV, January 4, 1994, in FBIS-EEU, January 4, 1994, 6.

33. *Narodna Obroda,* January 5, 1994, in FBIS-EEU, January 7, 1994, 16.

34. Fisher, "Meeting of Slovakia's Hungarians"; *Slovensky Dennik,* December 29, 1993, 1, in FBIS-EEU, January 4, 1994, 6.

35. STV, January 3, 1994, in FBIS-EEU, January 4, 1994, 6; *Slovensky Dennik,* December 29, 1993, 1, in FBIS-EEU, January 4, 1994, 6.

36. Czech Television Network (CTK), December 14, 1993, in FBIS-EEU, December 15, 1993, 23–24.

37. Fisher, "Ethnic Hungarians Back Themselves into a Corner," 60.

38. *Pravda* (Bratislava), June 9, 1994, 2, in FBIS-EEU, June 14, 1994, 15.

39. *Sme*, April 5, 1994, 4, in FBIS-EEU, April 7, 1994, 10–11.

40. *Slovensky Dennik,* February 2, 1994, 1, in FBIS-EEU, February 26, 1994, 11.

41. See interview with Duray in *Sme,* March 2, 1994, and interview with Bugár, Duray, and Nagy in *Sme*, April 5, 1994, 4, both in FBIS-EEU, April 7, 1994, 10–11.

42. Fisher, "Tottering in the Aftermath of Elections," 20–25.

43. *Sme*, April 5, 1994, 4, in FBIS-EEU, April 7, 1994, 11.

44. Ibid.

45. Ibid.

46. Quoted in *Pesti Hirlap,* March 16, 1994, 9, in FBIS-EEU, March 18, 1994, 6.

47. Interview with Duray in *Sme*, June 8, 1994, 1 and 4, in FBIS-EEU, June 14, 1994, 15.

48. *Sme*, May 12, 1994, 1, in FBIS-EEU, May 16, 1994, 7.

49. Ibid.

50. *Slovensky Dennik,* June 1, 1994, 1, in FBIS-EEU, June 6, 1994, 14. See also *Uj Szo*, May 17, 1994, 4, in FBIS-EEU, July 1, 1994, 10–12.

51. Comments by Bugár reported in *Slovensky Dennik,* July 25, 1994, 2, in FBIS-EEU, June 29, 1994, 8–9.

52. *Sme*, July 11, 1994, 2, in FBIS-EEU, July 13, 1994, 9–10.

53. *Slovenska Republika,* August 1, 1994, 3, in FBIS-EEU, August 4, 1994, 9; *Sme*, August 3, 1994, 3, in FBIS-EEU, August 9, 1994, 12–13.

54. *Sme*, July 30, 1994, 2, in FBIS-EEU, August 4, 1994, 9.

55. Abraham, "Early Elections in Slovakia," 90.

56. Fisher, "Ethnic Hungarians Back Themselves into a Corner," 61.

57. *Pravda* (Bratislava), May 15, 1995, 2, in FBIS-EEU, May 17, 1995, 8.

58. Jiri Pehe, "Slovak Hungarians Asked to Sign Declaration of Loyalty," *OMRI Daily Digest,* May 14, 1996.

59. *Magyar Hirlap,* September 9, 1995, 8, in FBIS-EEU, September 13, 1995, 8.

60. *Pravda* (Bratislava), February 1, 1995, 1, cited in Fisher, "Ethnic Hungarians Back Themselves into a Corner," 61.

61. *Sme*, July 7, 1995, 2, in FBIS-EEU, July 11, 1995, 10.

62. Anna Siskova, "Congress of Hungarian Civic Party in Slovakia," *OMRI Daily Digest*, October 29, 1996.

63. *Sme*, January 26, 1995, cited in Fisher, "Tottering in the Aftermath of Elections," 21.

64. *Nepszabadsag*, March 18, 1995, 3, in FBIS-EEU, March 22, 1995, 26–27.

65. *Pravda* (Bratislava), March 23, 1995, 2, in FBIS-EEU, March 27, 1995, 26.

66. Reuters News Service, March 27, 1995.

67. *Sme*, March 31, 1995, 3, in FBIS-EEU, April 5, 1995, 20. See also interview with Jozsef Kvarda, deputy chairman of Coexistence, in *Nepszabadsag*, April 5, 1995, 3, in FBIS-EEU, April 6, 1995, 12–13.

68. See Bugár's interview in *Sme*, March 15, 1995, cited in Fisher, "Treaty Fails to End Squabbles," 6.

69. Fisher, "Ethnic Hungarians Back Themselves into a Corner," 63. See also *Narodna Obroda*, July 26, 1995, 12, in FBIS-EEU, July 31, 1995, 6, and *Sme*, July 22, 1995, 4, in FBIS-EEU, July 27, 1995, 7.

70. *Narodna Obroda*, July 24, 1995, 3, in FBIS-EEU, July 28, 1995, 14.

71. *Magyar Hirlap*, September 9, 1995, 8, in FBIS-EEU, September 13, 1995, 10.

72. *Pravda* (Bratislava), November 11, 1995, 5, in FBIS-EEU, November 15, 1995, 11.

73. *Sme*, July 24, 1995, 2, in FBIS-EEU, July 27, 1995, 8.

74. *Pravda* (Bratislava), July 28, 1995, 1 and 4, in FBIS-EEU, August 1, 1995, 5.

75. *Kurrier*, July 8, 1995, 3, in FBIS-EEU, July 10, 1995, 7.

76. *Pravda* (Bratislava), November 11, 1995, 5, in FBIS-EEU, November 15, 1995, 24.

77. Fisher, "Ethnic Hungarians Back Themselves into a Corner," 63.

78. Alaina Lemon, "Slovak Parties Discuss Conditions for Supporting Minority Government," *OMRI Daily Digest*, June 25, 1996; Sharon Fisher, " . . . And Prepares to Form Minority Government," *OMRI Daily Digest*, June 21, 1996.

4

The Russophone Parties
in Estonia and Latvia

The disintegration of the Soviet Union in December 1991 left in its wake millions of Russophone "colonists" in the former republics of the USSR.[1] Nowhere has the treatment of these populations received more international attention than in the Baltic states, particularly in Estonia and Latvia. The arduous debate over citizenship for the Russophone residents has kindled charges of racism and fascism lodged against the governments of the newly independent countries. Yet despite the obvious ethnic tensions independence has generated in Estonia and Latvia, Russophone political activism has remained rather limited. This is not to say that there has not been a concerted effort to form organizations that could express the aspirations of the Russophone population, but not to the extent that has occurred with the Bulgarian Turks and the Slovakian Hungarians.

Unlike in either Bulgaria or Slovakia, where the minority populations have been included in the political process, in postindependence Estonia and Latvia, the Russophones have been all but excluded from political life. In neither case do significant ethnopolitical parties exist that represent the Russophone population. Nevertheless, exclusion has not bred the kinds of desires expressed by the Slovak Hungarians or the Bulgarian Turks.

Why has it been the case that the evolution of the Russophone political organizations in the Baltic states differs so greatly from either that of the MRF in Bulgaria or of the Hungarian parties in Slovakia? Indeed, as will be demonstrated shortly, the historical, economic, demographic, and political pressures on the Baltic Russophone population have been even more intense than on either the Hungarian population in Slovakia or the Turkish population in Bulgaria. But this has not led to the growing radicalization of the relatively weak Russophone political parties. What, then, are the primary factors that account for the lack of radical demands made by the Russophone parties in the Baltic states? Moreover, what accounts for the differences that exist between Estonia and Latvia themselves? For the level of political activity of the Russophone population is far greater in Estonia than in Latvia, and the demands made by the organizations purporting to represent the Russophone population in the former have been far greater than in the latter.

To address these questions, as in preceding chapters, the following sections will first identify the various pressures facing the Russophone populations in Estonia and Latvia. This chapter then identifies the political opportunities presented by the structural features of the post-Soviet Baltic political systems, as well as the structure of competition these parties face. The primary contention is that the Baltic Russophones have not yet formed the identity necessary to fuel the emergence of vibrant ethnopolitical parties, largely because of the recent nature of the community in the Baltics and the persistent influence of Russian politics on the Baltic scene. However, there are major differences that distinguish the evolution of the Russophone communities in Estonia and in Latvia, making the latter more likely to produce a more radical ethnopolitical party in the future than the former.

HISTORICAL BACKGROUND

The Russophone Community in the Baltic States

The present territories of the current Baltic states (Estonia, Latvia, and Lithuania) have long been the subjects of external pressures from powerful neighbors. The eastern Baltic littoral was conquered after the Crusades, and the local pagan peoples were Christianized and reduced to servitude by the Teutonic Knights in the thirteenth century. Subsequently, the region was governed by a confederation of princely estates of the Teutonic order. After the Reformation, the Teutonic order was reduced in significance, and the Baltic lands were subjugated by the Polish-Lithuanian kingdom, then Sweden, and then finally the Russian Empire. Throughout this period, the Germanic landowning nobility and the merchants of the Hanseatic League dominated political and economic life in the area, with the local peoples enserfed.[2] The conquest of the region by Peter the Great in 1721 did little to change the dominance of the Baltic Germanic nobility, who retained their privileges and political and cultural autonomy.[3]

After the Russian conquest of the region, Russians (mainly officials, soldiers, and merchants) began to populate Estland and Livonia, but only in very small numbers. However, in the middle of the nineteenth century, the tsarist government introduced measures to Russify the region—measures designed to undermine the power and influence of the German nobility.

Russification was also accompanied by the relocation of a large number of Russian peasants into what is now Estonia and Latvia. Many of these found their way to newly industrializing cities like Riga and Tallinn. As a result, the population of Riga by 1913 was only 39.8 percent Latvian while 20 percent was ethnic Russian. The Bolshevik revolution brought more refugees to the independent Baltic states, especially white officers, Russian-speaking Jews, and others who fled Bolshevik oppression. By the end of the 1930s, both Latvia and Estonia had substantial Russian populations (see Tables 4.1 and 4.2).

With the annexation of the Baltic states by the Soviet Union following the Molotov-Ribbentrop Pact, much of the local Russian population was systematically exterminated as enemy opposition communities in exile. The German occupation from 1941 to 1944 also reduced the number of local Russians. By the end of World War II, the great majority of the Russian community in the Baltics had been liquidated, eliminating "a group

Table 4.1 Ethnic Composition of Latvia, 1920–1989

Ethnic Group	1920 (%)	1939 (%)	1959 (%)	1989 (%)	1995 (% of Group Who Are Citizens)
Latvians	74.4	75.5	62.0	52.0	98.25
Russians	10.2	10.6	26.6	34.0	37.75
Germans	3.8	3.2	0.1	0.1	25.68
Jews	—	4.8	1.8	0.9	44.67
Poles	—	2.5	2.9	2.3	60.82
Ukrainians/ Byelorussians	—	1.4	4.3	8.0	5.99/19.22
Lithuanians	—	1.2	1.5	1.3	20.31
Total minorities	25.6	24.5	38.0	48.0	—

Sources: Lieven, *The Baltic Revolution,* 433; *Latvia Human Development Report,* chap. 2.

Table 4.2 Ethnic Composition of Estonia, 1934–1989

Ethnic Group	1934 (%)	1959 (%)	1970 (%)	1989 (%)
Estonians	88.2	74.6	68.2	61.5
Russians	8.2	20.1	24.7	30.3
Germans	2.2	0	0	0
Ukrainians/ Byelorussians	—	3.0	3.7	4.9
Others	1.4	2.3	3.4	3.3
Total minorities	11.8	25.4	31.8	38.5

Source: Lieven, *The Baltic Revolution,* 434.

which might later have built bridges between the Russian and Balt[ic] communities."[4]

Following the war, a massive influx of immigrants from various parts of the USSR flooded the Baltics, which more than made up for the wartime losses in the local Russophone population. The lure of jobs and the policy of the Soviet government to dilute the Baltic population in order to strengthen Soviet loyalties led to the rapid expansion in the number of ethnic Russians and other nationalities. Thus, for instance, although 75 percent of the population was ethnic Latvian in Latvia just prior to the war, by 1989, the proportion of Latvians in the population had been reduced to just over 52 percent. Ethnic Russians accounted for 10.6 percent of the population in 1939; by 1989, this had risen to 34 percent. In Estonia, the growth of the Russian portion of the population increased less rapidly, from 20.1 percent of the population in 1939 to 30.3 percent in 1989. By 1989, ethnic Estonians accounted for only 61.5 percent of the population.

As far as the patterns of residence in Latvia for the immigrant population are concerned, immigrants settled across Latvia, concentrating mainly in the cities. By 1989, immigrants constituted a majority in six of the major cities of the country, with the exception of Jelgava, where Latvians comprised a bare majority. Immigrants made up large portions of the populations of many rural districts, particularly in the eastern part of the republic (see Table 4.3).[5] The patterns of residence in Estonia, however, were quite different. Immigrants were concentrated in Tallinn and in the northeastern region of the country, particularly around the town of Narva (Table 4.4).

The immigrant population in the Baltic republics, though, was far from being a homogeneous entity. First, not all of the immigrants were ethnic Russians: Byelorussians and Ukrainians comprised a large proportion of the immigrant population. The immigrants were further divided not only by their loyalties and their ethnic identity, but also by socioeconomic class. Russophones in the Baltic states came from both the elites and the working classes. Moreover, the Russophone immigrants were drawn from a wide variety of regions, ultimately united by only their common residence. Thus, unlike either the Turks in Bulgaria or the Hungarians in Slovakia, the Russophones in the Baltic states did not represent a long-established minority community but, rather, immigrants who had arrived in the Baltics in the post–World War II period.

Thus, the Russophones in the Baltic states did not represent a stable community with easily identifiable characteristics to set them apart as a community. The symbols that bound them together derived from their connection to the Soviet multiethnic empire. With the collapse of the Soviet Union, these ties melted away, leaving the Russophones in the Baltics "on the whole a . . . demoralized lot, flung together from all over the Soviet

Table 4.3   Resident Population in Latvia by Nationality, City, and District, 1994

City or District	Latvians (%)	Non-Latvians (%)
Cities		
Daugavpils	13.8	86.2
Jelgava	50.7	49.3
Jurmala	45.1	54.9
Liepaja	42.1	57.9
Ventspils	45.2	54.8
Rezekne	38.4	61.6
Riga	37.5	62.5
Districts		
Aizkrakles	75.4	24.6
Aluksnes	78.5	21.5
Balvu	73.7	26.3
Bauskas	70.8	29.2
Cesu	83.8	16.2
Daugavpils	37.2	62.8
Dobeles	68.0	32.0
Gulbenes	81.8	18.2
Jelgavas	63.8	36.2
Jekabpils	64.7	35.3
Kraslavas	44.2	55.8
Kuldigas	85.6	14.4
Liepajas	83.5	16.5
Limbazu	87.4	12.5
Ludzas	54.5	45.5
Madonas	85.0	15.0
Ogres	83.0	27.0
Preilu	64.9	35.1
Rezeknes	53.5	46.5
Rigas	60.9	39.1
Saldus	81.4	18.6
Talsu	90.9	9.1
Tukuma	82.2	17.8
Valkas	77.8	22.2
Valmieras	80.9	19.1
Ventspils	93.2	6.8

Source: Latvijas Statistikas Gadagramata, 1993, 56–57.

Union. . . . without any cultural institutions or much sense of community."[6] Following Baltic independence, they sought to "fill the vacuum left by the obsolescence of Soviet identity."[7] Yet their seeming continuing attachment to symbols of the Communist past existed not because of an enthusiasm for Stalinism, but because of their opposition to the "nationalist" Baltic governments. Moreover, their system of symbols provided them with a sense of identity, a set of cultural symbols that distinguished them from Russians in Russia, with whom they felt little kinship.[8]

Table 4.4   Resident Population in Estonia by Nationality, City, and District, 1994

City or District	Estonians (%)	Non-Estonians (%)
Cities		
Kohtla-Jarve City	26.4	73.6
Narva City	4.9	95.1
Parnu City	74.1	25.9
Sillimae City	4.3	95.7
Tallinn-North	40.6	59.4
Tallinn-South	46.6	53.4
Tallinn-East	62.3	37.7
Tallinn-West	56.9	43.1
Tartu City	74.4	25.6
Districts		
Haapsalu	86.5	13.5
Harju	78.3	21.7
Hiumma	95.6	4.4
Jogeva	89.0	11.0
Kingiseppa	93.8	6.2
Kohtla-Jarve	68.1	31.9
Paide	92.6	7.4
Polva	93.5	6.5
Parnu	94.6	5.4
Rakvere	88.3	11.7
Tartu	84.1	15.9
Valga	92.1	7.9
Viljandi	90.4	9.6
Voru	93.5	6.5

Source: Taagepera, "Size and Ethnicity of Estonian Towns and Rural Districts," 105–127.

The Legacy of the Transition to Independence

Estonia. The period immediately prior to independence had a profound impact on setting the postindependence political stage. During the course of the political convulsions that rocked the two republics in the last years of Soviet rule, several organizations emerged that claimed to represent the non-Baltic, and primarily Russian, part of the population. In 1989, two such organizations were founded in Estonia: Ob'edinennyi sovet trudovykh kollektivov (OSTK), or the United Council of Labor Collectives, and Internatsional'noe dvizhenie trudiashchikhsia ESSR, or the International Movement of Workers in the Estonian Soviet Socialist Republic, known as Intermovement.[9] The OSTK was an organization initially created to coordinate protests against the government's wish to place all economic activity, including industry, under the control of republican, rather than all-union, authorities. The initial focus of the movement was primarily protecting the interests of non-Estonian workers, although the OSTK was founded mainly by directors of large plants and enterprises subordinate to the all-union ministries in Moscow. Intermovement, on the other hand, concentrated not only on the protection of economic rights, but also on the broader challenges presented by the resurgence of Estonian nationalism. The leadership troika of Intermovement included Vladimir Yarovoi and Igor Shepelevich, both of whom were factory directors, and Evgenny Kogan, an engineer.[10]

During the 1989–1990 period, these groups became more politically active, moving beyond their original goal of protecting the interests of the Russophone population in the direction of overt political activity. Thus, at its constituent congress on March 4–5, 1989, in Tallinn, Intermovement attacked the Communist Party of Estonia (CPE) leadership for its tolerance of the Estonian nationalists grouped in the Popular Front of Estonia (PFE).[11] In August 1989, largely in response to the adoption of what they claimed were discriminatory residence requirements for participation in the local election of December 1989, both the OSTK and Intermovement coordinated a series of republic-wide strikes. Approximately 18,000 workers from twenty-six enterprises took part. Although only 5 percent of the republic's labor force was involved, the action not only shut down supplies for all-union ministries, but interfered with transport and other local activities.[12] Whereas the strike itself was largely unsuccessful in paralyzing the Estonian economy, it did prompt the CPE leadership to acknowledge the political clout of the Intermovement-OSTK alliance. For example, Vaino Valyas, the head of the CPE, acknowledged in September that the CPE had failed to pay sufficient attention to the complaints of Intermovement and OSTK leaders.[13]

Latvia. In Latvia, non-Latvian political activity increased throughout 1988–1990, paralleling that of Estonia. On October 18, 1988, the foundation of Interfront marked the beginning of organized activity. The organization's founding charter was penned by directors of 153 all-union enterprises in the republic.[14] Coinciding with the creation of Interfront was the foundation of the Latvian Union of Workers (Soyuz Rabochikh Latvii), which was designed to organize all-union enterprises (as the OSTK did in Estonia).[15] Moreover, as in Estonia, it was the declaration by the Latvian Supreme Soviet in favor of the establishment of republican sovereignty that intensified the political activities of Interfront. At the fifteenth, and last, session of the Eleventh Latvian Supreme Soviet in February 1990, a resolution was adopted that called for the transformation of the "Latvian SSR [Soviet Socialist Republic] into an Independent Latvia." It established a commission that would prepare a referendum on the restoration of independence and draft treaties that would define Latvia's relations with other states.[16]

The leadership of Interfront was quick to condemn the action, and the group became particularly active in the establishment of strike committees in the spring of 1990 to protest the declaration of sovereignty. On Latvian television, Ivan Lopatin, Interfront chair and Communist Party of Latvia (CPL) member of the Supreme Soviet, condemned the decision, singling out Communists who had voted in support of the action:

> Today you have acted as the party of the representatives of those bourgeois parties of the twenties. Referring to the fact that, in 1940, the people of Latvia were not asked to decide on rejoining the Soviet Union, today also without asking the opinion of the people, you have taken a decision of a similar kind, to please the new ruling class which burst through in our republic, the creative and scientific intelligentsia of the leading clique of the Popular Front of Latvia. You have blatantly trampled on the views of those in the republic who do not agree with what has been proposed and the decisions adopted today. You have deliberately made a split in our society, and let this be on the conscience of those who today voted in favor of that split. I think that we will not have long to wait for a reaction to such decisions.[17]

The Legacy of the Dissolution of the Communist Parties

The subsequent push for full independence created a crisis in the ruling republican Communist parties, which fractured along pro- and anti-independence lines. This crisis came to a head in both the CPE and the CPL following the March 1990 republican elections. Those who favored independence argued for the establishment of republican parties that were independent from the Communist Party of the Soviet Union (CPSU). This was necessary because, as the first secretary of the CPE put it, "only an independent Communist Party of Estonia can efficiently participate in the new political life of Estonia, change tactics in a flexible way, form coalitions, and compete with other parties and movements."[18] Similarly, in Latvia, the first secretary of the CPL, Jan Vagris, contended that only through a "radically renewed" CPL could the party survive as the "key coalition for political stability and democratization."[19] However, the move to establish independent party organizations ultimately led to their division into independent and CPSU loyalist parties. In Estonia, the move to establish an independent CPE at the party's Twentieth Congress at the end of March 1990, led by Mikk Titma (the CPE secretary for ideology), resulted in the majority of delegates voting to declare the CPE independent from the CPSU. Immediately following the vote, the CPE split into two—the Independent CPE organization and a second CPE consisting of CPSU loyalists. Each organization elected its own Central Committee and its own leadership. In Latvia, at the party's Twenty-fifth Congress, the CPL also split along proindependence and loyalist lines, although the majority of the delegates supported the loyalist program.[20]

However, very different outcomes resulted from the Communist parties' splits—outcomes that were to have a profound impact on the future course of interethnic political relations in the Baltic states. First, unlike in Estonia, where the bulk of the organizational resources and personnel fell into the hands of the independence-minded faction of the CPE, in Latvia, the CPSU loyalists seized the bulk of the CPL's resources and elected an archconservative leadership under Alfreds Rubiks, former first secretary of the Riga party organization and chair of the republican strike committee organized by the Latvian Interfront. Second, the party split along ethnic lines in Latvia, with the bulk of non-Latvian membership remaining in the loyalist CPL; indeed, very few non-Latvians joined the Independent CPL.[21] In Estonia, in contrast, not all party organizations that represented Russophone-dominated areas of the republic joined the loyalist part. For instance, the Narva, Sillimae, and Kohtla-Jarve CPE organizations voted to join with the Independent Communist Party of Estonia shortly after the Twentieth Congress.[22] Third, the political rhetoric and activities of the CPL following the split at the Twenty-fifth Congress became more virulently opposed to political independence and adopted confrontational rhetoric that claimed that the proindependence political forces were pushing for the extermination of the non-Latvian portion of the population.[23] In Estonia, even the loyalist branch of the CPE was far more willing to reconcile its differences with the proindependence forces than the loyalist CPL, arguing that the Communist parties ought to use "civilized methods" to debate the issues regarding independence and that the "CPE-CPSU Program would be willing to join a coalition government" in Estonia.[24]

These developments were to have several effects on the course of preindependence Estonian and Latvian politics. With the victory of the "reformist" wing of the CPE and its move to maintain the party's multiethnic character, the threat posed by the CPE to the Popular Front government in Estonia, although not entirely eliminated, took on a less sinister edge. Moreover, the lessening of the threat posed by the CPE to the PFE contributed to the process of internal differentiation in the latter, leading it to moderate its demands concerning independence.[25] As a result, proindependence and anti-independence forces in Estonia did not align solely along ethnic lines.

In Latvia, the CPL, dominated as it was after March 1990 by a leadership with close ties to the virulently anti-independence Interfront, began to claim that the Popular Front government was intent on destroying the non-Latvian component of the population. Unlike the CPE, the CPL throughout 1990–1991 appeared increasingly more willing to employ "extralegal" means in order to forestall the drive toward independence. This led to the polarization of the main organized political forces, with very little room for maneuver between the two camps.

These developments were to have important consequences on the course of postindependence politics in both Baltic states. First, in Estonia, the moderation of the debate over independence did not lead one party or the other to claim that it represented the interests of one of the ethnic groups. This meant that the playing field was relatively open for the later entrance of non-Communist parties that were to claim to represent the interests of the non-Estonian portion of the population following independence. Second, in Latvia, the polarization of politics froze the party alignments, shrinking the political field; "pro-Soviet" became equated with pro-Russian, and for all intents and purposes, the CPL emerged as the self-annointed protector of non-Latvian political rights. Thus, at the moment of independence, Estonian and Latvian party development began at very different stages: Political parties in Estonia had already developed by the end of 1990, whereas Latvian parties remained weak and incoherent at that time.[26]

Economic Factors

Beyond the legacy of the past, the economic performance of the Baltic states following independence has also served to shape postindependence ethnopolitics. Since independence in 1991, the overall development of the economies of Estonia and Latvia has followed the patterns characteristic of most East European and post-Soviet states: an initial period of economic shock caused by the disruption of previous economic ties, followed by catastrophic declines in production, large-scale unemployment and underemployment, and rampant inflation. However, there a few noteworthy differences when comparing Estonia and Latvia. The shock for Estonia was far greater and more intense; it also came earlier than in Latvia. Thus, declines in real GDP occurred prior to Estonia's declaration of independence in 1991 and continued into 1992, whereas in Latvia, the greatest decline occurred after independence and especially throughout 1992–1993. Moreover, the extent of the recovery was far more dramatic for Estonia than Latvia, owing to the rapid adoption of privatization measures in the former (see Table 4.5).

Although there is little data that permits an accurate assessment of the status of different ethnic groups in Estonia and Latvia in the face of the difficult economic transition, some evidence suggests that there are indeed differences between Balts and non-Balts, as well as differences between Latvian and Estonian Russophones. Table 4.6 illustrates the pattern of unemployment for Latvia in the critical years of 1992 and 1993. At the beginning of 1993, although ethnic Latvians accounted for 53.5 percent of the population in Latvia, they accounted for only 45.2 percent of those unemployed. On the other hand, whereas ethnic Russians made up 34 percent of the population, they accounted for 41.6 percent of the reported unemployed at the beginning of the same year. Over time, however, this degree of disproportionality declined, with ethnic Russians accounting for only

Table 4.5   Macroeconomic Indicators and Degree of Regional Integration, Estonia and Latvia, 1990–1995

	1990	1991	1992	1993	1994	1995
Change in real GDP						
Estonia	–7.1	–22.1	–21.6	–6.6	6.0	4.0
Latvia	–1.2	–8.1	–35.0	–14.9	0.0	1.0
Unemployment						
Estonia	n.a.	n.a.	n.a.	4.3	4.5	4.1
Latvia	n.a.	n.a.	n.a.	6.0	6.5	6.6
Inflation						
Estonia	23.1	210.6	1,069.0	89.0	48.0	29.0
Latvia	10.5	124.4	951.2	109.0	36.0	25.0
Latvia						
Exports (% of total)						
To EC/EU	n.a.	1.7	35.6	24.7	n.a.	n.a.
To Russia and						
Eastern Europe	n.a.	78.7	44.4	46.1	n.a.	n.a.
Imports (% of total)						
From EC/EU	n.a.	2.5	24.8	20.2	51.49	n.a.
From Russia and						
Eastern Europe	n.a.	71.95	44.5	48.5	n.a.	n.a.
Estonia						
Exports (% of total)						
To EC/EU	n.a.	1.7	35.6	24.7	n.a.	n.a.
To Russia and						
Eastern Europe	n.a.	78.7	44.4	46.1	n.a.	n.a.
Imports (% of total)						
From EC/EU	n.a.	2.5	24.8	20.2	n.a.	n.a.
From Russia and						
Eastern Europe	n.a.	71.95	44.5	48.5	n.a.	n.a.

Sources: Eesti Pank Bulletin, nos. 1 and 9 (1995) and no. 5 (1996); *Economic Development of Latvia, Report.*

37.1 percent of the unemployed. In Estonia, although there is not comparable data on unemployment for 1994, figures for average income per person in a family are available from 1991 to 1993. In 1991, surveys indicated that 65 percent of Estonian Russians were in the highest income category, but this proportion had declined to only 39 percent by 1993; the largest increase occured in the lowest income category, where 21 percent of Estonian Russians fell in 1993 (as opposed to only 3 percent in 1991).[27]

Some evidence supports the contention that the economic lot of the Latvian Russian population has improved. In part, this recovery derives from the fact that non-Latvians continue to control the largest share of Latvia's business sector. Additionally, ethnic Latvians constitute a very small share of the population of the largest cities, especially Riga, so non-Latvians are in a better position to exploit contacts and are endowed with political and economic resources inherited from the past. Non-Latvians

Table 4.6   Unemployment Rates and Population by Nationality in Latvia, 1993–1994

Nationality	Unemployed Jan. 1993 (% of Total)	% of Population 1993	Unemployed Jan. 1994 (% of Total)	% of Population 1994
Latvian	45.2	53.5	48.7	54.2
Russian	41.6	34.0	37.1	33.1
Byelorussian	6.0	4.2	5.6	4.1
Ukrainian	2.5	3.2	2.9	3.1
Polish	1.7	2.2	2.6	2.2
Lithuanian	1.3	1.3	1.6	1.3
Jewish	0.4	0.6	0.3	0.5
Other	1.3	1.5	1.2	1.5

Source: Latvijas Statistikas Gadagramata, 1993, 55 and 82.

also control the transit trade from Russia, an industry where much profit can be made in a very short time. Another reason for the recovery is the high degree of complementarity of values held by the Latvian and Russo-phone managerial elite in Latvia. Indeed, as Gundar King, Thad Barnowe, and Svetlana Bankovskaya note in their 1994 study of the value orienta-tions of managers in Latvia, there is a higher degree of complementarity of values held by Latvian and Russophone managers than in either Estonia or Lithuania.[28] This suggests that part of the reason for the improved eco-nomic position of Latvian Russophones, especially the Russophone man-agerial class, is that this class has adapted rapidly to doing business in Latvia, unlike Russophones in the other Baltic states.

POLITICAL INCENTIVES

Estonia

In addition to historical and economic developments, political structures have contributed to the course of ethnic politics in both Estonia and Latvia. In Estonia, the basic framework of the political system was estab-lished by the 1992 constitution, which followed the basic structure of the pre-Soviet 1937 constitution. Cognizant of the rise of authoritarian rule in the 1930s, the designers of the constitution were careful to invest the sin-gle-chamber Riigikogu (State Assembly) with most of the political powers. The Parliament was to consist of 101 members elected to a four-year term by a variation of list proportional representation. The president was to be elected by the assembly through a two-thirds majority vote; it was largely a ceremonial post. However, in the 1992 election—a one-time exception to the constitutional structure—the president was directly elected, with the provision that if no candidate received an absolute majority, then the election of the president would be entrusted to Parliament. In this election, the popular ex-head of the Communist Party of Estonia, Arnold Ruutel, received 41.8 percent of the vote but nonetheless lost to the ex–foreign minister, Lennart Meri, who had received just 29.5 percent but was supported by the majority of the members of the Riigikogu in the subsequent runoff.

The election law that governed the Riigikogu elections of both 1992 and 1995 was a complicated system based upon party lists that nonetheless allowed individual candidates to run. Indeed, unlike in strictly PR party list systems (such as in the Netherlands), voters were afforded the opportunity to vote for individual candidates rather than party groupings. The country was divided into twelve electoral districts, the first four comprising the four municipal districts of Tallinn and the other eight comprised of two or three neighboring counties or cities combined. Every district, as in all PR systems, was multimandate.

Each party put forward a candidate list, and although voters could vote for individual candidates, they could vote for only *one* candidate. Once the votes were tallied, the candidate lists were rearranged according to the number of votes received by each, with the candidate receiving the largest number of votes placed at the top. Each list received as many seats in a district as the number of times the number of votes obtained in the district exceeded a simple quota. Individual candidates were elected only when their votes surpassed this quota. If there were any remaining mandates, these were distributed as compensation seats to the parties receiving at least 5 percent of the national vote or to those that had at least three candidates elected by simple quota. The parties then distributed these seats to the candidates they preferred most.[29]

One of the most important institutional factors for both Baltic states was the establishment of boundaries for political participation, particularly citizenship laws and voter enfranchisement. In Estonia, the initial citizenship law, adopted on February 23, 1992, was basically patterned after the 1938 citizenship law. The law granted automatic citizenship to all pre-1940 citizens and their descendants. For other residents (with some exceptions, such as those who worked for the KGB), the naturalization process involved a two-year residence requirement, a one-year waiting period, a fairly rigorous Estonian language test, and a loyalty oath.[30] The two-year residency period would begin on March 30, 1990, the day the Estonian Supreme Council declared the beginning of a transition to independence.

Latvia

In contrast to that of Estonia, the Latvian electoral system resembled a more traditional list proportional representation system. The country was divided into only five electoral constituencies, using party lists and a 5 percent threshold. Only registered parties or electoral associations could nominate candidates. Parties and coalitions submitted lists for each of the five constituencies. Certain categories of persons were excluded by law, which aroused a great deal of controversy. Specifically, persons were not eligible as election candidates if they had been active in the CPSU (after January 13, 1991), in Interfront, or in the All-Latvia Salvation Committee, as well as in other pro-Soviet organizations (including some veterans' associations). Several parties were affected by these provisions in 1995, most notably, two parties that were the successors to the CPL: the Labor and Justice Party and the Latvian Socialist Party (the latter lost twelve candidates to this clause, three of whom had been elected to the Saeima, or Parliament, in 1993). In all, thirteen candidates were removed from the party lists on this basis in the 1995 election.

Each voter received ballot papers for each party or coalition list of candidates. They chose the party for which they wished to vote by selecting that party's ballot paper. Having received the paper, the voter had the opportunity to reorder the party's list. They could place a mark next to a candidate's name, which indicated support for a particular candidate, or they could delete the candidate's name, or they could leave the ballot sheet unaltered. The candidate lists were reordered based upon voter preferences, and seats were awarded based on the number of votes received and the particular preferences the party's voters had for which candidates. In all, nine parties passed the 5 percent threshold in the 1995 election.

Although the current electoral systems in both Estonia and Latvia could be classified as proportional representation systems, there are some noteworthy differences, particularly in terms of the quality of representation. As discussed previously, Estonian voters are afforded the opportunity to base their choice on the qualities of individual candidates, rather than merely voting for a party label or program, while the Latvian system follows a more traditional PR format, where individual voters choose only parties and programs. Given this difference, we would expect that the development of ethnopolitics in Estonia would be qualitatively different from that in Latvia. Indeed, according to Paul Brass, the quality of representation is a key element in the promotion or mitigation of ethnic political conflict. Promoting individual competition and an individually based system of representation diffuses ethnic conflict by undermining "the segmental cleavages of plural societies and permit[s] inter-segmental alliances on other bases than inter-elite agreement."[31]

Most important, however, the initial Latvian citizenship law set almost insurmountable hurdles for Russophone citizenship. The issue of citizenship in Latvia had created tensions between the Latvians and Russophones, as well as with Latvia's neighbors, particularly Russia. The law was passed by the Latvian Supreme Council on October 15, 1991, and granted citizenship to those who could prove that at least one of their parents had been a citizen of the Republic of Latvia prior to Latvia's occupation on June 17, 1940.[32] All others were subject to provisions introduced for acquiring citizenship via naturalization, which entailed three requirements: a knowledge of spoken Latvian, continuous residence in Latvia for at least sixteen years, and the renouncement of citizenship of any other country. Particularly problematic was the language requirement, since most Russophones did not speak Latvian. The law was never confirmed, however, and action was postponed until after the election of the fifth Saeima in 1993.

In June 1994, the Saeima passed a new citizenship law that set strict quotas for naturalization. The law elicited considerable protest from Russia and local Russophones, as well as from Western Europe and the United States. The latter put considerable diplomatic pressure on the Latvian government to eliminate the quota provisions. In response, President Guntis Ulmanis decided not to sign the document and returned it to the Saeima for reconsideration. On July 22, the Saeima passed a revised bill that did not include the numerical quotas, which was then signed into law on August 11. Residents were eligible to become naturalized citizens if they had resided in Latvia for at least five years, had a command of the Latvian language, and renounced any previous citizenship. In March 1995, adopted amendments liberalized the law further by providing language certificates to persons who had obtained an education either in schools with Latvian as the language of instruction or in Latvian-language classes in mixed schools. Persons with such certificates would then receive automatic citizenship upon registration.[33]

Although Latvia and Estonia now have comparably restrictive citizenship laws, the two countries have differed in many ways regarding political citizenship. For instance, in Estonia, voting rights were extended to 170,865 noncitizens, or 19.6 percent of the electorate, for the local elections in 1993. This move might be viewed as evidence to support the contention that the Estonian government's position on the status of resident noncitizens (i.e., Russophones) has been relatively accommodating, as opposed to the more restrictive laws in Latvia, which limit voting rights to only citizens of the Latvian Republic.[34]

THE STRUCTURE OF COMPETITION

Estonia

Since independence, the pattern of party politics in the Baltic states has been quite different in Estonia and in Latvia. In Estonia, as one observer notes, "parties have, within a short period of time and with little trouble, assumed a dominating position in the political process."[35] Although there have been difficulties in institutionalizing the party system in Estonia, the maturation of the system since independence is very much in evidence. In 1992, the first free election in an independent Estonia in over fifty years was held; thirty-eight parties competed for 101 parliamentary seats, with nine parties and electoral unions winning seats (Table 4.7). Moreover, two parties (the Estonian Entrepreneurs Party and the Greens) were represented in the Riigikogu by virtue of individual candidates winning seats outright, despite the fact that their parties had not surpassed the 5 percent threshold. However, in the second election of 1995, the number of parties running decreased to thirty, with only seven parties and electoral unions winning seats and all of the parties surpassing the 5 percent threshold. Thus the 1995 election "reflected the development of more mature parties with well-organized election campaigns."[36] More significant was the victory in this election of the left-of-center Coalition Party–Rural Union alliance, which called for a "social market economy," favored European integration, and contained many former Communists. The organization was descended from the Safe Home (Kindel Kodu) alliance in 1992, which had unsuccessfully backed the presidential candidacy of Arnold Ruutel and had won seventeen seats in the parliamentary election. The biggest losers in the election were the government alliance made up of the right-of-center/ nationalist Fatherland (Isamaa) movement and the Estonian National Independence Party (ENIP), which together had won thirty-nine seats and 30.79 percent of the vote in the 1992 election. But by 1995, they were able to secure only eight seats and 7.86 percent of the vote, finishing a dismal fourth. One of the most noteworthy changes in 1995 was the electoral

Table 4.7 Election Results, Estonia, 1992 and 1995

1992			1995		
Party	% Vote	Seats	Party	% Vote	Seats
Fatherland	22.0	29	Coalition Party/Rural Union	32.23	41
Safe Home	13.6	17	Estonian Reform Party/		
PFE	12.25	15	Liberals	16.19	19
Moderates	9.73	12	Estonian Centre Party	14.17	16
ENIP	8.79	10	Fatherland/ENIP	7.86	8
Independent Royalists	7.12	8	Moderates	5.99	6
Estonian Citizens Party	6.89	8	Our Home Is Estonia	5.87	6
Estonian Entrepreneurs			Right-Wingers	5.00	5
Party	2.39	1			
Greens	2.62	1			

Sources: Vabariigi Presidendi Ja Riigkogu Valimised 1992; Ministry of Foreign Affairs, Republic of Estonia, *Final Election Results.*

breakthrough scored by the Estonian Russophone parties, which had grouped together as a coalition called Our Home Is Estonia (Meie Kodu on Eestimaa), and had garnered 5.87 percent of the popular vote and six seats in Parliament.

Latvia

The Latvian trend was quite different from Estonia's. Whereas parties appear to have firmly taken root in the latter, parties in Latvia remain relatively weak formations largely dominated by personalities. In fact, the winner of the 1993 parliamentary election, Latvian Way, was a loose grouping of personalities formed just prior to the election. It was viewed by many Latvians as a nomenclatural party because it included so many former Communists, yet it was also viewed as moderate by most Russophones. The party formed a governmental partnership with Harmony for Latvia, another alliance of personalities that had called for the coexistence of Latvians and non-Latvians. However, in the 1995 election, which was prematurely brought on by an extended governmental crisis in 1994, the government parties fared very poorly. Latvian Way won only seventeen seats (down from thirty-six in 1993) and 14.64 percent of the vote (down from 32.38 percent in 1993) (see Table 4.8). Harmony for Latvia (which became the National Harmony Party just prior to the 1995 election) was also a big loser, winning less than half the number of seats it secured in 1993. The Latvian Farmers Union (which had been part of the governing

Table 4.8 Election Results, Latvia, 1993 and 1995

1993			1995		
Party	% Vote	Seats	Party	% Vote	Seats
Latvian Way	32.38	36	Latvian Way	14.64	17
Latvian National			Democratic Party	15.15	18
Independence Movement	13.35	15	Peoples Movement		
Harmony for Latvia/Revival			for Latvia	14.89	16
of the Economy	11.98	13	Fatherland and Freedom		
Latvian Farmers Union	10.64	12	Union	11.93	14
Equal Rights Movement	5.77	7	Latvian Unity Party	7.15	8
Fatherland and Freedom			LNCP/Latvian Green		
Union	5.36	6	Party	6.32	8
Christian Democratic			National Harmony Party	5.55	6
Movement	5.01	6	Latvian Socialist Party	5.58	5
Democratic Centre Party	4.76	5	Latvian Farmers Union/		
			Latvian Christian Democratic		
			Union/Latgale Democratic		
			Party	7.15	8

Source: Sixth Saeima of the Republic of Latvia, *History of the Legislature.*

coalition and the exit of which in 1994 had initiated the governmental crisis) also fared poorly; even in conjunction with two other parties on a united list, the party won only eight seats and 7.15 percent of the popular vote, as compared to its 1993 respective figures of twelve and 10.64 percent.

The biggest winners in the 1995 parliamentary election were the parties of the extreme right. Both the ultranationalist and anti-Russian Latvian National Conservative Party (LNCP) and the Fatherland and Freedom Union had won seats in the 1993 elections (twenty-one between them), and they significantly improved their positions in 1995. The Fatherland and Freedom Union more than doubled its number of seats in Parliament, and the LNCP (formerly the Latvian National Independence Movement [LNIM]) formed an unlikely alliance with the Latvian Green Party in an attempt to moderate its image. Yet the LNCP did not fare well, with its popular support shrinking to only 6.32 percent of the vote and its number of seats declining to eight. However, the gains made by the extremist Peoples Movement for Latvia, which had been founded by the German neofascist and former LNCP MP Joachim Zigerists, further strengthened the position of the Latvian nationalists in Parliament. All told, the nationalist Latvian right after the 1995 parliamentary election controlled thirty-eight seats, seventeen more than in 1993. However, unlike in Estonia, where the Russophone parties had attained representation in Parliament, the major Russophone party in Latvia, the Russian Citizens of Latvia Party, received less than 3 percent of the vote and failed to pass the electoral threshold, gaining no representation in the 1995 Saeima.

DIFFERENCES AND SIMILARITIES BETWEEN ESTONIA AND LATVIA

In comparing the cases of Estonia and Latvia in terms of the historical legacy, the economic conditions of their Russian populations, and the structure of incentives, several noteworthy similarities and differences emerge. Perhaps the most noteworthy similarity is the high level of frustration on the part of both Russophone populations with the actions of the Baltic governments. As Graham Smith, Aadne Aasland, and Richard Mole have noted, the Russophones' condemnation of such actions as the citizenship laws and language requirements has been equally strong in Estonia and Latvia.[37] Richard Rose and William Maley have also noted a similar pattern, although the Estonian Russophones appear to view opportunities in Russia to be far more limited than do Latvian Russophones, which reinforces the sense that Estonian Russophones feel they have nowhere else to go (see Table 4.9).[38]

Table 4.9 Attitudes of Baltic Russians in Estonia and Latvia

Question: Would You Say That . . .	% Agree	
	Estonia	Latvia
The government treats Russians in this country fairly?	29	27
Noncitizens and minority nationalities are being treated badly here?	31	29
There are conflicts between Estonians/Latvians and Russians living here?	38	34
Conditions for your peers in Russia are worse than they are here?	53	34
This country offers better chances for improving living standards in the future than does Russia?	54	44

Source: Adapted from Rose and Maley, *Nationalities in the Baltic States.*

In terms of noteworthy differences between Estonia and Latvia, both countries suffered the burden of Soviet rule, but both were not similarly impacted by the residual legacy of the period immediately prior to independence. In Estonia, the transformation of the Communist Party into one that favored independence and the maintenance of a multiethnic coalition in the republic did much to allay the fears of the Popular Front leadership. In turn, this paved the way for the early development of political parties that began to act independently from the PFE. Thus, party development was quite extensive at the moment of independence in 1991. In Latvia, however, the polarization of politics set off by the hard-liners' capture of the CPL led to the squeezing out of alternative party organizations; in comparison to Estonia, then, Latvian party development at the time of independence was still in its infancy.

The two Baltic republics also differ in terms of institutional factors, such as election and citizenship laws. To be sure, the debate over citizenship laws was equally acrimonious in both countries, and the hurdles established for citizenship were equally daunting. In Estonia, the fact that noncitizens were afforded the right to vote in local elections as early as 1993 and that the Russophone parties were able to make an electoral breakthrough at the national level in 1995 stood in stark contrast to the virtual political exclusion of Russophones in Latvia.

Finally, the structure of competition has evolved very differently in both countries. In Estonia, the initial victory of moderate Estonian nationalists in the election of 1992 was soon surpassed by the victory of left-of-center parties in 1995. Estonian nationalists were therefore in a far weaker position in the Riigikogu than was the Latvian national right, which was able to make significant gains in 1995 despite that fact that the extremist Peoples Movement for Latvia was excluded from the governing coalition.

How did these factors affect the evolution of the Russophone parties in the Baltic states? Based upon the above, we would expect that the trend in Estonia, more so than in Latvia, would move over time in the direction of engaging in accommodative behaviors largely because of three conditions: (1) The period immediately prior to the transition in Estonia was characterized by much less interethnic party polarization; (2) the Russian parties had attained a higher level of organization and political representation in independent Estonia than in Latvia; and (3) the "threat" posed by the Estonian nationalist parties receded following the 1995 parliamentary election, whereas in Latvia, the rise of the extreme right has put added pressures on the Russophone population. The following sections assess the development of the Russophone parties in the Baltic states.

RUSSOPHONE PARTIES IN ESTONIA

The development of the Russophone political parties in Estonia followed a very different path from that in Latvia after 1991. In Estonia, the citizenship law, the adoption of legislation that limited certain jobs (such as judges and police officers) to only Estonian citizens, and the initial exclusion of the vast majority of Russian speakers from the electoral process in the parliamentary and presidential elections of 1992 increased interethnic tensions. Moreover, the adoption of such measures as the June 1993 Law on Foreigners, which denied legal residence permits to military pensioners and required that the majority of Russian-speaking noncitizens reapply for five-year temporary residence permits, made Russian speakers feel uneasy about the intentions of the new Estonian government; hence, their leaders began to organize to oppose such actions. One of these leadership organizations was the Russian Democratic Movement, which had been founded in 1991 and had ties with Prime Minister Edgar Savisaar, a former PFE leader. Originally supportive of independence, following 1992, the movement began to gravitate toward those who had been radically opposed to Estonian independence. By the summer of that year, the movement had entered into an alliance with the remnants of the OSTK, and a Coordinating Committee was established that was openly supported by members of the Russian-speaking managerial elite who had previously sponsored the efforts of local Communist authorities in opposing Baltic independence. This committee proclaimed that it would seek a special political status for the Russian-speaking majority regions of the northeast.[39]

The Coordinating Committee, which later renamed itself the Committee for the Autonomy of Northeastern Estonia, began to call for political and territorial autonomy for the Russian-speaking majority regions of the country. The committee accused former Soviet president Mikhail Gorbachev of "surrendering Baltic Russia which stretches from Narva river to Tallinn to Estonian Nationalists." To express support for the drive for political autonomy, the committee urged people to place stones in front of the city council building in Narva; however, it was reported that only five stones "the size of potatoes" were left by two pensioners by the end of the rally.[40]

At about the same time, another group was formed consisting of Russian speakers who qualified as citizens. Led by eight Russian-speaking deputies of the former Supreme Council, the Interregional Council was established in 1992, and it spearheaded the effort to convoke a Russian Representative Assembly patterned along the lines of the Estonian Congress, the alternative legislature to the Supreme Council established by the Estonian nationalists in 1990. Unlike the Coordinating Committee, which demanded political autonomy, the demands of the Russian Representative Assembly were rather moderate. As one of its leaders, Nikolai Yugantsev, remarked, the assembly did not have the intention to become "a parallel structure of legislative power," but only to "work within the Constitutional framework."[41] Further, the assembly expressed a willingness to initiate talks with the various political forces in Estonia, including the governing nationalist coalition of Isamaa and the ENIP.[42] Its goals were limited to those protecting the "human rights of Russians in the country," particularly in the northeastern region, not those pursuing political or territorial autonomy.[43] Nonetheless, the assembly's leaders pointed to the rise of "nationalism, interethnic animosity and moral degradation" and the fact that, in Estonia, the "seemingly eradicated fascism is again raising its head . . . hiding behind patriotic slogans and sometimes quite openly. . . . Not to notice it is dangerous; not to take action, criminal."[44]

However, with the passage of the language test requirements in February 1993 and the Law on Foreigners in June 1993, the more radical elements within the Russian-speaking community appeared to gain an edge over the more moderate assembly. The Coordinating Committee once again issued a call for the establishment of political autonomy, a call supported by the Russophone mayors of the northeastern cities of Narva and Sillimae. One of the more notorious leaders of the autonomy movement was Vladimir Chuikin, then mayor of Narva, who had been associated with the opposition to Estonian independence (although he claimed to have been on leave during the August 1991 coup). Chuikin had been linked to the "New Men" of the Gorbachev era and had built a solid base of local support in the Narva region, largely via his ability to distance himself from the Communist past and speak in terms of Estonian independence as a threat to Russian cultural life.[45] Chuikin was particularly active in the planning session for a referendum on territorial autonomy for the Russian-speaking majority region of the northeast, held on July 18–19, 1993. He argued that the referendum was necessary because of the discriminative laws passed by the Riigikogu, particularly the Law on Foreigners.[46] However, according to Chuikin, the referendum was being pursued only with great reluctance, for the Russian-speaking population had been forced into taking action; if the Riigikogu had "unambiguously made our rights equal to the rights of Estonian citizens, then the need for a referendum would disappear of its own accord."[47] The mayor of Sillimae, Aleksandr Maksimenko, went further, stating that autonomy was "the only peaceful possibility of bringing laws which discriminate against the Russian-speaking population into line with democratic norms. . . . We seek to amend . . . the law on citizenship and the law on language. Otherwise our city will forever remain a city of foreigners in Estonia and will not extricate itself from the political social and economic crisis."[48]

The controversial referendum, along with a similar one in Sillimae, was ruled illegal by the Estonian government as a violation of the constitution's guarantee of territorial integrity. Nonetheless, voting was held with a reported turnout of 54.8 percent of the electorate in Narva (97.2 percent of whom supported political autonomy) and of 61 percent in Sillimae (98 percent of whom supported autonomy).[49] The Estonian government, however, condemned the outcome of the referendums, claiming that there had been "irregularities" that rendered both invalid. One of these supposed irregularities was the accusation that groups of voters had been imported from across the border, specifically from Leningrad Oblast in Russia.[50] Another was the accusation that the referendum organizers had inflated the results and that less than 5 percent of the electorate had actually taken part.[51]

Despite these attempts at invalidation, the Estonian government relented and agreed to meet with the referendum organizers; thus Mayors Chuikin and Maksimenko convened with Prime Minister Mart Laar.[52] Both sides agreed that holding local elections in which Russian residents would participate (even if they were not citizens) was the best solution to the crisis.[53] Laar himself admitted that the government had not adequately dealt with the problems in the northeastern part of the country and vowed to cooperate with "constructive forces in the city councils [of Narva and Sillimae]."[54]

In October 1993, Estonia held its first post-Soviet local election, and for the first time since independence, substantial numbers of non-Estonians were able to vote. Although only citizens could be candidates, all permanent residents aged eighteen and older who had resided in the locality for five years were permitted to vote. The elections had two important effects on interethnic relations in Estonia. First, the parties in the ruling nationalist coalition fared very poorly in the local elections, especially in the larger cities. Second, the Russophone parties fared quite well. In Tallinn, the Russian Democratic Movement, which had moderated its position following the July referendum and had joined in an electoral alliance with the moderate Russian Representative Assembly, did particularly well. The assembly had campaigned on the platform that the best means to avoid ethnic tensions and conflicts among groups and the "formation [of] a closed society in Estonia with all of the negative consequences" was the extension of citizenship to as many Russian speakers as possible, as quickly as possible.[55] The assembly also promoted Estonian citizenship and stressed the importance of learning Estonian, adding that too many foreign citizens in Estonia constituted a threat.[56] Following the elections, the assembly formally established a political party, the Russian Party of Estonia.

Together, the Russophone moderates did quite well. The Russian Social Democratic Movement won seventeen of the sixty-four available seats, whereas the more radical group called Revel (the clear ideological descendant of Intermovement) won ten seats, with the remaining seats going to independents, most of whom were associated with the Russian Representative Assembly. The victory of the moderates was an encouraging sign. As Toivo Raun has noted, "these elections will prove to be a major step on the road to integrating those Russians and other non-Estonians who have made their peace with an independent Estonia."[57] Indeed, the victory of the moderates in the local elections in October, coupled with the low turnout (25 percent) among Russian citizens in Estonia for the December 1993 Russian parliamentary elections, was an encouraging sign that the majority of Russian speakers were rejecting radical solutions (although 48 percent of those who voted did so for Vladimir Zhirinovsky's Liberal Democratic Party). Nonetheless, the organizational presence of nationalist Russian organizations in Estonia was minimal, and cross-border ties between Russian speakers in Estonia and radical nationalist organizations in Russia were tenuous at best.[58]

Most encouraging of all, at least when looking at the likelihood of a complete bifurcation of politics along ethnic lines, was the formation and performance of the moderate Our Home Is Estonia electoral coalition. As mentioned earlier, the coalition was launched prior to the March 1995 election as an alliance of Russophone parties that included the Estonian United Peoples Party, the Russian Party of Estonia, and the Russian People's Party of Estonia; the Russian Democratic Movement declined to join the coalition. The movement continued to oppose the 1993 Estonian Law on Foreigners but expressed a willingness to cooperate with the Estonian parties in the new Center-Left coalition. Among the Russian speakers in Estonia, there appeared to be broad support for the moderate line put forward by the coalition.[59] Following the election, the alliance formed a parliamentary group called the Russian Faction (led by Viktor Andreev, Sergei Kuznetsov, and Aleksei Semenov). The Russian Party of Estonia later absorbed the Russian People's Party in 1996 and remained the leading member in Our Home Is Estonia.[60]

Russophone Parties in Latvia

When comparing the development and behavior of the Estonian Russian-speaking parties with those in Latvia, it is apparent that efforts to organize the Russian-speaking community in Latvia were far less successful than in Estonia. Most of these efforts focused on the creation of loosely structured nonpolitical economic or cultural associations, as opposed to explicitly political movements. As early as 1988, the Baltic-Slavic Society of Cultural Cooperation was founded, uniting Russian Byelorussian and Ukrainian cultural centers. Subsequently, these groups initiated the Russian Community of Latvia Organization in the fall of 1991, and soon it established a private technical university. Following the abortive coup and the declaration of Latvian independence, the Economic Association of Russian Citizens of Latvia was also established, consisting of descendants of Russians who were citizens of the interwar Latvian state. The primary goal of the association was to regain property owned by Russian-Latvian citizens before the annexation by the USSR, although the association had a political purpose as well. According to the organization's chairman, Vladimir Sorochin, the association represented the interests of those Russian speakers who were repulsed by the antics of Interfront, and he proclaimed his group's special loyalty to an independent Republic of Latvia.[61] Although a party of Russian speakers had run in the 1995 parliamentary election, the party failed to surpass the electoral threshold and did not make any significant inroads into Latvian politics.

Since independence, as in Estonia, the Russian-speaking community's initial support for independence has soured, particularly concerning the government's 1993–1994 actions regarding citizenship, the denial of political representation, and the coming to power of a nationalist right-wing coalition in 1995. Further, many Russian speakers felt that they had nowhere else to go: They and their children were born in Latvia, and there were few economic opportunities awaiting them in Russia. Taken together, these sentiments have led to a growing sense of frustration and anger within the Russian-speaking community vis-à-vis the independent Latvian government, which appears less and less sympathetic to the plight of "stateless" persons in Latvia, even those who were initially strong supporters of independence. This attitude was reflected by Katya Borschova, formerly a Latvian Russian journalist for the Popular Front of Latvia's Russian-language newspaper.

> We feel under constant pressure because of the continual barrage in the Latvian press . . . ; the constant talk of "colonists," "aliens," "fifth columnists," "illegal immigrants"; the constant stress on a Latvian Latvia; the exaltation of everything Latvian; the denigration of everything Russian.

This is especially irritating when it comes from individuals who only a year ago were stressing that this was not a national struggle. Russians here are now saying to us, "[Y]ou see Interfront was right after all . . . and you deceived us." Among Russian intellectuals there is a tendency to look down on the Latvians as "little children pretending to be [a] nation." But yes, a certain mood of hatred for the Latvians is also growing because of the pressure, even among Russians who are ashamed of this feeling.[62]

Despite the growing sense of frustration over the Russian-speaking community's plight in Latvia, the level of political organization within the community remains very low, particularly when compared to the level of organization in Estonia. To a large extent, the only political parties that have purported to represent the Latvian Russian population since independence have been Harmony for Latvia and the Latvian Socialist Party (formerly the Equal Rights Movement). However, neither party regards itself as representative of the Russophones exclusively, though each has made dialogue and reconciliation among groups one of its main goals. Although there have been some efforts to form political organizations to represent the Latvian Russophone community—such as the founding of the League of Apatrides in Latvia in January 1994, which claims to represent about 40,000 Russophone noncitizens, and the Russian Citizens of Latvia Party, which contested the 1995 parliamentary election—these efforts have been relatively unsuccessful in either mobilizing the Russophone population or securing representation in the Saeima. Moreover, these efforts have met stiff resistance from the Latvian right, which has been unwilling to recognize Russophone representatives as legitimate negotiating partners.[63]

Two explanations for the lack of Russophone political mobilization in Latvia as compared to that in Estonia stand out. Juris Dreifelds contends that because the Russian-speaking community in Latvia represents a "mass society" with few linkages between the primary family and friendship levels with the power elites, there is very little in the way of community solidarity and only a vestigial ethnic consciousness among the various groups, whose main links are those of Russian language and Soviet culture. Moreover, there are only a very few non-Latvian representatives in the political and bureaucratic elites. The economic elites, on the other hand, many members of which have arisen from the Russian-speaking milieu, have not yet fully taken on the mantle of intermediaries for local ethnic groups. For Dreifelds, this isolation represents a dangerous situation: The paucity of intermediary groups and representation "inevitably heightens alienation, discontent and a sense of unfair treatment by Latvian authorities, and could presage the availability of this population to populist mobilization or more critically outside interference and agitation."[64]

Another explanation relates to the legacy of the immediate preindependence period. Prior to independence, the major organizations that claimed to represent the interests of the Russian-speaking population (Interfront and the CPL) had relied upon ties to Moscow rather than a popular mandate for power. Further, the organizational successor to the CPL, the Latvian Socialist Party, which claims to represent the "internationalist" population in Latvia and be the self-annointed guardian of the Russian-speaking population, has made it difficult for political replacements to emerge. In contrast, in Estonia, the pro-Moscow forces had been considerably weakened within the CPE prior to independence, leaving open the possibility for political replacements to the Communist Party to emerge.[65]

Whatever the case, the potential for future difficulties in interethnic relations is far greater in Latvia than in Estonia, especially if Latvian nationalist forces, bolstered by their political success in 1995, begin to target "foreign speculators," Russophone professionals ignorant of the Latvian language, and unemployed industrial workers. As Anatol Lieven notes, since there is a higher proportion of educated Russians in Latvia than in Estonia who have become the driving force in business and technology, in the future it is likely that "Russian resistance in Latvia would be more formidable than in Estonia, not simply because they are more numerous, but because they would be better and more articulately led."[66]

DISCUSSION AND CONCLUSION

The evolution of the Russophone parties in Estonia and Latvia since independence represents patterns of development that are different from either those exemplified by the MRF in Bulgaria or those of the Hungarian parties in Slovakia. Despite similarities to the cases of Bulgaria and Slovakia in terms of the presence of an ethnic kin state that has taken an active interest in the Russophone population, the legacy of the previous multiethnic empire, the territorial compactness of the Russophone population, and the economic hardships suffered by the minority population following independence (although this is more pronounced in Estonia than in Latvia), there are significant differences as well. First, unlike in either Bulgaria or Slovakia, where the minority population has been a long-standing and continuous community within these states, in Estonia and Latvia, the Russophone population is made up of relatively recent arrivals to the Baltics. Moreover, whereas the multiethnic Ottoman and Austro-Hungarian Empires had ended in Bulgaria and Slovakia long before the democratic transition, the demise of the multiethnic empire coincided with the democratic transition in the Baltic states. This has meant that the Russophones in the Baltics, unlike the Turkish population in Bulgaria and the Hungarian minority in Slovakia, lack a clear and fully developed identity as a community, beyond some lingering attachment to symbols of the Soviet past.

Thus, on the whole, the Russophone parties in Estonia and Latvia are less developed than both Bulgaria's MRF and Slovakia's Hungarian parties.

Estonia and Latvia differ from each other as well. In Estonia, the level of ethnopolitical party development has been far higher than in Latvia, despite similarly high levels of discontent on the part of Russophones with the activities of their respective governments regarding language and citizenship issues. To a large extent, this differential level of development is due to different experiences regarding the evolution of transitional politics prior to independence, marked by the emergence of a partially articulated party system prior to independence in Estonia and the lack of one in Latvia.

Moreover, the Russophone political parties have generally been more aggressive in Estonia than in Latvia in making demands for political autonomy for regions where Russophones comprise a majority of the population (particularly around Narva and Sillimae), most evidenced when the local government sponsored a referendum on political autonomy in 1993. In Latvia, though, Russophones have thus far been content with focusing on the defense of language, educational, and cultural rights without seeking fundamental restructuring of the postindependence political system.

However, the potential for more radical demands on the part of Russophones is probably far greater in Latvia than in Estonia. This is because Russophones in Estonia have not only gained representation (and hence a voice) in post-Soviet Estonian politics, especially after the 1993 local and 1995 parliamentary elections, but also because the parties that represent the most moderate elements there have emerged to become the political voice of the Russophone population. In contrast, Latvian Russophones remain essentially excluded from the political process—they have neither an independent voice nor moderate political parties that can channel demands into constructive directions. Furthermore, whereas the Estonian nationalists, who had pushed for the most onerous legislation on language and citizenship (at least from the perspective of the Russophone population), suffered a political setback in the parliamentary election in 1995, the Latvian nationalists made significant gains in 1994. Thus the Russophone parties in Latvia have little recourse other than to continue to rely on other organizations to defend the interests of the Russophone community or, more ominously, to increasingly depend on the intervention of Moscow to promote their interests in postindependence Latvian politics. Although the leadership of the Russophone population in Latvia does not appear to be currently inclined toward making demands for the fundamental restructuring of the Latvian state, this is due to the fact that the Russophone population has yet to develop its consciousness as a distinct group and the organizations to articulate its growing dissatisfaction with the present regime.

NOTES

1. We use the term "Russophone" here rather than "Russian" because the populations in the newly independent states are made up of not only ethnic Russian, but Byelorussians, Ukrainians, Armenians, and so forth.

2. von Rauch, *The Baltic States*; Misiunas and Taagepera, *The Baltic States*, 2–3.

3. Raun, *Estonia and the Estonians*; Haltzel, "The Baltic Germans," 111–120.

4. Lieven, *The Baltic Revolution*, 183.

5. Zvidrins, "Changes in the Ethnic Composition in Latvia," 359–368.

6. Lieven, *The Baltic Revolution*, 66.

7. Kirch, Kirch, and Tuisk, "Russians in the Baltic States," 173–179.

8. Lieven, *The Baltic Revolution*, 178; Aasland, "The Russian Population in Latvia," 240–250.

9. Shafir, *Immigrants and Nationalists,* 193–202.

10. On the origins of Intermovement, see *Moscow News,* April 8–15, 1990, 11. Kogan was injured in an auto accident shortly before the Congress of Peoples' Deputies elections in June 1989, and his physical plight apparently aroused much sympathy among voters. Indeed, Kogan claimed that this greatly affected his political style and that he "learned and appreciated the value of scathing words . . . that wrench tears of sympathy from kind hearts."

11. Statement on Intermovement by Vanio Valyas reported in *Sovetskaya Estoniya,* May 5, 1989, 1.

12. *Moscow News,* September 3–10, 1989, 9.

13. *London Financial Times,* August 17, 1989, 2

14. Dreifelds, "Latvian National Rebirth," 77–94.

15. Moscow Domestic Service, September 18, 1989, in Foreign Broadcast Information Service–Soviet Union (Central Eurasia) (hereafter referred to as FBIS-SOV), September 18, 1989, 61.

16. This resolution brought Latvia in line with similar declarations by the Supreme Soviets of Estonia and Lithuania on November 12 and 23, 1989. See Bungs, "A Further Step Towards Latvian Independence," 25.

17. Quoted by Riga Domestic Service, February 15, 1990, in FBIS-SOV, February 20, 1990, 94.

18. TASS (Moscow news agency), March 23, 1990, in FBIS-SOV, March 26, 1990, 131.

19. Bungs, "Latvian Communist Party Splits," 19.

20. Ishiyama, "Founding Elections and the Development of Transitional Parties," 277–299.

21. See report by Ivars Kezbers, first secretary of the Independent CPL, in Vilnius Domestic Service, June 28, 1990, in FBIS-SOV, July 6, 1990, 45.

22. Tallinn Domestic Service, March 29, 1990, in FBIS-SOV, March 30, 1990, 92–93.

23. TASS, December 14, 1990, in FBIS-SOV, December 16, 1990, 91.

24. See speech by Lembit Annus, first secretary of CPE-CPSU program, reported in MAYAK (Russia private news agency), April 28, 1991, in FBIS-SOV, April 29, 1991, 41.

25. Ishiyama, "Founding Elections and the Development of Transitional Parties," 292–293.

26. Bungs, "People's Front of Latvia"; Bungs, "A Further Step Towards Latvian Independence"; Kionka, "Identity Crisis in Estonian Popular Front."

27. Kirch, Kirch, and Tuisk, "Russians in the Baltic States," 175; Rose and Maley, *Nationalities in the Baltic States.*

28. King, Barnowe, and Bankovskaya, "Complementary and Conflicting Personal Values," 255–260.

29. *Vabariigi Presidendi Ja Riigkogu Valimised 1992.*

30. Lieven, *The Baltic Revolution,* 310; Kionka, "'Alternative' Plebiscite in Estonia," 26.

31. Brass, *Ethnicity and Nationalism,* 340.

32. Dreifelds, *Latvia in Transition,* 97–98; Karklins, *Ethnopolitics,* 145–151.

33. *Latvia Human Development Report,* chap. 2.

34. See Girnius, "The Baltic States," 5–6.

35. Rosimannus, "Political Parties and Identification," 29.

36. *Estonia Today,* July 18, 1996, 1.

37. G. Smith, Aasland, and Mole, "Statehood, Ethnic Relations, and Citizenship," 194–197.

38. Rose and Maley, *Nationalities in the Baltic States.*

39. Lieven, *The Baltic Revolution,* 309.

40. ITAR TASS (Russian news agency), January 17, 1993, in FBIS-SOV, January 19, 1993, 88–89.

41. FBIS-SOV, March 8, 1993, 80.

42. FBIS-SOV, February 17, 1993, 79.

43. FBIS-SOV, March 8, 1993, 80.

44. Baltic News Service (hereafter referred to as BNS), February 4, 1993, 44.

45. Lieven, *The Baltic Revolution,* 189–193.

46. FBIS-SOV, July 7, 1993, 63.

47. *Izvestiya,* July 13, 1993, 2.

48. *Izvestiya,* July 20, 1993, 1–2.

49. FBIS-SOV, July 21, 1993, 66.

50. *Rahvaa Haal, Paevaleht,* July 20, 1993, 1 and 3, in FBIS-SOV, July 21, 1993, 66. See also comments by Prime Minister Mart Laar in FBIS-SOV, July 21, 1993, 66–67, and ITAR TASS, July 23, 1993, in FBIS-SOV, July 23, 1993, 78.

51. *Pravda* (Moscow), July 24, 1993, 2; *Izvestiya,* July 20, 1993, 1–2.

52. ITAR TASS, July 23, 1993, in FBIS-SOV, July 26, 1993, 87.

53. FBIS-SOV, July 26, 1993, 88.

54. ITAR TASS, July 23, 1993, in FBIS-SOV, July 23, 1993, 78.

55. Semenov, "The Formation of a Legal State," 241.

56. Estonian Telegraphic Agency, October 9, 1993, in FBIS-SOV, October 23, 1993, 98.

57. Raun, "Post-Soviet Estonia," 74–75.

58. BNS, January 22, 1994.

59. Norgaard et al., *The Baltic States After Independence,* 207–208.

60. *VM Info,* February 22, 1995.

61. Karklins, *Ethnopolitics,* 80–81.

62. Quoted in Lieven, *The Baltic Revolution,* 308.

63. Norgaard et al., *The Baltic States After Independence,* 209–211.

64. Dreifelds, *Latvia in Transition,* 101.

65. Metcalf, "Outbidding to Radical Nationalists," 213–234.

66. Lieven, *The Baltic Revolution,* 188.

5

The Volksunie and the Vlaams Blok in Belgium

Within the Flemish movement, there have long been differences of opinion regarding its end goal and ideology. The experiences of Flemish-speaking troops serving under French-speaking officers in the trenches at the IJzer Front during World War I convinced many Flemish soldiers to support a movement that sought to enhance the rights and opportunities of their people but left unclear what the ultimate aim should be: Moderates desired greater autonomy, whereas radicals desired political independence. The first Flemish ethnopolitical party to gain seats in Parliament dates from the first election after that war. Earlier, in the second half of the nineteenth century, Flemish nationalists had endeavored to get their voices heard within existing parties and had close ties with the left. During the interwar years, the first independent Flemish ethnopolitical party began to associate itself with Nazi ideology.

This gave the Flemish movement a dual heritage that still divides the movement today: left-leaning ideological ties as well as extreme rightist views. These differences were contained within one party until the emergence of the Vlaams Blok in 1978. Although the Vlaams Blok initially remained a small party, it was able to gain representation in Parliament relatively easily, for Belgium's proportional representation system allows such access to new parties.

The seeds of ethnopolitics were present at the inception of the Belgian state. It is one of the younger states of Western Europe, gaining its independence in 1830 after a revolt against Dutch rule, which had begun only about fifteen years earlier. At the conclusion of the Napoleonic Wars, the Low Countries were united into one kingdom. The north had been a sovereign entity since 1648, whereas the south was known first as the Spanish Netherlands, then as the Austrian Netherlands. The adoption of French as the Belgian national language in 1830 may have been a logical reaction to years of Spanish, Austrian, and, most immediately, Dutch dominance, but as time passed, the Flemish segment of the population became more vocal in its demands for recognition of its language and cultural heritage.

French was spoken by the elites and the population of the southern part of the state, Wallonia. Dutch dialects were spoken by the population in the northern part of the state, Flanders. Yet the conflict between the Flemish- and French-speaking communities that came to define politics in Belgium was not necessarily inevitable. Flemish ethnopolitics arose in reaction to the efforts of the French-speaking elites to create a French-speaking Belgian state and initially remained a sociocultural movement among select Flemish elites.

The conflict can thus be said to reflect the failure of the dominant group to impose its language and culture on the entire country. Perhaps too many factors conspired against its success: As one of Europe's younger states, it attained its independence through the intervention of the Concert of Europe and acquired a German prince as its king.[1] This, coupled with Wallonia's early industrialization while Flanders remained agricultural and, later, Flanders' economic rise while Wallonia's industry declined, did not make it easier to weld a unified nation out of such different parts.

HISTORICAL BACKGROUND

Since its early days, Flemish ethnopolitics has focused on linguistic issues to express the unequal status of Flemish- or Dutch-speaking versus French-speaking Belgian citizens.[2] Yet the issues that divide the two groups are not fundamentally about the right to use Flemish in official environments: Language became the metaphor that expressed the Flemish sense of exclusion within their own country.[3]

Using language to express political grievances was perhaps a logical choice for the Flemish movement. First, King William I used the Dutch language in his efforts to unify the Low Countries. According to Arthur Vermeersch, this king "estimated the value of the Dutch language as a unifying factor to be very high" and instituted a language policy that reflected this view.[4] Dutch was declared to be the official language, although its use was not initially compulsory. However, Flemish elites had increasingly adopted French and often regarded Dutch with disdain. Furthermore, the declaration of Dutch as the official language created employment problems for those in the bureaucracy who had not mastered this language. Although other issues played a role as well, the perceived cultural affront and the loss of employment contributed to the grievances that eventually led to the revolution in the southern Netherlands and the subsequent creation of the Belgian state in 1830.[5]

Second, the leaders of the Belgian revolution stressed French and declared that Flemish was not a language, but a dialect.[6] The right to use this dialect in education, the military, the courts, public administration, and so on, became the centerpiece of the Flemish movement's efforts to gain equal status with French-speaking Belgium. More important than language, however, was the Flemish perception of second-class citizenship. This perception was rooted in the widespread poverty that plagued Flanders while Wallonia industrialized.

The Flemish movement began as a sociocultural movement of Flemish elites. It stressed the use of the Flemish language and fought against the perception of it as a collection of dialects spoken only by the uneducated masses. Flemish was promoted as a worthy instrument of literature and, by extension, culture.

There were some cautious attempts to move into the political arena after the founding of the Vlaamsch Verbond (Flemish Union) in 1861, but the Flemish movement was not yet associated with a particular party at this time. Instead, Flemish nationalists were activists within the existing parties. Notable among them was Camille Huysmans, a member of Belgian Workers Party, for whom the emancipation of workers and of the Flemish were closely intertwined: "As an internationalist and as a Belgian, Flemish separatism founded on the supposition of Flemish nationalism and a Flemish 'race' did not appeal to him. His ideal was cultural autonomy within the unitary state and the economic framework of the Belgian nation."[7]

Despite these initial forays into politics, the movement remained largely elite based and sociocultural in focus until the introduction of universal suffrage in 1893, which brought a large number of exclusively Flemish-speaking men into the electorate.[8] Developments since that time have given Flemish ethnopolitics a dual historical heritage: It was associated with the left early on, yet it also associated itself with Nazi ideology during World War II. In addition, Flemish ethnopolitics in its infancy developed moderate and radical strains. Both this dual heritage and these two strains can be recognized in the two Flemish ethnopolitical parties today.

The first attempt to found a Flemish party dates from the 1890s, but it found little support. A more durable Flemish political party emerged from the Front movement during World War I among the soldiers in the trenches at the IJzer Front, where mostly Flemish soldiers served under officers who were often not just French-speaking, but anti-Flemish as well. Under these conditions, the attraction of a movement that promised greater autonomy was quite understandable. Yet the movement also took advantage of the German occupation to advance its cause, and it became difficult to distinguish between collaborators and Flemish nationalists. Instead of being rewarded for their bravery with concessions to Flemish demands, those who had been involved in the movement found themselves in jail if they had not managed to flee abroad.[9]

Nevertheless, many veterans joined the Verbond der Vlaamse Oudstrijders (Union of Flemish Veterans). This organization played a major role in the creation of a new political party called the Vlaamsche Front (Flemish Front, or Frontpartij). It participated in the national elections of 1919 and won five seats. This was the first election to be contested using single, universal male suffrage and proportional representation.[10] Prior to that time, the upper classes had been able to cast multiple votes, which affected the extent to which the "common man" could influence elections. Hence, it is no surprise that the Frontpartij entered the national Chamber of Representatives at that time. The upper classes tended to be more tied into the French-speaking elite structure, whereas the ordinary Flemish person more clearly felt the disadvantages of belonging to a language group whose rights were not recognized.

Two strands had developed early on within the Flemish movement, which are commonly referred to as "minimalist" and "maximalist."[11] Minimalists generally sought to advance the Flemish cause within existing political parties. However, such parties also focused on other issues, and the specific problems of the Flemish were not necessarily the highest priority. For the Frontpartij, the Flemish question did have priority, but whether it was truly maximalist is another matter. Maximalists did not merely make the Flemish cause a high priority; those classified into this category tended to question the very existence of Belgium. The Frontpartij stood for some form of self-government, but it was not yet clear what shape that would take. In 1917, the leaders at the front had demanded that Flanders be granted self-government after the war. This demand was translated in various ways: Some wanted a federal state, some favored disbanding Belgium, and others preferred incorporation into the Netherlands.[12]

The Frontpartij was clear on its left-wing and antimilitarist stances. The party consisted of individuals with a desire to change the world for the better, some of whom identified themselves as socialist or communist. The party received 2.6 percent of the vote and entered Parliament with five seats in 1919. In the election of 1929, it managed to obtain eleven seats, but it subsequently lost votes and three seats in the election of 1932. In this same time period, the rightists within the party gained more strength.[13]

In some cases, individual party supporters also changed their views. Joris van Severen, for example, had supported the Frontpartij, but during the 1920s became enamored of Mussolini. In 1931, he formed the Verbond van Dietsche Nationaal-Solidaristen, or Verdinaso (League of Dutch-Speaking National Solidarists). Although this group never gained many followers, it was one of the factors that influenced the reorganization of the Frontpartij after its electoral debacle of 1932. In 1933, the party renamed itself the Vlaamsch Nationaal Verbond (VNV; Flemish National Union) and adopted a totally revised program: Once left-wing and democratic, it was now right-wing and authoritarian. A Catholic teacher and veteran of World War I, Staf de Clerq, became the leader of the new VNV. Although he was not himself an ideologue, he allowed himself to be influenced by fascist thinkers.[14]

The VNV was present in Parliament for the entire interwar period, gaining its highest level of representation in the elections of 1939 with seventeen seats. Largely as a result of its association with Nazi ideology and its collaboration with the Nazi occupation, there was a decline in support for Flemish nationalism in the immediate post–World War II period.[15]

THE VOLKSUNIE AND THE VLAAMS BLOK

The Volksunie

The Flemish ethnopolitical movement in the period immediately following World War II included many individuals who had been collaborators or who had been accused of collaboration. It is therefore noteworthy that the executives of the newly created Volksunie were all individuals who did not have such a past. In fact, Hugo Gijsels argues that the group was carefully chosen to allow the new party to dissociate itself from the extreme right sympathies of some in the movement, although such individuals could be found among the members of the Volksunie.[16] Some waited before joining the new party. Karel Dillen, for example, who had a long-standing association with the extreme right and later became the founder of the Vlaams Blok, joined the Volksunie three years after its creation, having initially remained outside it.[17]

At its founding in 1954, the Volksunie set two main goals: (1) It aimed to reform the Belgian state into a federal structure; and (2) it hoped to change the political structures and political culture more generally. The first goal relates directly to the ethnopolitical agenda: Through federalization, the party aimed to secure greater autonomy for Flanders. In concrete terms, this meant greater control over policymaking in all matters that affected Flanders, from language rights to unemployment benefits and the building of roads. The second goal was not so much to reform the formal institutional framework but, rather, to change how politics was conducted within that framework. The consensus-oriented political practices of the traditional parties were faulted because they created a system that was relatively impenetrable to outsiders. In addition, the traditional parties were able to maintain their power bases through patronage. Membership in political parties has long remained higher in Belgium than in the surrounding democracies, and one reason is that tangible benefits, such as jobs, often depended on such affiliations.[18] Despite the criticism of the political practices of the traditional parties, the emphasis of the Volksunie was first and foremost on Flemish interests, that is, the federal goal.

The party significantly improved its performance in 1965 when it gained 6.7 percent of the vote, doubling its support from the previous election. It built on that success and polled around 10 percent of the vote in the next four elections (see Table 5.1). In that same time period, it participated in government coalitions, first in the period 1977–1978 and again in 1988–1991.[19] In each case, the coalition was broad and inclusive. The first coalition included both Flemish and Walloon Christian Democrats (i.e., Catholieke Volkspartij [CVP], or Christian Peoples Party, and Parti Social Chrétien [PSC], or Christian Social Party) and Socialists (i.e., Parti Socialiste and Socialistische Partij); the Front Démocratique des Francophones Bruxellois (FDF), a party claiming to represent the interests of the French-speaking Brussels population; and the Volksunie. The second coalition consisted of the same parties, minus the FDF. In both cases, nationalist parties were perhaps natural coalition participants, because the issues concerned the transformation of the Belgian state from a unitary to a federal system in response to the communitarian problem. In both cases also, constitutional changes were on the agenda that required two-thirds majorities and, to secure these, larger than usual coalitions.[20]

Finally, in both cases, coalition participation entailed significant consequences for the Volksunie. At the end of its first coalition participation, Dillen and a number of others left the party to form the Vlaams Blok. They considered the Volksunie to have added too much water to its ideological wine in making compromises regarding constitutional changes. Thus, starting with the 1978 elections, the Volksunie had to compete with a second Flemish ethnopolitical party that occupied space to the former's ideological right. The latter did not gain strong voter support initially, but it meant a split in the Flemish movement nonetheless. Whereas the Volksunie had been the single representative of Flemish ethnopolitics within Parliament since 1954, there were two such voices after 1978.

The second coalition participation of the Volksunie had equally important consequences. For one, the party experienced heavy losses in the 1991 elections. It polled only 5.9 percent of the vote, down from 8.1 percent in 1987. In the aftermath of this electoral disaster, a number of the Volksunie's MPs defected to the liberal party, the Partij voor Vrijheid en Vooruitgang (PVV), or the Party for Freedom and Progress. Among them was Jaak Gabriels, former chairperson of the Volksunie. The liberal party itself was in some turmoil, as it had once again failed to gain voters or to become part of the government coalition. The liberals soon reinvented themselves to become Vlaamse Liberalen en Democraten (VLD), or the

Table 5.1 Flemish Nationalists in the Belgian Parliament

Election	Party	% Vote	No. Seats
November 16, 1919	VNV	2.6	5
November 22, 1921	VNV	3.0	4
April 5, 1925	VNV	3.9	6
May 26, 1929	VNV	6.3	11
November 27, 1932	VNV	5.9	8
May 24, 1936	VNV	7.1	16
April 1, 1939	VNV	8.3	17
February 17, 1946	—	—	—
June 19, 1949	Flemish Nationalists	2.1	0
June 4, 1950	—	—	—
April 11, 1954	Flemish Nationalists	2.2	1
June 1, 1958	Volksunie	2.0	1
March 26, 1961	Volksunie	3.5	5
May 23, 1965	Volksunie	6.7	4
March 31, 1968	Volksunie	9.8	20
November 7, 1971	Volksunie	11.1	21
March 10, 1974	Volksunie	10.2	22
April 17, 1977	Volksunie	10.0	20
December 17, 1978	Volksunie	7.0	14
	Vlaams Blok	1.4	1
November 8, 1981	Volksunie	9.9	20
	Vlaams Blok	1.1	1
October 13, 1985	Volksunie	7.9	16
	Vlaams Blok	1.3	1
December 13, 1987	Volksunie	8.1	16
	Vlaams Blok	1.9	2
November 24, 1991	Volksunie	5.9	10
	Vlaams Blok	6.6	12
May 21, 1995	Volksunie	4.7	5
	Vlaams Blok	8.0	11

Sources: de Winter, *Elections et Gouvernements*; Inbel, *Belgium;* Belgium Ministerie van Binnenlandse Zaken, *Parlementsverkiezingen.*

Flemish Liberals and Democrats, co-opting the Flemish ethnopolitical agenda in an effort to appeal to a wider range of voters.[21] The fact that it has chosen to do so may constitute evidence of the importance of ethnopolitics in Belgium; it may constitute a "contagion of ethnic politics."[22]

After participating in two coalitions, the Volksunie had lost both party members and voters, and it had gained competition for the nationalist vote from both the radical Vlaams Blok and the liberal VLD. So in 1993, the Volksunie attempted to give itself a clearer profile with a renewed and progressive program. Flemish ethnopolitics is still an important focus of the party, and it is still defined in terms of a federal goal. However, this federal goal is now set against the backdrop of the European Union (EU) and a "Europe of peoples and regions" that is to supersede the current states. Domestic goals include the quest for federalization of social welfare policy and a guaranteed minimum existence for every Belgian citizen over eighteen years of age. The party wants to integrate immigrants into the society and views them as an enriching element. In addition, the Volksunie pleads for an independent Ministry of Development Cooperation, one with a bigger budget and separated from Belgian commercial interests.[23] Together, these program points indicate a left-leaning brand of ethnopolitics that incorporates solidarity with outgroups, be they immigrants within Belgian borders or citizens of Third World states.

Although the Volksunie started out as the sole political voice of Flemish ethnopolitics and incorporated different viewpoints, across time, the more moderate and left-leaning nationalists became central. The departure of Karel Dillen and others who formed the Vlaams Blok also meant that the Volksunie was less compelled to cater to all aspects of its complex heritage: It was no longer necessary to cater to those with extreme right views, who also tended to be those who took an all-or-nothing view toward Flemish autonomy. The departure of Gabriels and the more liberal-oriented members of the Volksunie allowed the party to strengthen the socialist-leaning aspects of its program.

The party's governance structure consists of a congress, a party council, and a party executive. The congress is officially the highest decision-making organ and decides all important questions, including whether or not to participate in government coalitions. The party council is more important than the councils of Belgium's other political parties: It meets once a month and determines the strategy of the party; it also elects the party executive and the chairperson. The executive group is responsible for the day-to-day governance of the party and meets weekly. Another important feature of the Volksunie is that it was created as a nonprofit organization, a legal construction that has, so far, been mirrored only by the Greens.[24]

The Vlaams Blok

The Vlaams Blok represents both a reaction to the Volksunie's willingness to compromise with the mainstream political parties and the extreme right-wing component of Flemish nationalism. It tends to take a maximalist view regarding the movement's goals; its official program calls the Belgian state a "historical error" and demands it be abolished.[25]

The party was founded in 1978 in protest to what was regarded as too much flexibility on the part of the Volksunie. For instance, during its coalition participation in 1977–1978, the Volksunie had accepted the Egmont Pact, which concluded a compromise regarding the adaptation of the constitution to which the Vlaams Blok objected. Starting in the 1980s, the Vlaams Blok also strongly objected to immigrants, who they perceived as culturally and economically detrimental to Flanders.[26] The party's slogan,

"*Eigen volk eerst*" (own people first), was pasted on large billboards along the roads in Flanders. Given the long-standing sympathies with the radical right by the party's main leader, Dillen, this attitude toward nonindigenous populations is not surprising. Although some authors classify the party as exclusively on the extreme right, it is a nationalist party: It arose from the Flemish movement and represents an intolerant form of nationalism.[27]

The Vlaams Blok captured only about one or two seats each election prior to the 1991 election, when it suddenly jumped to a twelve-seat win. Put differently, it had won less than 1.5 percent of the vote in earlier elections, but increased its share to 6.6 percent in 1991. In 1995, the party improved slightly, and it now holds 7.3 percent of the seats versus the 5.7 percent of the total number of parliamentary seats it held after the 1991 elections.

The party's program states that it aims to transform Flanders into an independent state. Its pro-Flemish stand is coupled with an exclusivist stance regarding all others, as reflected in such program points as the desire to have taxes collected in Flanders benefit only the Flemish, to have unemployment benefits and other social services operate on the "own people first" principle, and to ensure that jobs, as well, go to the Flemish first.[28]

Like the Volksunie, the Vlaams Blok positions itself as a party that protests traditional political parties and the "politics as usual" approach. However, whereas the former has been willing to reform the system through participation in it, the latter takes a hard-line stance vis-à-vis the traditional political parties. In other words, the Vlaams Blok would categorize the Volksunie as such a traditional party and would present itself as an alternative. It attempts to appeal to "common sense" and, in that manner, fits comfortably among the recent wave of extreme nationalist parties.[29]

The party's governance structure consists of a congress, a council, and an executive. All members of the party have access to the party congress, which functions primarily as a forum for discussion.[30] The council is more important in decisionmaking and is the highest organ of the party. It meets monthly and makes all decisions regarding policy and strategy. In addition, the executive determines the daily governance of the party. The statutes dictate that the current party chairperson himself appoints his successor. After much speculation, the seventy-year-old Dillen finally made his choice known at the party's congress in June 1996: He selected Frank Vanhecke, a thirty-seven-year-old with convictions similar to Dillen's.[31]

In short, the current Vlaams Blok leadership is seeking to preserve the "purity" of its ideology. It is unlikely to change into a more moderate and tolerant ethnopolitical party anytime soon.

Structure of Incentives

The Flemish and Walloon communities inhabit geographically distinguishable portions of the Belgian state. The exact boundaries of the Flemish- and French-speaking regions have shifted across time, which has contributed to the definition of socioeconomic and political issues in linguistic terms. In fact, research on Belgium's political divisions has placed undue emphasis on linguistic aspects and ignored many others factors that have shaped the political importance of segmentation within this state.[32] The conflict never was about language alone. There were and are distinct economic differences between the two regions. Although the social barriers that once motivated Flemish ethnopolitics have been substantially removed, perceptions of inequality linger. Moreover, modifications to the constitution have acknowledged and institutionalized the communitarian differences.[33]

One issue of contention remains the allocation of governmental resources. A strict focus on the equity of such allocations has led to a profusion of useless and wasteful public works, which have been chronicled in several books.[34] This equity has not diminished Flemish/Walloon antagonism because the Flemish object to evenly divided allocations while contributing more than one-half of the tax base. In a sense, the meticulous pursuit of equity has provided the fodder for further demands for regional autonomy.

Social and Economic Pressures

Economic prosperity has never visited Flanders and Wallonia simultaneously. The differential growth patterns of the two regions have been cited as a factor that has contributed to the emergence of communitarian conflict.[35]

Prior to the Peace of Westphalia in 1648, over two centuries before the establishment of the Belgian state, Flanders was urbanized and prosperous.[36] The heritage of this early time still graces the architecture of many Flemish cities. However, this early economic success was not carried over into the industrial era. Wallonia industrialized as Flanders stagnated.

Belgium was the first state on the European continent to industrialize, but this affected mainly the Walloon provinces of Liège and Hainaut. The coal deposits of this region facilitated the creation of a steel and metalworking industry. In addition, textiles were an important facet of the industry in this region. As a historically very open economy, Belgium has been strongly affected by changes in the world economy, and in the post–World War II era, Wallonia's industry was hit especially hard. Although Flanders had begun its rapid industrialization in the earlier part of the twentieth century, its economy emerged as the more prosperous one only in the period after World War II.[37]

The differential economic experiences of the two regions are reflected in the fact that the employment structures of the Flemish and Walloon regions are still different. As Table 5.2 shows, industrial employment tends to be higher in the Flemish provinces, whereas employment in services tends to be higher in Wallonia: The former employs 33 percent in industry and 64 percent in services, whereas the comparable figures for the latter region are 26 and 71 percent. Moreover, unemployment tends to be higher in the Walloon provinces than in the Flemish region. Although unemployment in the Flemish provinces of Antwerp and Limburg approximates that of some Walloon provinces, on average, Flanders is much better off: 5.5 percent versus 10.8 percent unemployment in Wallonia. Interestingly, the two Flemish provinces with relatively high unemployment rates have also tended to support nationalist politics more strongly. Note that election results reported in Table 5.3 show that in the elections just before (1987) and after (1991) the year for which unemployment figures were observed in Table 5.2 (1990), the two provinces of Antwerp and Limburg reveal stronger support for nationalist parties than any of the other Flemish provinces. Thus there appears to be at least some relation between high unemployment rates and nationalist votes.

Antwerp and Limburg also have higher percentages of foreign residents than the remaining Flemish provinces—excluding Brabant, the

Table 5.2 Structure of Employment in Belgium

Region	Employment (1989)			% Unemployment (1990)
	% Agriculture	% Industry	% Services	
Flanders	3	33	64	5.5
Antwerp	2	33	65	6.5
Flemish Brabant	3	25	73	4.2
Limburg	3	37	60	8.8
East Flanders	4	35	62	5.3
West Flanders	5	34	61	3.7
Wallonia	3	26	71	10.8
Walloon Brabant	3	24	73	6.1
Hainaut	3	27	70	13.1
Liège	3	28	70	11.0
Luxembourg	9	18	73	5.9
Namur	4	21	75	9.9
Belgium	3	27	70	7.6

Source: Eurostat, *Portrait of the Regions,* vol. 1.

Table 5.3 The Flemish Ethnopolitical Vote by Province, 1978–1995[a]

Province	1978	1981	1985	1987	1991	1995	Province: Mean St.D.
Antwerp	13.0	18.1	16.3	18.3	24.6	25.2	19.3
							4.8
Flemish Brabant	10.5	14.0	11.6	12.5	15.0	15.6	13.2
							2.0
Limburg	14.5	18.1	16.9	19.6	21.7	17.7	18.1
							2.4
East Flanders	13.8	18.0	14.0	14.3	17.9	19.0	16.2
							2.4
West Flanders	13.8	17.8	13.5	13.4	14.9	15.1	14.8
							1.7
Year:							
Mean	13.1	17.2	14.5	15.6	18.8	18.5	16.3
St.D.	1.6	1.8	2.2	3.1	4.3	4.1	3.4

Source: Belgium, Ministerie van Binnenlandse Zaken, *Parlementsverkiezingen.*
Note: a. Figures represent votes for the Volksunie plus the Vlaams Blok divided by the total valid poll for the Flemish provinces.

province in which the capital region of Brussels is located.[38] Belgium has seen an influx of foreign residents since 1950 that has doubled the percentage of the Belgian population.[39] However, these residents are concentrated in the capital region and Wallonia, where they make up 28.5 and 11.4 percent of the population; in Flanders, they constitute just 4.5 percent of the population.[40] Moreover, a sizable proportion of their presence relates to Belgium's central position within the EU: A large proportion of foreign residents are citizens of other EU countries.[41] The Vlaams Blok militates not so much against the presence of these foreigners as against those from beyond the borders of Europe. The xenophobia of this party should therefore be considered as part and parcel of its extreme right rhetoric and as only tangentially related to the objective presence of foreign residents within Belgium.

Economically, Belgium is very open and has a high dependence on trade with the European Union and Europe more generally. Table 5.4 shows that about three-quarters of Belgian exports are destined for EU countries and over 80 percent have European destinations. Belgian imports exhibit a similar pattern of interconnectedness with the EU and Europe at large. The Volksunie's rhetoric recognizes this fact, whereas the Vlaams Blok ignores it. The former clearly positions Flanders within the European Union; the latter is much more skeptical.[42]

The economic growth of Flanders in the post–World War II era gave the Flemish a degree of clout they had not experienced before. As the standard of living increased, so did the demands Flemish nationalists made on

Table 5.4   Belgian Trade with Europe, 1991

Trade	% of Total
Exports to the EU	75.2
Imports from the EU	72.8
Exports to all of Western Europe (including the EU)	82.8
Imports from all of Western Europe (including the EU)	81.3

Source: The International Yearbook and Statesman's Who's Who.

the political system. Initially, these demands centered on linguistic parity. French had been the official language in Belgium, which meant that Flemish citizens needed to master French if they aspired to a university education or government job.

Political Incentives

Political Structures.   The fortunes of the Volksunie, the Vlaams Blok, and the traditional Belgian political parties have been played out against the background of a series of constitutional changes that have gradually transformed Belgium from a unitary state into a complex, quasi-federal structure. Currently, the division is twofold: The country is divided into three regions and three communities that overlap. First, there are the Flemish, Walloon, and Brussels capital regions, each having its own legislative council. Second, the Flemish-, French-, and (small) German-speaking communities, each with its own council as well. The Flemish Parliament fuses the regional and community councils into one body, but it denies voting rights to the representatives from the Brussels region for matters concerning the Flemish region. In other words, when discussing legislation that concerns the Flemish region, only those representatives elected from constituencies in that region have voting rights; but when legislation concerns the Flemish community as a whole, the representatives from both the Flemish and Brussels regions vote. This complicated structure allows for representation on the basis of geographic and economic regions, as well as linguistic and cultural communities.

The division of competencies between the regions and the federal government is complex. Some policy areas have been delegated to the regions, but certain components of it remain in the federal government's hands. For example, the regions may set economic policy, but labor law is made by the federal government.[43] In some cases, the retention of such powers by the federal government must be seen in the context of the European integration. In sum, however, the federal government is in charge of foreign and defense policy, the judiciary, and monetary policy.

The federal structure as it currently stands is the result of the fourth constitutional revision of 1993. The four constitutional revisions of 1970,

1980, 1988, and 1993 all addressed issues surrounding the communitarian conflict, with the latter three progressively changing Belgium from a unitary to a federal state.[44]

An additional feature of the political structure is the electoral system. The Belgian system is a proportional representation system that provides relatively easy entry for new parties, especially given the low threshold. The country is divided into twenty voting districts for the 150 seats of the Chamber of Representatives, allocated on the basis of the relative population size of the districts. This yields districts that vary in size from two to twenty-two seats. Seats are allocated at two levels: first in the voting district, and second at the provincial level. Parties cannot automatically participate in the provincial division of seats; they must have reached the threshold in at least one voting district within the province. This threshold is set at one-third of the quota, which is calculated using the d'Hondt method.[45]

The Structure of Competition. Although a PR system does not necessarily lead to a proliferation of political parties, Belgium has experienced a fractionalization of the party system as a result of the mobilization of the Flemish community.[46] Not only did ethnopolitical parties such as the Volksunie and the Vlaams Blok obtain parliamentary representation, the traditional political parties fragmented along communitarian lines as well. The Christian Democrats split in 1968 into the CVP and the PSC. The Liberals broke in 1971 into the PVV and the Parti Réformateur Libéral (PRL), or the Liberal Reform Party. The PVV became the VLD after the 1991 elections. The Socialists were the last to fragment: In 1978, they split into the Socialistische Partij and Parti Socialiste. This essentially leaves Belgium without any truly national political party organizations,[47] although the ideological "sister" parties of the Flemish and Walloon communities have thus far chosen to join or leave coalitions in tandem.

Without considering the entry of new parties into Parliament, the split of the three main parties led to a doubling of the number of parties to six. In addition to the above-mentioned parties, the Belgian Communist Party was represented until it lost its last seats in the 1985 election. The Volksunie has been represented in Parliament since 1954, whereas the joint list of the FDF and the Rassemblement Wallon (RW) first obtained seats in 1968. After the Vlaams Blok and an antitaxes, anti-immigrant party called Respect voor Arbeid en Democratie/ Union pour la Démocratie et la Respect du Travail (RAD/UDRT) entered Parliament with one seat each in 1978, the number of parties had increased to eleven. In the subsequent election of 1981, a Flemish and a Walloon Green Party entered Parliament, bringing the total number of parties to thirteen. Since that time, the number and identity of the parties in Parliament have fluctuated with each election. Some of the new parties disappear after only one election; others hang on a little longer. The RAD/UDRT disappeared from Parliament in 1987 after having obtained one or more seats in the previous three elections. A party called Rossem entered Parliament in 1991 but disappeared again in 1995. The Front National entered Parliament in the same year and doubled its presence to two seats in 1995. After losing ground, the FDF affiliated itself with the PRL in 1995, reducing the number of parties to eleven in 1995. In addition to the parties that manage to gain representation in Parliament, many others have run for election at least once. In 1991, forty-one different parties ran, and in 1995, there were sixty different lists on the ballot.[48] The majority of these aspirants have not gained representation, but their presence suggests that the Belgian party system remains in flux. This flux has contributed to openings for more radical ethnopolitics.

The rise of ethnopolitical parties in Belgium has been described both as a cause and as a symptom of the breakdown of the consociational party system.[49] The rigidity of the consociational system may have contributed to the rise of new parties to represent these emerging nationalist interests. Yet the rise of these new parties also contributed to the fragmentation of the traditional mass parties into Flemish and Walloon counterparts. Only the Communist Party maintained a single national party structure until its demise in 1985. The breakup of the Socialist Party essentially completed the communitarization of the political parties in Belgium.

The Flemish ethnopolitical parties have had two aims—one substantive and the other process oriented. The former entails a demand for greater autonomy for the region and linguistic community. The latter entails a challenge to consociationalism that, the new parties claim, did not respond adequately to certain political problems faced by the society—specifically, the socioeconomic differences between Flanders and Wallonia.[50] As such, the ethnopolitical parties can be seen as mobilizing parties that seek to attract voters on the basis of a "program that stresses new issues and looks at old issues from a new ideological vantage point."[51] The consequence of Flemish ethnopolitical representation in Parliament has been a restructuring of the entire party system along communitarian lines and the demise of national parties.

EVOLUTION OF THE VOLKSUNIE AND THE VLAAMS BLOK

As stated earlier, the emergence of the Flemish movement was not only about linguistic issues, yet language structured Flemish ethnopolitics in important ways. Although the Flemish are not in numbers a minority population—they constituted just over 55 percent of the population in 1965, and their share of the population then grew to almost 58 percent by 1993 (see Table 5.5)—they have historically constituted a political minority. The French-speaking or Walloon population has shrunk slightly, but it remains at around 32 percent of the population. The German-speaking minority has remained stable as well. In the past, the Flemish were the most likely of these three groups to become fully bilingual: French acted as a ticket to university education, a desirable career, and membership in the elite. The Francophone population may have been exposed to Flemish in school, but it often cared little to become truly conversant in it.[52] As the Flemish movement gained ground and effected constitutional changes, identifying oneself as Flemish became more attractive than a bilingual identification. Indeed, Table 5.5 shows a drop in the percentage of the population identifying itself as bilingual.

There have been other issues that have demanded attention, but the communitarian conflict is the thread that consistently runs through the history of the Belgian state. In the early post–World War II years, the "Royal Question" divided citizens; and in the 1950s, the so-called School Conflict did likewise. The former revolved around the acceptability of Leopold III as the king of Belgium. The king had spent the war years in the custody of the Germans and was for many associated with collaboration. A referendum did not settle the question. A majority nationally wished the king to return, but the vote was divided unevenly between the two regions: The Flemish tended to favor the king's return, and the Walloons did not.[53] In August 1950, the king proposed to abdicate in favor of his son Boudewijn, and the issue was thus settled.

Soon after, Belgium was embroiled in another debate. This time, the issue was secondary education. At issue was the fact that the cost of Catholic secondary schools often precluded parents from choosing freely whether they preferred an "official" (or public) or a "free" (private or Catholic) education for their children. The problem was complicated by

Table 5.5 Composition of the Belgian Population, 1965–1993

	1965	1970	1975	1980	1985	1991	1993
Flemish (%)	55.4	56.1	56.5	57.0	57.5	57.8	57.9
French (%)	32.7	32.3	32.2	32.1	31.9	32.0	32.0
Bilingual (%)	11.3	11.0	10.7	10.2	9.9	9.6	9.4
German (%)	0.6	0.6	0.6	0.7	0.7	0.7	0.7
Total population[a]	9,499,234	9,650,944	9,788,248	9,863,374	9,858,895	9,986,975	10,068,319

Source: Statesman's Yearbook.
Note: a. Population figures are estimates, except for the 1970 figure, which is based on a census.

the fact that the Catholic schools were more plentiful than public ones in Flanders. The School Pact of 1959 settled the issue by making secondary education free, with the state paying the salaries of teachers in both public and private schools and increasing the number of public secondary schools, especially in Flanders.[54]

Additional consequences of the School Pact were a qualitative improvement in education and a coherent educational policy. A by-product of greater access to education has been that the composition of the Belgian elite has changed to include more Belgians of Flemish heritage.[55] Increased inclusion of Flemish Belgians into elite ranks was indeed the result of the changed circumstances, but it also strengthened Flemish ethnopolitics. Thus, although Flemish and French Belgians have achieved parity in educational levels, the French still have an advantage that derives from (family) connections with the elite.[56] In other words, while the pool of candidates for elite positions is now equivalent across the two communities, the Flemish still perceive French Belgians to have an advantage. A sense of cultural inferiority has been difficult to overcome, despite real and significant change in the region.

An improved economic base and enhanced educational opportunities have nevertheless allowed more Flemish to join the ranks of the elite. Simultaneously, the Flemish movement gained a firm foothold in Belgian politics; although it had obtained five seats in 1961, its electoral support strengthened significantly in 1965, when it lost one seat but received a much larger share of the vote than it had in the previous election (see Table 5.1 above).

Gaining representation in Parliament may have served to strengthen the ethnopolitical cause, because it evidenced voter support for the movement and encouraged others who were sympathetic to express that sympathy electorally. Strengthening voter support beyond the initial base, however, often meant appealing to a broader audience. The Volksunie chose to do so and is now represented about equally in the Flemish provinces. The Volkunie's first electoral success came in Antwerp; but as the party gained more seats, the distribution of its support diffused among the provinces.

Participation in a government coalition, the next step taken by the Volksunie, proved to be a double-edged sword. On the one hand, participation allowed the party to play a role in the conduct of government and to influence decisions. On the other hand, it necessitated compromise, which became difficult for the party's membership and voters to accept. Thus, in keeping with Kris Deschouwer's contention that "new parties begin to lose as soon as they are perceived as being part of the 'traditional game,' which certainly happens when they accept an offer to join the government,"[57] the give-and-take of coalition politics readily led to the perception that the Volksunie failed to protect the interests of the group. The resulting loss of support from the group the party represented was very difficult to recoup.[58]

The Volksunie lost seats in the elections immediately following its coalition participation in two coalition governments. In 1978, at the end of its first taste of coalition government, it lost six seats, which it was able to regain in the subsequent election of 1981. The aftermath of its second coalition participation turned out quite differently. In 1991, the party again lost six seats, but instead of regaining these in the subsequent election, the party continued to slide to five seats in 1995. This loss of seats looks more dramatic than it actually was: The Parliament used to consist of 212 seats but was reduced to 150 seats in the 1995 election. Ten seats in 1991 translated to 4.7 percent of the total, whereas five seats in 1995 translated to 3.3 percent of the total number of seats.

Despite the Volksunie's voting losses, the total ethnopolitical vote fluctuated little. Since the Volksunie's rise to almost 10 percent of the vote in the 1968 election, the ethnopolitical vote has been around 10 percent of the national total. It reached a low in 1978, with 8.4 percent, and a high in 1995, with 12.7 percent. Across the ten elections between 1968 and 1995, the ethnopolitical vote averaged 10.5 percent, with a standard deviation of 1.369. By this measure, all but the 1978, 1991, and 1995 elections fell within 1 standard deviation of the average.

The greatest benefactor from the Volksunie's decline has been the Vlaams Blok. Since 1978, the latter received enough votes to obtain one or two seats and initially was of secondary importance compared to the Volksunie. However, in the 1991 elections, the Vlaams Blok gained significantly in support, polling 53 percent of the ethnopolitical vote and leaving the Volksunie just 47 percent. Despite this increased electoral strength, the Vlaams Blok has remained a party that is thoroughly entrenched in the province of Antwerp. As Table 5.6 shows, in both the 1991 and 1995 elections, about half of the Vlaams Blok's support came from that province. Put another way, the party has done less to broaden its appeal than the Volksunie did at a comparable stage in its evolution. In concrete terms, this means that the Vlaams Blok has moderated its message only slightly, which is also evident from a comparison of the party's 1991 and 1995 programs. The Vlaams Blok has continued to favor an independent Flemish nation-state and maintains a virulently anti-immigrant stance.[59]

Thus, while the face of Flemish ethnopolitics is changing, much remains the same: The socialist and extreme right traditions continue to be found in Flemish nationalism. The first is associated with the Volksunie and the latter with the Vlaams Blok. In addition, the former represents a moderate and the latter a radical ethnopolitics. The Volksunie stresses autonomy within the now-federal Belgian state and eventually in a "Europe of nations and regions," whereas the Vlaams Blok argues for an independent Flanders.[60]

Table 5.6   Distribution of Volksunie and Vlaams Blok Parliamentary Representation in Flemish Provinces

		Province				
Year	Antwerp	Vlaams Brabant[a]	Limburg	East Flanders	West Flanders	Total
Volksunie						
1954	1	—	—	—	—	1
1958	1	—	—	—	—	1
1961	2	1	—	2	—	5
1965	4	1	—	4	3	12
1968	6	3	2	5	4	20
1971	7	3	2	5	4	21
1974	7	4	2	5	4	22
1977	6	4	2	5	3	20
1978	3	3	2	3	3	14
1981	5	4	2	5	4	20
1985	4	3	3	3	3	16
1987	4	3	3	3	3	16
1991	3	2	3	2	—	10
1995	1	1	1	1	1	5
Vlaams Blok						
1978	1	—	—	—	—	1
1981	1	—	—	—	—	1
1985	1	—	—	—	—	1
1987	2	—	—	—	—	2
1991	6	2	1	3	—	12
1995	5	2	1	2	1	11

Sources: Annuaire Statistique de la Belgique, 1991; Belgium, Ministerie van Binnenlandse Zaken, *Parlementsverkiezingen.*
Note: a. Includes seats won in the voting district of Brussel-Halle-Vilvoorde.

What has changed is that Flemish ethnopolitics now affects all Flemish political parties. All have been forced to pay attention to ethnopolitical issues. The Liberals have perhaps gone the furthest in adopting aspects of the ethnopolitical agenda, indicated by their name change to Flemish Liberals and Democrats after the 1991 election. This name change also indicated an adoption of a moderate Flemish ethnopolitical agenda. The current fraction leader of the VLD in the Flemish Parliament, André Denys, has argued for greater autonomy for Flanders, although he also clearly states that he is not a separatist and does not want to do away with the Belgian state.[61]

As the VLD has moved to adopt some of the Flemish ethnopolitical agenda, some former members of the Volksunie have joined its ranks. André Geens, who was minister of development cooperation during the 1988–1991 coalition of Christian Democrats, Socialists, and the Volksunie, has since exchanged his Volksunie membership for membership in the VLD's party executive. Another former Volksunie member, Jaak Gabriels, has similarly joined the VLD.[62]

As the political representation of the Flemish movement was split between the Volksunie and the Vlaams Blok, the former adopted a more left-
oriented platform, while the latter built on the far-right tradition of the
movement. Moderate Flemish nationalists who were not comfortable with
the radical and far-right aspects of Flemish ethnopolitics, but also did not
feel at home with the increasingly socialist orientation of the Volksunie,
found a home in the VLD.

The Vlaams Blok has continued to gain in strength, but its future may
be in question as it has recently resorted to what was described in the press
as a "coup attempt" and likened to tactics used by Nazi storm troopers.[63]
In response to the riot created by a group associated with the Vlaams Blok
at the annual commemoration of the Flemish war experience at the IJzer
Front during the last weekend of August 1996, a split occurred within the
party: Jan Caubergs and several other Vlaams Blok politicians quit the
party in protest. Caubergs will remain a member of Parliament, but he will
now be an independent, rather than the representative of a party. The others held office at the provincial and local levels.[64]

This split brings home the message that there are limits to how radical
the Vlaams Blok can become. Extralegal or antisystem activities may be
tolerated by some in the movement, but they will also create tensions
within the party and hamper its effectiveness. The actions of the Vlaams
Blok at the IJzer commemoration also highlight the party's quest to become the sole voice of the Flemish movement. Ironically, the message that
its riot drowned out was a speech that stressed dialogue and cooperation
among the politicians of Flanders and an injunction to develop a common
vision regarding the meaning and the priorities for the autonomy that has
been achieved thus far.[65]

DISCUSSION AND CONCLUSION

A series of constitutional changes reformed Belgium from a unitary state
to a complicated federal one. Despite substantial grants of autonomy to the
Flemish and Walloon regions, the debate continues. The Flemish ethnopolitical parties continue to receive support, together polling a more or less
steady proportion of the national vote since about 1968.

That does not mean that the phenomenon of Flemish ethnopolitics has
remained unchanged across time. Economic disparity between the two regions has existed throughout Belgium's history and has provided the seeds
of discontent. However, the rise of the Flemish economy coincides with
the increasing strength of the Flemish ethnopolitical parties (Expectation
2a in Chapter 1). The gap between Flanders and Wallonia initially nar-
rowed, as the former's economy started catching up with the latter's, and

then widened in Flanders' favor. It must be noted that while the Volksunie maintained a moderate stance, the Vlaams Blok emerged as the mouthpiece of a more extreme ethnopolitics. If the two parties are considered jointly, it may be concluded that Flemish ethnopolitical demands did indeed radicalize as Flanders emerged economically.

Furthermore, in those areas in Flanders that have experienced higher unemployment, support for the ethnopolitical parties tends to be stronger. This gives some credence to the notion that economic downturn creates an environment that is responsive to more extreme ethnopolitical demands (Expectation 2b).

The Flemish ethnopolitical parties emerged in a country in which consociational traditions favored cross-party agreement. The elites of both communities were represented in the traditional political parties. However, these elites, whether of Walloon or Flemish descent, also tended to speak French and to be highly interconnected with each other. Thus, the perception that the French-speaking community dominated Belgian politics was not difficult to substantiate (Expectation 5). Flemish ethnopolitical demands were geared to breaking open this relatively closed system of elite interconnectedness, thus providing greater opportunities for upward mobility for an emerging Flemish middle class. In short, Flemish ethnopolitical demands reacted not only to the overrepresentation of the French-speaking community in government, but also to a relatively closed elite structure.

NOTES

1. Kossmann, *The Low Countries*, 164; Fishman, *Diplomacy and Revolution*, 85.

2. The distinctions between modern Dutch and Flemish are comparable to those between British and American English. References to either are used interchangeably, except for those to historical situations: King William I meant to create a unity of language; the French-speaking leaders of the newly independent Belgium meant to be derogatory about the Flemish language.

3. Wils, "Introduction," 1–39.

4. Vermeersch, *Vereniging en Revolutie*, 32.

5. Witte, Craeybeckx, and Meynen, *Politieke Geschiedenis van België*, 58; Luykx and Platel, *Politieke Geschiedenis van België*, 44; Wils, "Introduction," 5; Kossmann, *The Low Countries*, 123; Fishman, *Diplomacy and Revolution*, 23; Vermeersch, *Vereniging en Revolutie*, 52, 88–92; Geyl, *Noord en Zuid*, 195.

6. Witte et al., *Politieke Geschiedenis van België*, 58.

7. Kossmann, *The Low Countries*, 469. See also Witte et al., *Politieke Geschiedenis van België*, 101, 142–143, and Luykx and Platel, *Politieke Geschiedenis van België*, 126–127.

8. Kossmann, *The Low Countries*, 465; Witte et al., *Politieke Geschiedenis van België*, 122.

9. Kossmann, *The Low Countries*, 470, 542–544; Luykx and Platel, *Politieke Geschiedenis van België*, 265; Witte et al., *Politieke Geschiedenis van België*, 149–150.

10. Witte et al., *Politieke Geschiedenis van België*, 181; Kossmann, *The Low Countries*, 607, 638; Deschouwer, "Small Parties," 137; de Winter, *Elections et Gouvernements*, 77; Dewachter, *De Wetgevende Verkiezingen*, 22.

11. Witte et al., *Politieke Geschiedenis van België*, 182–185; Luykx and Platel, *Politieke Geschiedenis van België*, 271–274; Kossmann, *The Low Countries*, 637.

12. Kossmann, *The Low Countries*, 542–543, 638; Clough, *A History of the Flemish Movement*; Witte et al., *Politieke Geschiedenis van België*, 184.

13. Witte et al., *Politieke Geschiedenis van België*, 184; Kossmann, *The Low Countries*, 639; de Winter, *Elections et Gouvernements*, 88, 93.

14. Witte et al., *Politieke Geschiedenis van België*, 210, 215; Kossman, *The Low Countries*, 639–640.

15. de Winter, *Elections et Gouvernements*, 108; Urwin, "Social Cleavages," 320–340; Deschouwer, "Small Parties," 138. In the meantime, Dutch historian Pieter Geyl helped draft a 1931 bill proposing to reorganize Belgium as a federal state (Kossmann, *The Low Countries*, 643). Despite his actions, Geyl did not think this plan was realistic, and neither did the minimalist Flemish nationalists within the Catholic and socialist parties. They favored linguistic parity and a bilingual central administration instead. However, the proposal is of interest because more than sixty years later, Belgium has, after four constitutional revisions, indeed become a federal state.

16. Gijsels, *Het Vlaams Blok*, 49–50.

17. Ibid., 50.

18. Deschouwer, "The Decline of Consociationalism," 102–103.

19. de Winter, *Elections et Gouvernements*, 176, 204–205.

20. Deschouwer, "Small Parties," 146–148.

21. Ibid., 90.

22. Horowitz, *Ethnic Groups in Conflict*.

23. Volksunie, *Met Hart en Ziel voor Vlaanderen*.

24. Deschouwer, "De Politieke Partijen," 127; Deschouwer, "The Decline of Consociationalism," 91.

25. Vlaams Blok, *Nu Afrekenen!*; Vlaams Blok, *Uit Zelfverdediging*.

26. Deschouwer, "De Politieke Partijen," 130. See also Deschouwer, "Small Parties," 138.

27. Gijsels, *Het Vlaams Blok*, 46–49; Desolre, "The Far Right in Belgium," 245–257.

28. Vlaams Blok, *Nu Afrekenen!*; Vlaams Blok, *Uit Zelfverdediging*.

29. Deschouwer, "De Politieke Partijen," 130.

30. Ibid., 131.

31. Derk Jan Eppink, "Bijtklare Vanhecke Houdt Blok Ultra-rechts," *De Standaard*, June 10, 1996.

32. Huyse, "Politiek-Wetenschappelijke Publikaties over België," 193–206; Frognier, Quevit, and Stenbock, "Regional Imbalances," 251.

33. Dunn, "The Revision of the Constitution," 143–163.

34. Folkert Jensma, "De Belg, Hij Lééft," *NRC Handelsblad*, February 5, 1994, sec. Boeken.

35. Frognier et al., "Regional Imbalances," 274; Wils, "Introduction," 1; Dewachter, "Elite Circulatie," 199–258.

36. Wils, "Introduction," 2; Frognier et al., "Regional Imbalances," 253.

37. Wils, "Introduction," 1, 12–13; Frognier et al., "Regional Imbalances," 252, 254; Kossmann, *The Low Countries*, 635; Witte et al., *Politieke Geschiedenis van België*, 139; Katzenstein, *Small States in World Markets*.

38. Inbel, *Belgium*, 14.

39. *Statesman's Yearbook*, various years.

40. Matthijs, "Bevolking," 50–58.

41. Eurostat, *Portrait of the Regions*, vol. 1, 156.

42. Volksunie, *Met Hart en Ziel voor Vlaanderen*; Volksunie, *Iemand Moet z'n Nek Uitsteken*; Vlaams Blok, *Nu Afrekenen!*; Vlaams Blok, *Uit Zelfverdediging*.

43. Van Nieuwenhove, "De Bevoegdheidsverdeling," 200.

44. Lamberts, "Staatsvorming via Conflictbeheersing," 43.

45. Dewachter, *De Wetgevende Verkiezingen*, 353; Deweerdt, "Verkiezingen," 274–277.

46. Powell, *Contemporary Democracies*, 101. See also Deschouwer, "The Decline of Consociationalism," 84. The nationalist movement was primarily a Flemish one, but it did draw a response from the Walloon community in the form of the FDF and the RW (Deschouwer, "Small Parties," 135–151). Although the two together polled around 10 percent of the national vote in the early 1970s, they have not been able to sustain that electoral success in the subsequent decades.

47. Deschouwer, "Small Parties," 144.

48. Belgium, Ministerie an Binnenlandse Zaken, *Parlementsverkiezingen*.

49. Urwin, "Social Cleavages," 340; Deschouwer, "The Decline of Consociationalism," 82–83. Deschouwer includes the FDF and the RW in his analysis, as well as the Flemish and Walloon Green Parties.

50. Deschouwer, "The Decline of Consociationalism."

51. Rochon, "Mobilizers and Challengers," 421. The concept of a mobilizing party is similar to G. Bingham Powell's extremist contender, in the sense that such parties "promise radical changes" (*Contemporary Democracies*, 93).

52. Recently, *De Standaard* reported that more Francophone Belgians are now learning Dutch or Flemish; they are beginning to view it as an economic necessity (June 24, 1996).

53. Witte et al., *Politieke Geschiedenis van België*, 246–252; Luykx and Platel, *Politieke Geschiedenis van België*, 449.

54. Luykx and Platel, *Politieke Geschiedenis van België*, 488–489.

55. Witte et al., *Politieke Geschiedenis van België*, 264; Dewachter, "Elite Circulatie," 224.

56. Dewachter, *De Wetgevende Verkiezingen*, 233–234.

57. Deschouwer, "The Decline of Consociationalism," 106.

58. Horowitz, *Ethnic Groups in Conflict*, 344.

59. Breuning and Ishiyama, "The Rhetoric of Nationalism."

60. Volksunie, *Met Hart en Ziel voor Vlaanderen;* Volksunie, *Iemand Moet z'n Nek Uitsteken;* Vlaams Blok, *Nu Afrekenen!;* Vlaams Blok, *Uit Zelfverdediging*.

61. Boudewijn Vanpeteghem, "Meer Autonomy of België ontploft," *De Standaard*, September 13, 1996.

62. Janssens, Fiers, and Vos, "Vlaamse Politieke Partijen," 503–559.

63. Derk Jan Eppink, "Vlaams Blok doet couppoging op IJzerweide," *De Standaard*, August 26, 1996.

64. "Ruzie over IJzerbedevaart," *NRC Handelsblad*, September 3, 1996.

65. Guy Tegenbos, "'Soevereiniteit' moest Vlamingen herenigen," *De Standaard*, August 29, 1996.

6

The Scottish National Party
and Plaid Cymru in
Great Britain

The ethnopolitical challenge to the British state has been a persistent, if marginal, feature of the relations between what is called the "Celtic fringe" and the English core. Although there are commonalities between the ethnopolitical parties of Scotland and Wales today, they originate from different social and political circumstances and have followed different trajectories across time. Devolution is now a fact, but it is more widely supported in Scotland than in Wales. Moreover, the Scottish Parliament has more significant powers, including the ability to vary the tax rate from that set by the central government in London, than does the Welsh Assembly.

The Scottish National Party (SNP) emerged in a Scotland where identification as a nation separate from England was rooted in history and culture, but not in language. Early Scottish ethnopolitics did have its share of romantics who favored the Gaelic language, but so few among the Scots spoke it that it was difficult to structure political demands around linguistic issues. Pragmatism, centered on the observation that Scottish socioeconomic needs were neglected by Parliament, became dominant within the SNP initially. The party has consistently favored constitutional methods. However, the British electoral system has made it difficult for third parties to gain representation in Parliament. In claiming to speak on behalf of Scottish interests, then, this has resulted in two problematic goals for the SNP: first, to convince Scots to vote in large numbers for a party that is unlikely to have much of a voice in government and, second, to convince the central government in London that it is a force with which to be reckoned. In response to these difficulties, the SNP, while remaining committed to the principles of democratic government and negotiated change, has also radicalized its rhetoric: It now demands independence for Scotland. Nevertheless, the SNP has expressed a willingness to accept autonomy, at least for the time being.

Plaid Cymru, by contrast, emerged in an environment where Welshness and language were more closely connected, even as the proportion of the population actually speaking Welsh continued to decline. Linguistic preservation and language rights were long central to the party, which on occasion expressed its frustration at its lack of success through extraconstitutional acts. Its association with such acts not only slowed its transformation into a political party fully committed to constitutional means, but it also slowed the diffusion of voter support among the population of Wales. The marginal support for the Welsh Assembly showed that, despite the strength of Welsh identity, Plaid Cymru's demands have not taken hold among the region's voters.

In both the Scottish and Welsh cases, ethnopolitics sought to reverse absorption into one British whole. Scotland preserved some of its unique institutions after the Act of Union with England in 1707, whereas Wales lost its institutions in its Act of Union with England in 1536. Conversely, Wales managed to keep its Welsh language alive, whereas Scotland all but lost its Gaelic. Despite the unique ability of a language to tie a people together, Scottish ethnopolitics has politically been more successful.

HISTORICAL BACKGROUND

Scotland

Scottish ethnopolitics has deep roots and has been an enduring facet of the relations between Scotland and England. It has been argued that "Scottish nationalism is as old as the Scottish nation," and the Declaration of Arbroath of April 6, 1320, has been cited as an early and significant event in the formation of a Scottish national identity. This declaration predated the union of 1707 with England, which stirred the nationalist imagination in literary circles in the eighteenth century; but this literary movement largely failed to capture the enthusiasm of the Scottish masses.[1]

Historically, Scottish ethnopolitics has lacked a readily definable feature around which grievances could be structured. Linguistic or religious grievances have not played a role, as neither reliably differentiates the Scottish and English peoples. More important, on the political front, Scots have long enjoyed representation in the British government; the 1707 union resulted in the parliamentary representation of Scotland with forty-five members in the House of Commons and sixteen peers in the House of Lords. This gave the Scottish people a voice at the center of government, the lack of which often becomes a source of ethnopolitical grievances. Moreover, the union stimulated both economic and intellectual development. This does not mean that the relations between Scotland and England functioned smoothly from the start. The first half century was a period of adjustment and considerable discontent, because the expected expansion of Scottish commerce and industry was slow to materialize. Once the economic expansion took hold, however, discontent largely vanished, and the union went basically unchallenged for about a century.[2]

Toward the latter part of this period, the Reform Act of 1832 redrew district boundaries and extended the franchise. Scotland gained a system of free elections, and for the next fifty years its MPs were almost exclusively Whig or Liberal. While Scottish politics thus played itself out through the mainstream political parties, there also emerged a recurrent criticism of the union.[3]

As early as 1828 there was a call for the creation of a Scottish Office to handle Scottish affairs. Scottish nationalism did not emerge until the middle of the nineteenth century, however. H. J. Hanham argues that three distinct groups were attracted by nationalist ideas at the end of the 1840s: The first was made up of practical reformers and businesspeople in Glasgow, who argued that Scottish needs were neglected by the Parliament at Westminster. The second comprised the Scottish literary establishment in Edinburgh, which emphasized the need to restore Scotland to its former glories. Many among this group favored Gaelic, which was spoken by less than 2 percent of Scots. In fact, most of the Gaelic speakers were bilingual. Third, there were the few radical thinkers who wanted Scotland to stand on its own two feet.[4] The first group, while using the symbols of ethnic politics, represented issues central to all political decisionmaking: who gets what share of the government's resources. It represented moderate demands. The second and third groups represented romantic notions of the nation and potentially more radical demands. Crosscutting the birth of ethnopolitics was the emergence of socialism, which had a profound effect on the political outlook of many Scots.[5] However, since class interests extended beyond national boundaries, they also tempered nationalist demands.

Most important, it was difficult to formulate the sort of grievances that compel people to join the nationalist cause. English rule was not particularly exploitative, and the government showed "a capacity and a willingness to respond, albeit slowly and reluctantly, to Scottish pressures."[6] Nevertheless, the Scottish people did not perceive themselves as part of a single, integrated British nation. In fact, public opinion was generally favorably disposed toward the idea of greater autonomy for Scotland.[7] But this support did not frequently translate into political demands.

In 1853, the first nationalist organization emerged: the National Association for the Vindication of Scottish Rights (or the Scottish Rights Society). The group's support came primarily from literary and radical sources. One of its supporters was the Reverend James Begg of Edinburgh, who had earlier called for a stronger representation of Scotland at Westminster and for a secretary of state for Scotland. The group's activities came to a halt when the Crimean War broke out in 1854.[8]

Toward the end of the nineteenth century ethnopolitics reemerged. Now, demands for home rule were voiced in both Scotland and Ireland. In 1886, Prime Minister William Gladstone decided to support home rule for Ireland. The issue caused a split in the Liberal Party. In Scotland, one group saw it as a dangerous precedent: The implications of land tenure reforms and the consequences for business worried landowners and businesspeople. The other group saw it as an opportunity: It made home rule for Scotland seem acceptable and feasible. It is no surprise, then, that the very same year, the Scottish Home Rule Association was founded. However, the Irish question took precedence for the Liberal Party at Westminster, and Scottish home rule was supported more in word than in deed. In this time period, home rule became a popular idea among radical and labor leaders. Indeed, Hanham goes so far as to argue that the debate "brought to the fore a new type of working-class nationalism."[9]

Between 1892 and the outbreak of World War I in 1914, proposals to grant Scotland a separate Parliament were introduced on a number of different occasions. There was support for the idea of a federal structure, not only by Liberals, but on the part of the Conservatives as well. Toward the end of World War I, a new Home Rule Association was formed. In the period subsequent to the war, the Labour Party emerged as one of the main bodies in Britain and Scotland. Although it was initially supportive of home rule, that support began to weaken in the early 1920s. Part of the problem was that the Labour Party in England needed the votes of its Scottish and Welsh counterparts. Devolution away from the unitary government in London would weaken the party's support. Thus, it was not in the interest of the Labour Party to support devolution or home rule. Additionally, the Scottish Trades Union Congress, which had earlier supported the call for autonomy, increasingly emphasized solidarity with the international working-class movement, rather than with ethnic politics.[10]

As the Labour Party's support for Scottish autonomy began to weaken in the 1920s, the movement's reliance on mainstream parties to achieve it began to look less and less promising. Up to this point, Scottish nationalists had worked within the established parties. Now, however, voices emerged within the Scottish Home Rule Association in favor of running independent Scottish candidates.[11]

After the failure of yet another home rule debate in Parliament in 1924, Roland Muirhead, a small businessman who had been active in the pre–World War I Home Rule Association, became convinced that the existing political parties would never support the nationalist cause. He initiated talks with various organizations in Scotland to try to establish a Scottish ethnopolitical party. At first, there was little interest. Each organization had a different purpose. The Scots National League stood for breaking up Britain as soon as possible, whereas the Scottish Home Rule Association advocated autonomy within the existing structure of Britain. The Glasgow University Scottish Nationalist Association, which had been the by-product of a rectorial election at the university, eventually provided the catalyst necessary to bring the rival groups together. The result was the National Party of Scotland (NPS), which held its inaugural meeting on June 23, 1928, and entered the political arena as a left-leaning party with complete independence from England as its goal. The party almost immediately announced four candidates for Parliament and contested its first elections in 1929. The party did not do very well in those elections, partly because it had not yet built a grassroots organization that could support the campaign efforts.[12]

The NPS became increasingly dependent upon John MacCormick, who had led the Glasgow University Scottish Nationalist Association and who was the only person within the organization endowed with a talent for organizing electoral campaigns. MacCormick was a moderate: He favored autonomy rather than independence, and under his leadership, the NPS became associated with this goal. He aimed to win broad public support for his party and displayed an impatience with the more radical literary men within the party.[13]

In the meantime, a second, more moderate party emerged, the Scottish Party (SP), which favored autonomy over independence. Prior to its creation, its leaders had consulted with MacCormick, and an eventual merger of the two parties was likely from the start. MacCormick saw the emergence of this second party as a way to broaden his party's base and to steer the latter solidly in the direction of the moderate goals he preferred. He initiated a debate about the future of the NPS, and although his position initially looked precarious, he eventually won out: The radicals were expelled from the party, and on April 30, 1934, the two parties merged to form the Scottish National Party.[14]

Wales

The incorporation of Wales into Britain proceeded differently from that of Scotland and took place at an earlier date. Toward the end of the thirteenth century, King Edward I of England had conquered Gwynedd. This event was the culmination of the conquest of Wales, which had taken place during the preceding two centuries. English control over Wales resulted in socioeconomic changes, such as the replacement of gavelkind, or equal shares inheritance, with primogeniture. Social upheaval accompanied these changes. The most notable of these was the revolt led by Owain Glyndwr at the start of the fifteenth century. For a decade, he controlled an independent state in Wales. Although his defeat marked the definitive end of Welsh independence, some today trace Welsh ethnopolitics back to Glyndwr's actions.[15]

The Act of Union of 1536 consolidated English control over Wales. It was part of a series of acts that not only affected Wales, but also centralized government control more generally, and hastened the end of feudalism. However, the end result was that Wales, in contrast to Scotland, lost its indigenous political and social institutions. In addition, the Act of Union specified that non-English-speaking persons were prohibited from holding office. Consequently, the Welsh elite became anglicized, but the peasantry did not. It is important to note that the requirement for office-holders to speak English was not a deliberate attempt to suppress the Welsh language; rather, it was an administrative convenience.[16]

These English actions concerning Wales yielded a different situation than that experienced in Scotland. As a consequence, Welsh ethnopolitics was founded on different bases, with Welsh language and the prevalence of nonconformist religions being central features. The two are intertwined here, for during the eighteenth century, missionaries taught the Welsh to read the Bible in their own language, which resulted in both a religious awakening and a revival of the Welsh language. The same era also witnessed the formalization of the Eisteddfod, a folk festival with competition in Welsh poetry, prose, and music. This annual event became a focal point for development of Welsh ethnopolitics.[17]

Although the enclosure of land had been possible in Britain since the late seventeenth century, Wales did not experience enclosures on a significant scale until the nineteenth century. The changes the enclosures wrought on the rural, agrarian society caused much discontent, which expressed itself in the Rebecca Riots of the early 1840s and other protests. In the same century, industrialization made inroads. Technological improvements allowed the iron industry to prosper and made local coal reserves usable in its manufacture. As a result, the rural areas rapidly depopulated as people shifted to the locales of the coal and iron industry.[18]

These economic changes were accompanied by changes in religious affiliation. At the start of the nineteenth century, most Welsh belonged to the established church, but half a century later, nonconformity was dominant. It spread especially rapidly after the Calvinistic Methodists formally broke with the established church in 1811. By some accounts, three-quarters of the population belonged to various nonconformist denominations at midcentury. These denominations played a role in Welsh ethnopolitical sentiment, which coalesced around efforts to disestablish the church in Wales. A first attempt was made through a private member's bill in 1870 and was followed by several others; the disestablishment of the church finally materialized in 1920. Ethnopolitical sentiment thus focused on religious issues rather than political ones, and the first home rule for Wales bill was not introduced until 1914—as disestablishment appeared to be forthcoming by that time—somewhat later than Scottish efforts to attain a measure of self-government.[19]

The Reform Act of 1832 served to increase Welsh influence in the British Parliament slightly and produced a small extension of the franchise, but the balance between county and borough representation was not changed. According to Gareth Jones, it was "deliberate policy in England and Wales to reinforce the landed interest despite population changes."[20] Yet the 1867 Representation of the People Act resulted in more fundamental change. The subsequent election of 1868 gave Wales its first nonconformist MP, Henry Richard, who was elected in the industrial constituency of Merthyr Tydfil. More generally, this election increased the Liberal Party's share of the vote. However, only after the introduction of the secret ballot in 1872 did the Liberal Party solidly take hold in Wales.[21]

Gladstone's support for home rule for Ireland had a somewhat different impact on Wales than it did on Scotland. According to Jones, Gladstone was sympathetic to Wales on many issues, and such Welsh politicians as Tom Ellis and David Lloyd George rose to prominence and succeeded in obtaining some special legislation for Wales. Both also played important roles in the Cymru Fydd (Wales to Be) movement of the 1890s, which was the first Welsh ethnopolitical organization. Self-government was its main objective, although it had been established as a cultural and literary organization. Founded in London, it consisted primarily of Welsh intellectuals who resided there, and it later established branches in Wales. Cymru Fydd aimed to influence the Liberal Party to adopt the goal of self-government for Wales. After this failed, the group's leaders pursued their political careers within the Liberal Party. Lloyd George eventually became prime minister of Britain in 1916. Although he surrounded himself with prominent Welsh Liberals, this was not an era of Welsh ethnopolitical activism: Disestablishment had been achieved, and the influence of the landed estates on politics had eroded substantially.[22]

In the early twentieth century the Labour Party grew rapidly and gained influence, especially in the industrial areas of Wales, and came to dominate Wales from about 1922 to 1974. Although Wales' first Labour MP, Keir Hardie, was a supporter of Welsh national identity, cultural differences were de-emphasized during this time of Labour dominance in favor of class differences.[23] For many in industrial Wales in the 1920s, unemployment and other economic issues took precedence. This same pattern of sympathy for ethnic aspirations but emphasis on class issues was found in early Flemish ethnopolitics as well.

Meanwhile, in 1925, six Welshmen met during the National Eisteddfod at Pwllheli, in the northern Wales region of Gwynedd, to create Plaid Genedlaethol Cymru (Nationalist Party of Wales), with the objective of obtaining dominion status for Wales. The party's name was changed to Plaid Cymru (Party of Wales) after World War II because of the stigma attached to the term "nationalist." Its founding was the result of a merger of several groups, none of which were political parties: Byddin Ymroelwyr (the Welsh Home Rule Army), Byddin Yr Iaith (the Language Army), Y Gymdeithas Genedlaethol Gymreig (the Welsh National Society), and Y Mudiad Cymreig (the Welsh Movement). One additional group, Plaid Genedlaethol Cymru (Nationalist Party of Wales), had existed only since December 1924. Although this last group called itself a party, it never contested an election, and it functioned more like a pressure group. All these groups were small and their memberships overlapped.[24]

THE SCOTTISH NATIONAL PARTY

The debate within the NPS prior to the merger with the SP set the SNP on a moderate course, but the debate between moderate and more radical elements within the party continued to simmer. In 1942, the Scottish role in the war industrial effort, and the party's reaction to it, became the catalyst for a split within the party. This time, MacCormick left the SNP to form the Scottish Convention, which aimed at a federal Britain. The SNP now became a more radical party that began to include once again some of those who had been expelled from the NPS prior to its merger with the SP.[25] However, at the conclusion of World War II, the SNP took a course for moderation under the leadership of Robert McIntyre.

In a by-election in 1945, McIntyre briefly held the parliamentary seat for Motherwell district for the SNP until it was lost again in the general election that followed six weeks later. He became party chairman in 1947 and remained in that position until 1956. Even before he rose to that position, he influenced the party with the argument that it should decide where it stood and then remain committed to that position.[26]

McIntyre was successful in unifying the various voices within the party behind his program, and the party did stay on the course outlined in its 1946 policy statement. This statement was libertarian in tone and emphasized small-town democracy. Most significant, it did not contain a section on Scottish culture because the party's appeal was to the smallholder and lower-middle-class Scot "to whom culture was something that he had already."[27] In other words, the audience to which the party sought to appeal took for granted that it had a distinct way of life—this did not need to be asserted. This audience was also inherently suspicious of the state, so the claim that Scotland was not always well served by decisions made in London did not fall on deaf ears. The focus on local decisionmaking prompted the SNP to concentrate its efforts in municipal elections and to contest parliamentary elections only in districts where it already had a solid base.[28] The period of McIntyre's leadership was one of relative unity, but success in the general elections remained absent. The party contested only a few districts during this period, winning none of them, and its support remained at around 0.5 percent of the vote (see Table 6.1).

In the early 1960s, the SNP changed course again when a group of younger men took over the leadership. More pragmatic in orientation than the radicals earlier in the century, these men exploited economic grievances to rally the Scottish people to demand independence, giving the party a vaguely left-of-center line. They changed the internal workings of the party as well and built an effective publicity machine. Two men in particular played a central role in this transformation of the SNP: William Wolfe and Ian Macdonald. The former was later to become the chairman of the party.[29]

The SNP began to contest elections in more districts and started to improve its showing at the polls: In the 1964 general election, it contested fifteen districts, and although it did not win any seats, it gained a larger percentage of the vote than it ever had. In the subsequent general election of 1966, the party ran an even larger number of candidates and doubled its percentage of the vote. The twenty-three SNP candidates who were on the

Table 6.1 Scottish National Party Election Results, 1929–1997

Election	Party	% Scottish Vote	No. Seats	No. Contested	No. of Constituencies in Scotland
1929	NPS	0.5	0	2	71
1931	NPS	1.0	0	5	71
1935	SNP	1.3	0	8	71
1945	SNP	1.2	0	8	74
1950	SNP	0.4	0	4	71
1951	SNP	0.3	0	2	71
1955	SNP	0.5	0	2	71
1959	SNP	0.5	0	5	71
1964	SNP	2.4	0	15	71
1966	SNP	5.0	0	23	71
1970	SNP	11.4	1	65	71
February 1974	SNP	21.9	7	70	71
October 1974	SNP	30.4	11	71	71
1979	SNP	17.3	2	71	71
1983	SNP	11.7	2	72	72
1987	SNP	14.0	3	71	71
1992	SNP	21.5	3	72	72
1997	SNP	22.1	6	72	72

Sources: Butler and Sloman, *British Political Facts;* Hanham, *Scottish Nationalism;* Kellas, *Modern Scotland;* Lutz, "Diffusion of Nationalist Voting"; Scottish National Party, *A Short History;* British Election Pages.

ballot in 1966 contested seats primarily in the industrial heartland of Scotland; the party concentrated its efforts there rather than in the Celtic fringe, as had been the case for its predecessor, the NPS.[30] Nevertheless, it still did not net a seat in Parliament.

The breakthrough came in a 1967 by-election when Glasgow lawyer Winifred Ewing won the Hamilton seat. Like McIntyre's seat earlier, it was lost again in the following general election. Still, the Hamilton by-election had given the party a renewed confidence.[31] By 1970, the party won the seat for the Western Isles district in the general election and, more important, once again doubled its voter support.[32] The more significant breakthroughs came in the 1974 general elections. In the February election, the SNP netted seven seats in Parliament, and in October, it increased its parliamentary presence to eleven seats. This success, however, was to be short-lived.

In response to the SNP's success in the late 1960s, the Labour Party in 1969 had appointed a Royal Commission on the Constitution. The report of this commission was released in 1973. It paved the way for the 1978 Scotland Act, which provided for an elected Scottish Assembly with limited powers.[33] However, a condition had been attached to the bill specifying that it could be implemented only if it secured the endorsement of 40 percent of the electorate at a referendum. On March 1, 1979, the Scottish electorate voted on this referendum. Although 51.6 percent of the votes cast favored the provisions of the Scotland Act, this fell short of the necessary support, for it constituted 32.9 percent of the electorate, just shy of the 40 percent the law required. In effect, not voting in the referendum was counted as equivalent to a negative vote.[34]

The subsequent general election of May 1979 brought another blow to the SNP. After it had voted with the Conservatives to bring down the Labour government, it was presented with a crushing defeat: Voter support fell dramatically, and representation in Parliament was reduced to two seats. All in all, 1979 became the most traumatic year in the SNP's history. It resulted, not surprisingly, in struggles within the party to determine its identity and direction. These struggles were personified in the form of the 79 Group, which was originally called the Interim Committee for Political Discussion. It consisted of middle-class professionals who were generally younger than most other SNP members. The group assumed that its voters had defected to the Labour Party, although there was evidence that the SNP lost support across the political spectrum. This assumption dictated the group's subsequent strategy, which aimed at the Labour vote with a socialist platform. The 79 Group did not succeed in capturing control of the party and in 1982 was asked to disband. Some of its committee members were expelled from the party, among these Stephen Maxwell and Alex Salmond, who later rose to prominence within the SNP.[35] The expulsion was subsequently turned into a six-month suspension, but the party had clearly taken a position against a too obviously socialist platform.

The next election, in 1983, saw a continued decline of the SNP's voter support, although the party managed to hold on to its two seats. The decline was halted in the 1987 election, which gave the party a net gain of one seat. The three seats it captured in this election actually represented two new seats and the loss of its only urban constituency of Dundee East. A by-election in 1988 netted the party yet another seat. Jim Sillars won the Labour stronghold of Glasgow-Govan.[36]

The party interpreted this by-election result as an endorsement of its new strategy—specifically, independence in Europe. Britain had become a member of the European Union in 1973, and the SNP's argument in the late 1980s centered on the premise that, as part of the EU, Scotland would be able to avoid the problems of being a small, independent state, while gaining representation at the European center, and be part of decisionmaking there, rather than to rely on the London government to do its bidding.[37] Independence in Europe would thus present Scotland with the benefit of gaining representation at the European level, while also affording continued access to the European market.

In the period leading up to the 1992 general election, several other by-elections were held. Although the SNP in each case performed respectably, it did not win any additional seats. It did, however, gain a fifth MP as a result of Dick Douglas's defection from the Labour Party. Both his seat and the one won by Sillars in the Glasgow-Govan by-election were regained by the Labour Party in the 1992 general election. The SNP maintained the three seats it had won in the previous general election, all in rural areas, rather than in the urban centers of Scotland. Each of the urban seats it has held, usually as the result of a by-election, it lost again in the subsequent general election. In short, "Each success in the urban industrial belt has proved an unreliable indicator of the SNP's future prospects."[38] Without the support of the urban centers, the SNP is unlikely to present a serious challenge to the status quo. Part of this problem may be explained by the difficulty the British electoral system presents for a third party, but the structural impediments to gaining representation do not entirely explain the SNP's lack of success.

PLAID CYMRU

The six founding fathers of Plaid Cymru were Moses Gruffydd, H. R. Jones, Fred Jones, Saunders Lewis, Lewis Valentine, and D. E. Williams. Of these, two were ministers and one was a former quarryman who had become a grocery salesman. Saunders Lewis was the most distinguished of the lot: A former librarian, poet, novelist, and lecturer in Welsh at the University of Wales College at Swansea, he went on to become president of Plaid Cymru in 1926 and remained in that position until 1939. The party's leadership agreed on the importance of preserving the Welsh language and expressed a preference for dominion status for Wales. Under Lewis's leadership, the party was primarily a single-issue pressure group that idealized a pre-English and preindustrial rural Wales.[39] In short, the party espoused a cultural and linguistic ethnopolitics.

It contested very few seats and won none. In 1929, Reverend Lewis Valentine became the first Plaid Cymru candidate in a parliamentary election. In the subsequent general elections of 1931 and 1935, the party contested two seats and one seat, respectively, but again to no avail. Four years later, in 1939, Saunders Lewis's presidency of the party ended. In the years that followed, J. E. Daniel and Abi Williams took their turns as president of Plaid Cymru. On the whole, the party seemed to suffer from disillusionment during this period, which was perhaps best expressed by its foray into violence. In 1936, three top leaders of the party, Lewis, Valentine, and D. J. Williams, went to jail after burning some buildings at the construction site for a new air force bombing school in Wales.[40]

Plaid Cymru charted a new direction under the leadership of Gwynfor Evans. He had joined the party as a student and had learned Welsh as a second language. Having been vice president during Abi Williams's tenure, Evans was just thirty-two years old when he was elected to the party's presidency in 1945. Under Evans, the party began to move away from the influence of Saunders Lewis and to contest elections more widely. However, it was not until 1959 that Plaid Cymru contested the majority of seats in Wales, as is shown in Table 6.2.[41]

In the meantime, Plaid Cymru engaged in formal and informal cooperation with other organizations to further its aims. One such example was its involvement in the Parliament for Wales campaign, which was modeled after the movement for a Scottish covenant in 1949–1950. Only toward the end of the 1950s did the party begin to concentrate its efforts on strengthening its own organization. Although it had not yet won any seats, the results of two by-elections prior to the 1955 general election had bolstered the party's morale. The party now also began to contest elections in the urbanized and largely English-speaking regions of south Wales. This was the result of a conscious decision by the party to leave behind its previous, exclusively Welsh-speaking image, which was also reflected in the new focus on a bilingual Wales and a demand for a Welsh Parliament.[42]

The results of the 1959 general election, in which the party for the first time contested more than half the seats in Wales, proved disappointing: The vote was scattered, and no seats were won. The equally disappointing results in a subsequent by-election in 1962 led to internal dissension and,

Table 6.2 Plaid Cymru Election Results, 1929–1997

Election	% Welsh Vote	No. Seats	No. Contested	No. of Constituencies in Wales
1929	0.0	0	1	35
1931	0.2	0	2	35
1935	0.3	0	1	35
1945	1.2	0	7	35
1950	1.2	0	7	36
1951	0.7	0	4	36
1955	3.1	0	11	36
1959	5.2	0	20	36
1964	4.8	0	23	36
1966	4.3	0	20	36
1970	11.5	0	36	36
February 1974	10.7	2	36	36
October 1974	10.8	3	36	36
1979	8.1	2	36	36
1983	7.8	2	38	38
1987	7.3	3	38	38
1992	9.0	4	38	38
1997	9.9	4	40	40

Sources: Butler and Sloman, *British Political Facts;* Craig, *British Electoral Facts;* Lutz, "Diffusion of Nationalist Voting"; British Election Pages.

again, a resort to violence. This time, two members of the party attempted to sabotage the power supply at the site where the dam for the Tryweryn Reservoir was under construction. This reservoir would submerge part of Wales, but it would benefit industrial development in Liverpool.[43] The party's constitutional strategy appeared to be failing, and its leadership began to lose control over its members. The party's attitude toward violent action remained ambivalent: Emrys Roberts, Plaid Cymru's general secretary at the time, declared that the party was not in favor of violent action in general, but that it was justified if used "to force the Government to respect the wishes of the people of Wales."[44]

However, violence damaged the cause and the party. Increasingly, the leadership began to dissociate itself from violence in favor of constitutional methods, but its control over its membership and the separate organizations that were formed was weak. In the meantime, the party began to formulate more clearly its stance regarding the economic problems of Wales and to discuss the role of the Welsh language in its politics.[45]

The most notable transformation of the party came as the result of a by-election held several months after the 1966 general election in which the Labour Party had won a comfortable majority. In Carmarthen, a constituency with a large proportion of Welsh speakers, Plaid Cymru won its first seat. Gwynfor Evans thus became the party's first MP.[46] Plaid Cymru had now shown itself a credible alternative to the major parties. However, it did not win subsequent by-elections in 1967 in Rhondda West or in 1968 in Caerffilli, although it did receive a respectable proportion of the vote in each. The party's membership increased, and it made organizational changes. One of these was the establishment of the Research Group, initially based in London, which was to aid in policy formulation. In 1969, the party produced for the first time a platform that was strongly oriented toward economic issues. Its focus was on the economic problems of the industrial south, rather than the rural north. In addition, it now specifically stated a bilingual Wales as its objective, rather than the previous emphasis on a return to an all-Welsh-speaking Wales. In 1971, it also created a more centralized administrative structure based in its Cardiff office.[47]

Although Plaid Cymru lost its one seat in the 1970 general election, for the first time it contested all Welsh constituencies and more than doubled its electoral support. It did enter Parliament again after the 1974 general election, winning two seats in February and three in October. It has had a continuous presence in Parliament since. Yet, while the SNP saw its support climb to just over 30 percent of the vote in the October 1974 general election, Plaid Cymru's support continued to hover around 10 percent. On the other hand, the SNP's support fell dramatically after the 1979 referendum, whereas Plaid Cymru's support declined only modestly. The latter also lost only one of its three seats in Parliament. Support for devolution was much less strong in Wales: Only 20.3 percent of those voting, or 11.9 percent of the electorate, voted for the Wales Act.[48]

Although the referendum is often described as a humiliating defeat for ethnopolitics in Britain, Plaid Cymru was not devastated by it. In its aftermath, the party completed its transformation from a cultural organization to a political party with a socialist orientation. A leading advocate of this new direction was Dafydd Elis Thomas, who would serve as Plaid Cymru's president from 1984 to 1991.[49]

Plaid Cymru maintained its two seats in Parliament in the 1983 election and added one in each of the following two elections. Interestingly, its 1987 gain of one seat was achieved as a result of the concentration of the vote, because its overall proportion of the vote was smaller than in the previous election. The party's 1992 gain of one seat was matched by a gain in terms of its overall proportion of the vote. Although the party did gain more votes in the 1997 election, it remained at four seats. Of these, one is held by Dafydd Wigley, who succeeded Thomas as president in 1991.

Despite the party's transformation to a socialist-oriented political party, it has made few inroads into the traditional industrial areas dominated by Labour. Like the SNP, Plaid Cymru's support is based in rural, rather than urban, areas. However, whereas the SNP has held urban seats for short periods of time, usually as a result of a by-election, Plaid Cymru has had more consistent success with its rural constituency.

Like the SNP also, Plaid Cymru suffers from the structural impediments the British single-member district system presents to third parties. Plaid Cymru's vote is more concentrated than the SNP's: In the aftermath of the 1979 referendum, it has consistently matched or exceeded the SNP in terms of seats with a substantially lower proportion of the vote. In other words, Welsh ethnopolitics is a less widely shared sentiment than its Scottish counterpart.

STRUCTURE OF INCENTIVES

Social and Economic Pressures

Scotland. Scotland and Wales, as well as Ireland, are part of the so-called Celtic fringe of the British Isles. Although each has a well-defined and separate identity, they share Celtic roots, and it is these roots that set each apart from the Anglo-Saxon heritage of the English. Nevertheless, taken together, they are only a small proportion of the British population: The Scots constitute about 10 percent and the Welsh about 5 percent of the population of Britain (see Table 6.3).

Despite the common heritage of the two regions, Scottish and Welsh ethnopolitics are different. For example, language does not play a role in Scottish ethnopolitics, as it does in the Welsh ethnopolitical movement; too few Scots speak Gaelic to successfully employ language as a political instrument. Furthermore, the problems of Northern Ireland have had an impact on the Scottish: The SNP's anti-English statements are quite moderate, the party does not condone any form of political violence, and it is committed to democratic and electoral avenues to achieve its goals. There is some indication that the Scottish people, while intensely proud of their distinctive identity, would not support violence to assert that identity politically.[50]

The explanation for such moderation lies in part in the economic opportunities the union with England brought to Scotland. Initially, these

Table 6.3 Composition of the British Population, 1951–1991

	1951	1961	1971	1981	1991
Scottish (%)	10.4	10.1	9.7	9.5	9.2
Welsh (%)	5.3	5.2	5.1	5.2	5.2
English (%)	84.3	84.7	85.3	85.4	85.6
Total population	48,854,303	51,283,892	53,978,538	54,147,300	54,156,067

Source: Statesman's Yearbook, 132nd ed., 1995–1996.

opportunities provided a powerful incentive to understand, and to accul-
turate to, the culture, politics, and intellectual life of England. However,
the benefits derived from the Act of Union did not remain so obvious when
Scottish industry lagged during the interwar period. All of Britain was affected, but Scotland was hit especially hard since its main market was
England and the economic depression there had a severe impact. In addition, Scotland was strongly focused on traditional heavy industry, such as
coal, steel, and shipbuilding. Toward the end of the 1930s, the economic
problems of Scotland were eased by the efforts of the Economic Committee and the Scottish Development Council, which helped to bring new industries to Scotland. Early on, this mainly involved the manufacture of
munitions as part of the wartime industrial effort, but it also led companies
to locate high-technology production facilities in the region.[51] In the immediate postwar period, the Marshall Plan helped maintain economic investment, but around the mid-1950s, the economy slowed down once again.

Scotland's economy has historically relied on foreign investment and
British government spending in the form of regional subsidies, a practice
that continues today. Scotland has been termed both a "branch-plant economy" and an "economic colony."[52] This meant that decisions of crucial
importance to the Scottish economy are not made in Scotland. Tom Gallagher argues that this reliance on the British state and foreign investment
created "a culture of dependency resistant to the nationalist project which
could easily be depicted as entailing a great deal of risk and uncertainty."[53]
However, although Scotland lacked indigenous entrepreneurs and depended on subsidies, its economic structure was not very different from
that of Britain. Scotland therefore lacked the sort of economic grievances
and subsequent successes that fueled Flemish ethnopolitics in Belgium. In
short, the lack of indigenous Scottish industry made ethnopolitics less attractive than it otherwise might have been. Moreover, the British economy
is not strongly interconnected with Europe. Trade with the EU accounts for
just over half of both its exports and imports. If trade with the rest of Europe is included, the figures are about ten percentage points higher (see
Table 6.4). In contrast, the Belgian economy is more thoroughly integrated
in the European economy.

During the 1950s and 1960s, the competencies of the Scottish Office
were gradually extended. This office did not have policymaking powers
and reflected a decentralization of bureaucratic functions instead. Although the office was intended to have a purely administrative role, its
secretary of state and senior civil servants became an effective lobby for
Scottish interests. However, the effects of the decline of the British economy had severe repercussions for Scotland: It lost a large proportion of its
manufacturing labor force, had an unemployment rate nearly double that
of Britain, and a per capita income substantially lower and a cost of living

Table 6.4   British Trade with Europe, 1990

Trade	% of Total
Exports to the EU	52.9
Imports from the EU	52.3
Exports to all of Europe (including the EU)	61.9
Imports from all of Europe (including the EU)	64.8

Source: The International Yearbook and Statesman's Who's Who.

significantly higher than that of Britain. Yet these economic circumstances did not result in a surge in nationalism. National sentiment was important in sociocultural terms, but the Scottish did not perceive their economic situation as a justification for ethnopolitical action; they did not perceive their economic situation in terms of oppression.[54]

Meanwhile, large deposits of natural gas and oil were discovered in the North Sea, which was to have important effects on the economies of Scotland and Britain during the 1970s. By the end of that decade, natural gas had supplanted the use of coal as an energy source. Oil was first discovered in 1969, and in little over a decade, Britain was to become an exporter, rather than an importer, of this energy source. The first oil came ashore in 1975. Five years later, Britain was self-sufficient in oil, and a year after that a net exporter. The commercial development of North Sea oil had been made feasible by the Organization of Petroleum Exporting Countries price increases of 1973–1974. North Sea oil was most important as a source of revenue to the central government and its positive effects on Britain's balance of payments. It did not generate large numbers of jobs in Scotland, and although its effects were not insignificant, North Sea oil did not make up the earlier loss of jobs in the manufacturing sector. Overall, the oil industry had rather limited effects on the remainder of the Scottish economy and did not lead to its regeneration.[55] Although unemployment is lowest around Aberdeen (Grampian), the center of the oil industry, Scotland's unemployment rate is still markedly higher than that of Britain as a whole (see Table 6.5). Despite this higher unemployment, Scotland's labor force is structured similarly to the British average, although there are marked variations among the different regions. Moreover, the areas with the highest unemployment are not the ones in which the SNP has won seats (cf. Tables 6.5 and 6.6).

The discovery of oil did have an impact on Scottish politics: It was argued that it was "Scotland's oil" and should therefore benefit Scotland primarily. Indeed, support for the SNP has been strongest where the oil industry has had its clearest impact, in Grampian and Tayside. The central

Table 6.5 Structure of Employment in Scotland

Region	% Agriculture	% Industry	% Services	% Unemployment (1990)
		Employment (1989)		
Borders	6	39	55	5.0
Central	1	34	66	9.3
Fife	1	39	60	8.7
Lothian	1	25	74	7.4
Tayside	2	28	70	8.7
Dumfries and Galloway	8	32	60	7.5
Strathclyde	1	30	69	11.2
Highland	4	21	75	9.2
Islands	5	28	67	7.3
Grampian	2	35	63	4.7
Scotland	2	30	68	9.2
United Kingdom	1	30	69	6.3

Source: Eurostat, *Portrait of the Regions,* vol. 2.

government, in contrast, assumed that the oil revenue should benefit Britain as a whole.[56] While the Scots would have liked to benefit to a greater extent from the revenues of "their" oil, Scottish dependence on investment and subsidies from England militated against acting on this desire.

Wales. Language has long been a feature of Welsh ethnopolitics. Although Welsh is certainly more widely spoken in Wales than Gaelic is in Scotland, there has been a definite decline in the number of Welsh speakers over time. At the turn of the century, about half the population of Wales were Welsh speakers. By the 1990s, this had declined to one-fifth. These Welsh speakers are not uniformly distributed across Wales: In parts of northwest Wales, as much as 80 percent speaks the language.[57] Welsh speakers are thus predominant in the areas of Wales least touched by industrialization. Accordingly, Welsh ethnopolitics has long been colored by romantic notions of the Welsh countryside and folklore.

It is therefore not surprising to find that support for Plaid Cymru is strongest in the most rural areas (see Table 6.8). The rural regions of Gwynedd and Dyfed have elected Plaid Cymru candidates to Parliament. In the industrial south, Plaid Cymru's support is strongest in Mid Glamorgan, which has experienced the highest unemployment in the south of Wales. The last couple of decades have witnessed a dramatic transformation of the Welsh industrial economy. The recession of the early 1980s had a particularly strong impact on the Welsh steel industry. Since then, substantial restructuring has taken place, and although the region has suffered

Table 6.6 Scottish Election Results by Region, 1983–1997

Region	Year	SNP % Vote	SNP No. Seats	Labour % Vote	Labour No. Seats	Conservative % Vote	Conservative No. Seats	Liberal Democrats % Vote	Liberal Democrats No. Seats	Other % Vote	Other No. Seats	Total Valid Poll
Borders (2)	1983	3.8	0	7.5	0	34.5	0	54.2	2	0	0	60,474
	1987	6.8	0	10.0	0	33.6	0	49.6	2	0	0	62,534
	1992	13.4	0	9.7	0	33.1	0	43.8	2	0	0	64,614
	1997	14.2	0	21.3	0	22.7	0	39.1	2	2.7	0	74,733
Central (4)	1983	13.4	0	43.1	3	26.8	1	16.5	0	0.2	0	146,149
	1987	15.8	0	48.6	3	23.1	1	12.5	0	0	0	161,661
	1992	22.3	0	45.5	3	25.3	1	6.7	0	0.2	0	164,725
	1997	23.9	0	51.7	4	18.5	0	5.4	0	0.5	0	166,687
Fife (5)	1983	8.2	0	35.5	4	28.6	1	26.8	0	0.9	0	186,767
	1987	10.4	0	44.6	4	23.4	0	21.6	1	0	0	201,766
	1992	18.1	0	40.8	4	23.6	0	17.3	1	0.1	0	199,328
	1997	18.6	0	47.6	4	14.6	0	17.9	1	1.3	0	190,584
Lothian (10)	1983	7.4	0	35.6	6	30.4	4	26.2	0	0.3	0	422,908
	1987	10.2	0	41.6	8	27.3	2	20.5	0	0.4	0	449,026
	1992	18.4	0	38.8	8	27.4	2	13.8	0	1.5	0	446,650
	1997	18.2	0	46.6	9	19.3	0	14.5	1	1.5	0	425,178
Tayside (5)	1983	29.8	1	21.1	1	34.2	3	14.7	0	0.3	0	215,701
	1987	31.6	1	26.7	2	30.6	2	11.0	0	0.1	0	226,499
	1992	34.3	1	24.2	2	32.7	2	8.1	0	0.6	0	225,596
	1997	36.3	3	30.3	2	24.2	0	7.5	0	1.6	0	212,553
Dumfries and Galloway (2)	1983	20.5	0	16.3	0	44.6	2	18.6	0	0	0	81,347
	1987	22.5	0	19.3	0	41.2	2	16.4	0	0.7	0	85,921
	1992	24.8	0	21.9	0	42.6	2	10.3	0	0.4	0	93,388
	1997	26.8	1	33.4	1	29.4	0	9.0	0	1.4	0	90,979
Strathclyde (33/32)[a]	1983	8.9	0	44.1	26	24.2	6	22.5	1	0.3	0	1,309,477
	1987	11.5	0	53.3	30	19.3	2	15.7	1	0.2	0	1,357,058
	1992	20.4	0	49.8	30	20.0	2	8.9	1	0.9	0	1,247,290
	1997	20.4	0	55.5	31	13.7	0	8.1	1	2.3	0	1,218,556

(continues)

Table 6.6 continued

Region	Year	Party SNP % Vote	SNP No. Seats	Labour % Vote	Labour No. Seats	Conservative % Vote	Conservative No. Seats	Liberal Democrats % Vote	Liberal Democrats No. Seats	Other % Vote	Other No. Seats	Total Valid Poll
Highland	1983	11.4	0	14.2	0	29.5	0	44.8	3	0	0	103,291
(3)	1987	17.9	0	29.4	0	28.8	0	22.6	3	1.3	0	77,255
	1992	21.2	0	19.8	0	22.4	0	35.3	3	1.2	0	114,171
	1997	24.3	0	30.6	1	13.6	0	29.3	2	2.3	0	116,895
Islands	1983	32.1	1	20.3	0	18.8	0	28.8	1	0	0	35,578
(2)	1987	12.4	0	29.2	1	16.6	0	32.5	1	1.0	0	37,816
	1992	22.5	0	32.1	1	16.1	0	27.6	1	1.7	0	36,656
	1997	21.8	0	34.6	1	9.8	0	30.6	1	3.3	0	36,771
Grampian	1983	16.6	0	18.9	2	37.8	3	26.6	1	0.1	0	252,682
(6/7)a	1987	19.7	2	22.5	2	32.6	1	25.1	1	0.1	0	277,520
	1992	25.4	2	18.9	2	36.1	1	19.4	1	0.1	0	284,802
	1997	25.2	2	25.6	3	25.0	0	22.6	2	1.6	0	283,448
Total	1983	11.8	2	35.2	42	28.5	20	24.3	8	0.3	0	2,814,374
(72)	1987	14.2	3	42.8	50	24.3	10	18.3	9	0.2	0	2,937,056
	1992	21.7	3	39.0	50	25.4	10	13.2	9	0.8	0	2,877,220
	1997	22.1	6	45.6	56	17.1	0	13.0	10	1.9	0	2,816,384

Source: British Election Pages.

Note: Numbers in parentheses under each region indicate the number of districts within that region.

a. As a result of redistricting, Strathclyde lost one seat and Grampian gained one. The total number of seats for Scotland remains the same in the 1997 general election.

substantial unemployment, it is now closer to the British average and markedly lower than in Scotland.[58] Furthermore, unemployment differences among the various regions of Wales are less stark than those among the various Scottish regions (cf. Tables 6.5 and 6.7).

Yet the lower unemployment figures obscure the fact that, on average, the standard of living is lower in Wales than in Britain: Household incomes are significantly below the British average, and Welsh households spend a greater proportion of their incomes on basic necessities. Like many other areas that once depended largely on mining and heavy industry, the Welsh economy experienced substantial restructuring in the post–World War II era. Heavy industry was replaced with light manufacturing and the growth of the service sector. Particularly in south Wales, these new industries have not always compensated fully for the job losses in the older industrial sectors. Much of the new investment in Wales has come from foreign companies, whereas the development of the service sector has largely resulted from an increased role of the state in the economy.[59] Like Scotland, Wales has depended on subsidies from England. Unlike Scotland, however, Welsh ethnopolitics does not constitute a straightforward reaction to the region's economic dependency.

Political Incentives

Political Structures. The history of both the SNP and Plaid Cymru is in part the story of the difficulties faced by a third party in a single-member district system with a plurality rule. This system has also been characterized as "first past the post": The candidate with the largest number of votes wins

Table 6.7 Structure of Employment in Wales

Region	Employment (1989)			% Unemployment (1990)
	% Agriculture	% Industry	% Services	
Clwyd	2	39	58	5.8
Dyfed	7	23	69	6.7
Powys	10	28	62	3.7
Gwynedd	4	24	72	8.5
Gwent	1	40	59	6.9
Mid Glamorgan	1	42	57	7.7
South Glamorgan	0	20	80	7.1
West Glamorgan	1	32	68	6.8
Wales	2	32	66	6.9
United Kingdom	1	30	69	6.3

Source: Eurostat, *Portrait of the Regions,* vol. 2.

Table 6.8 Welsh Election Results by Region, 1983–1997

Region	Year	Plaid Cymru % Vote	Plaid Cymru No. Seats	Labour % Vote	Labour No. Seats	Conservative % Vote	Conservative No. Seats	Liberal Democrats % Vote	Liberal Democrats No. Seats	Other % Vote	Other No. Seats	Total Valid Poll
Clwyd (5/6)[a]	1983	3.7	0	29.5	2	39.5	3	27.3	0	0	0	228,655
	1987	3.4	0	38.3	3	38.9	2	19.5	0	0	0	246,959
	1992	3.9	0	44.6	4	38.6	1	12.4	0	0	0	257,784
	1997	5.6	0	53.9	6	26.3	0	10.6	0	3.4	0	237,882
Dyfed (4/5)[a]	1983	14.0	0	28.5	2	33.0	1	23.5	1	1.0	0	193,515
	1987	12.7	0	36.0	2	28.5	1	22.2	1	0.6	0	209,138
	1992	19.8	1	38.5	3	27.1	1	14.2	0	0.3	0	219,434
	1997	22.6	1	44.7	4	18.8	0	10.9	0	3.1	0	208,173
Powys (2)	1983	3.3	0	17.8	0	45.1	1	32.7	1	1.1	0	67,550
	1987	2.7	0	21.1	0	36.3	0	39.9	2	0	0	73,293
	1992	2.6	0	20.4	0	34.7	1	41.2	1	1.2	0	77,326
	1997	3.0	0	23.4	0	27.8	0	43.0	2	2.8	0	74,806
Gwynedd (4)	1983	32.7	2	17.3	0	33.0	2	17.1	0	0	0	138,965
	1987	36.1	3	18.1	0	30.9	1	14.8	0	0	0	145,250
	1992	35.2	3	21.4	0	29.1	1	13.2	0	1.1	0	148,035
	1997	34.8	3	30.8	1	19.1	0	12.8	0	2.5	0	140,075
Gwent (6)	1983	2.3	0	45.6	4	28.2	2	24.0	0	0	0	252,162
	1987	2.0	0	54.2	5	27.9	1	15.7	0	0.2	0	263,302
	1992	5.5	0	60.5	5	27.2	1	9.7	0	0.2	0	270,666
	1997	3.0	0	64.1	6	19.4	0	9.9	0	3.6	0	245,761
Mid Glamorgan (7)	1983	7.7	0	52.9	6	18.6	1	19.7	0	1.1	0	300,359
	1987	5.8	0	63.9	7	17.8	0	12.0	0	0.5	0	313,201
	1992	8.1	0	65.8	7	17.6	0	8.3	0	0.3	0	316,126
	1997	8.1	0	68.9	7	10.7	0	9.5	0	2.8	0	285,823

Party

Region	Year	Plaid Cymru		Labour		Conservative		Liberal Democrats		Other		Total Valid Poll
		% Vote	No. Seats	% Vote	No. Seats	% Vote	No. Seats	% Vote	No. Seats	% Vote	No. Seats	
South Glamorgan (5)	1983	2.0	0	29.0	1	42.2	4	26.5	0	0.2	0	209,770
	1987	1.5	0	37.2	2	40.7	3	20.6	0	0	0	226,670
	1992	2.0	0	46.8	3	38.3	2	12.3	0	0.6	0	238,461
	1997	3.3	0	52.3	5	26.7	0	12.8	0	4.9	0	227,332
West Glamorgan (5)	1983	4.1	0	49.1	5	25.3	0	21.1	0	0.3	0	211,124
	1987	3.3	0	57.4	5	23.8	0	15.3	0	0.2	0	220,345
	1992	5.4	0	61.6	5	22.9	0	9.5	0	0.6	0	220,309
	1997	5.8	0	65.7	5	14.3	0	10.8	0	3.3	0	199,685
Total (38/40)	1983	7.8	2	37.3	20	31.2	14	23.3	2	0.4	0	1,602,100
	1987	7.3	3	45.1	24	29.5	8	17.9	3	1.2	0	1,698,158
	1992	9.0	4	49.5	27	28.6	6	12.4	1	0.5	0	1,748,141
	1997	9.9	4	54.7	34	19.6	0	12.4	2	3.4	0	1,619,537

Source: British Election Pages.

Note: Numbers in parentheses under each region indicate the number of districts within that region.

a. As a result of redistricting, Clwyd and Dyfed each gained one seat, bringing the total number of seats for Wales to forty in the 1997 general election.

the seat, irrespective of whether this represents a majority of the votes cast. Such a system makes it difficult for third parties to gain representation because voters often choose to vote for the candidate who can win, rather than the one they prefer.[60] Third parties, like the SNP and Plaid Cymru, nevertheless do emerge and can gain seats, provided their support is concentrated enough to secure the plurality of votes within a specific district. This presents these parties with a strategic dilemma: On the one hand, the party will not win seats unless its support is concentrated in specific districts. On the other hand, concentrated support will not gain the party credibility as the representative of its region's interests. Only broad-based support can achieve the latter, but it has the drawback of gaining the party fewer seats and, thus, less political clout.

Interestingly, the SNP and Plaid Cymru since the 1979 referendum have done about equally well in terms of seats, but not in terms of overall support. The SNP receives a higher proportion of the Scottish vote than does Plaid Cymru of the Welsh vote. In addition, the Plaid Cymru vote has not fluctuated a great deal since the 1970s, whereas the SNP has received between 30 (1974) and 12 (1983) percent of the vote. The SNP has also steadily improved its share of the vote since the 1983 election.

As a comparison of Tables 6.6 and 6.8 shows, support for the SNP is more evenly spread among the various Scottish regions, whereas Welsh support for Plaid Cymru is clearly concentrated in Gwynedd and Dyfed. Despite their current similarities as left-leaning ethnopolitical parties, the SNP clearly has a more broad-based support than Plaid Cymru. Thus, the former more easily claims to speak for the Scottish than the latter for the Welsh.

In addition to the structural impediments that single-member district systems pose for third parties, the elections are held at irregular intervals. Parliaments may last a maximum of five years, but they can be dissolved earlier if the government wishes to do so. The incumbent party can thus call an election at a time that it perceives as advantageous to its own fortunes, increasing the difficulties faced by the opposition, including such ethnic parties as the SNP and Plaid Cymru.

The Structure of Competition.

Scotland. Despite the fluctuations across time in the Labour movement's stance on Scottish autonomy, it is still the case today that the majority of Scottish constituencies elect Labour MPs. For example, the 1992 general election returns showed the Labour Party winning fifty of seventy-two Scottish constituencies (see Table 6.6 above), which amounts to 69.4 percent of Scottish seats. In Great Britain overall, the Labour Party won 271 out of 651 constituencies, or 41.6 percent of the seats in Parliament. While the contrast between Labour's performance in Scotland and Britain changes somewhat depending on the results of any specific election, Labour has generally performed better in Scotland than in Britain more generally. The Labour Party has nevertheless often played into Scottish ethnopolitics when in the opposition. Once in government, however, there have always been matters of higher priority pushing Scottish demands onto the back burner. The party assumed that while Scottish voters supported the idea of home rule in the abstract, they were not committed enough to this issue in practice to have it determine their vote.[61]

In the early 1960s, the Liberals also played the ethnopolitical card. William Wolfe, the SNP's chairman at the time, offered the Liberals a pact. The goal was to make the Liberals take a clear stance on the priority they attached to Scottish autonomy. The Liberal Party turned down the offer, but in the subsequent election of 1964, the two parties did not contest the same districts.[62]

In 1987, the SNP did not contest the seats for the Western Isles, but it made a pact with the Orkney and Shetland Movement (OSM), which contested the election for that district. Its candidate obtained 14.5 percent of the vote, about the same as the SNP candidate in the previous election and a little more than the SNP candidate who contested the subsequent election.

In the 1974 elections, the SNP appeared to have broken through as a viable alternative. Although its share of the vote had increased prior to those elections, in 1974, it first won seven and later eleven seats. The party's support in the 1992 election is comparable to the proportion of the vote it received in the first election of 1974, but it received far fewer seats. This means that the SNP's support among the Scottish electorate is now more diffused than in 1974. Fiona Davidson notes that since 1987, support for the SNP has become more evenly distributed. In addition, she notes that its support in the 1992 election increased most substantially in areas where it was traditionally weak.[63] This diffusion of support is underscored by the fact that the party was the second-largest vote getter in thirty-five districts in the 1992 election and in forty-three districts in the 1997 election. However, the first past the post system means that a second-place performance does not net the party any representation in Parliament.

Broadened support for the party emerged in the aftermath of the 1979 devolution referendum, but this was part of a trend that started in the early 1960s: A new generation of moderate leaders steered the party to a vaguely left-of-center line that the party has never abandoned. As a result, the policy positions of the SNP and the Labour Party often are quite similar.[64] The main difference is the ethnopolitical aspect of the SNP. As long as it is phrased in sufficiently moderate tones, the SNP is likely to remain a viable competitor to the Labour Party in Scotland.

Wales. In Wales, too, the Labour Party has long been the main competition for Plaid Cymru. In 1992, twenty-seven of the thirty-eight seats went to Labour—71.1 percent of the Welsh seats. Hence, Wales repeats the pattern seen in Scotland: Labour does better in both areas than it does in Great Britain as a whole. Also, in Wales, Labour has often been ambivalent about devolution. The political ambition of some Welsh MPs, such as Neil Kinnock, led them to openly oppose devolution in 1979.[65]

Plaid Cymru never attained as high a share of the vote as the SNP, but neither did it experience as precipitous a drop in support after the 1979 referendum. More problematic is the fact that Plaid Cymru's support is concentrated in specific regions of Wales—Gwynedd and Dyfed, both mostly rural areas with high proportions of Welsh speakers. Although the party has never attained a seat in Mid Glamorgan, it has received some support there. The latter area has experienced the highest unemployment among the industrial regions of Wales. Hence, despite broadening its appeal to non–Welsh speakers and pursuing a left-of-center line, Plaid Cymru has only marginally broadened its voter support. In 1992, it won four seats and came in second in two additional districts. In 1997, the party did not win any additional seats but came in second in four districts.

Plaid Cymru has continued to represent an ethnopolitics that contains a stronger cultural element than the SNP. Yet attachment to a separate Welsh identity has not led to electoral support for Plaid Cymru, largely because the party has been associated with extremism and violence. There is also some indication that, even among Welsh identifiers, there is less support for self-government in Wales than in Scotland.[66]

Evolution of the Scottish National Party and Plaid Cymru

Scottish National Party

The election of 1979 not only brought the SNP a crushing defeat, it also brought to power the Conservative Party and Margaret Thatcher. Her politics affected the attitudes of many Scottish voters toward the central government. Thatcher dismissed the idea of devolution, and as a result of her policies, it now became easier to perceive the London government as oppressive. This did not immediately translate into greater support for the SNP, but it did lead to the Campaign for a Scottish Assembly (CSA). Its objective was to gain cross-party agreement on, and support for, a strategy to create a Scottish representative body. Eight years after its formation, in 1988, the CSA published a report titled "A Claim of Right for Scotland." It recommended the creation of a Constitutional Convention, which would serve several purposes: One, it would show the strength and unity of Scottish dissatisfaction with the government in London; two, such a unified movement could put pressure on the government to enter into negotiations with Scotland; three, it would serve as "a forum for drawing up a new constitution for Scotland."[67] The report thus focused on autonomy rather than independence. While it did not rule out the latter option, it certainly did favor a strategy of gradual and negotiated change.

The Constitutional Convention proposed in the report held its first meeting in March 1989. The convention brings together a wide array of social groupings. Among its member organizations are churches, trade unions, business organizations, ethnic minority groups, women's movements, local authorities, and a number of political parties such as the Labour Party, the Scottish Liberal Democrats, the Social Democratic Party, the OSM, and the Scottish Green Party.[68] Many of these parties have not fared very well under the current electoral system. Only the Labour Party and the Liberal Democrats have seats in Parliament. The Orkney and Shetland Movement contested the 1987 election for the Western Isles seat in an agreement with the SNP, but it did not win the seat.

The Labour Party chose to participate in the Constitutional Convention to underscore its concern with Scotland's welfare. The Conservative Party declined to participate early in the process, a stance that was to be expected: Since the mid-1970s the party has consistently argued that Scotland is an integral part of Britain. The SNP did participate in some of the preparatory work, but it eventually chose not to join the Constitutional Convention. Its nonparticipation is on the surface more surprising. Gallagher notes that the SNP perceived the Labour Party's decision to participate in the convention as a threat. Although Labour has indeed often appealed to the very same constituency to which the SNP appealed, the apprehensions of the SNP probably run even deeper: The Constitutional Convention complicates the ethnopolitical landscape in Scotland. The SNP is no longer the only option available to voters who wish to express their support for Scottish autonomy. In other words, the Constitutional Convention has broken the SNP's monopoly as the representative of Scottish political aspirations.[69]

The Constitutional Convention stresses autonomy. Importantly, issues such as national security, foreign affairs, and social security and economic policy would remain in the hands of the London-based government. The Parliament proposed by the Constitutional Convention builds on the current parliamentary districts, with the exception that Orkney and Shetland would become two separate constituencies. In addition, the eight constituencies currently in use for the election of representatives to the European Parliament would be used to elect seven additional members for each of those eight districts. The Scottish Parliament would thus consist of 129 seats. Of these, seventy-three would be directly elected using a single-member district plurality rule. The remaining fifty-six would be elected using a party list system, with the aim of making the final result more proportional to the share of the vote cast for various parties in each district. In assessing proportionality, the results from both the single-member district and party list elections will be considered.[70] The Constitutional Convention thus seeks to maintain the traditional Scottish districts while achieving a greater degree of proportionality than is possible under the current system.

The SNP, on the other hand, has emphasized independence. In other words, the SNP's aim is an independent Scotland within the framework of the European Union. Robert McCreadie argues that the attraction of this scheme stems primarily from the fact that the EU umbrella would assure Scotland a political status it could not attain on its own.[71] It nevertheless remains to be seen whether the Scottish are committed enough to this idea to support the SNP in sufficiently large numbers to allow that party to make its case convincingly to the London government. An opinion poll published in February 1992 showed that 50 percent of the respondents supported full independence, but far fewer voted for the SNP in the subsequent general election.[72] Although later opinion surveys have shown continued support for a change in the way Scotland is governed—three-quarters of Scots support either devolution or independence, according to poll results—less than one-fifth claim it is the most important issue facing Scotland. In addition, a 1994 poll showed that of the 82 percent of Scottish voters who favor constitutional change, 44 percent support devolution, whereas 38 percent favor independence.[73] In short, although support for change is strong, more Scots favor autonomy than independence.

Alex Salmond, the SNP's current leader, appears to be well aware of this. He has made clear that his party intends to participate in elections for a Scottish Parliament. Moreover, he has stated that he will aim to win a mandate for the SNP in such a body to use as a springboard toward Scottish independence. In the aftermath of the September 11, 1997, referendum, Salmond was quick to position his own party for the planned 1999 elections for a Scottish Parliament. The centerpiece of the SNP's manifesto will be an independent Scotland, which the SNP's leader now believes will be achieved in his lifetime. Indeed, the 1997 referendum yielded results quite different from those of 1979: 74.2 percent voted in favor of a Scottish Parliament, and 63.5 percent supported tax-varying powers. Moreover, a majority within each local authority area supported the proposed Parliament, and only two out of a total of thirty-two local authority areas did not support taxation powers for it.[74] Whether the Scottish electorate is prepared to move beyond autonomy to demand outright independence is an open question. Indications are that autonomy suits most Scots just fine, but much will depend not only on attitudes within the Scottish electorate and the central government in London, but also on the further evolution of the European Union.

Plaid Cymru

The election following the 1979 referendum did not result in as dramatic a loss for Plaid Cymru as it did for the SNP. Nevertheless, voter support continued to decline slightly until the 1992 election, when the party won its fourth seat in Parliament. Plaid Cymru now held more seats than the SNP, which had remained at three. Yet, while the SNP's platform reflected widely shared sentiments in favor of self-government, Plaid Cymru found itself at the margins of Welsh politics. At the same time, both public discourse and public opinion shifted in its favor, and its current platform consequently reflects demands and arguments that are now much more broadly held than in the past. The long dominance of the Conservative Party has also had an impact, as Plaid Cymru claimed Wales to be suffering from "Tory colonial suppression" and the "dictatorial domination by sleazy right wing politicians."[75]

The Labour and Liberal Democratic Parties both called for a Welsh Assembly by the 1990s and thus played to Plaid Cymru's goal of self-government. In addition, pressure groups such as Cymdeithas yr Iaith Gymraeg (the Welsh Language Society), which had been founded in 1963, successfully campaigned for language rights. A Welsh television station was created in 1982, Welsh acquired a more prominent role in the education system, and by the 1990s, the use of Welsh was on the rise after many decades of decline.[76] In sum, the competition faced by Plaid Cymru largely took the form of extraparliamentary action focused on cultural and linguistic rights, rather than on political autonomy.

Interestingly, Plaid Cymru has consistently used terms like "self-government" as opposed to "independence." Even though one of its principal aims has remained the desire to secure for Wales the right to become a member of the United Nations, the party is now focused on a place for Wales in the "Europe of the Regions." The difference from the SNP's approach is subtle but significant: Whereas the SNP has expressed a desire for "independence in Europe," Plaid Cymru has avoided such terminology altogether in favor of an emphasis on localized decisionmaking powers and democracy. Welsh ethnopolitics has thus become an argument for subsidiarity (or decisionmaking at the smallest appropriate unit of government), rather than for nationalism under its traditional definition. This was perhaps a logical step for a party that operates in a region where ethnic identity has manifested itself primarily in cultural and linguistic, as opposed to political, terms.[77] However, this development must also be seen against the backdrop of the party's previous association with militant extraparliamentary action: Plaid Cymru has had a greater need than the SNP to convince its electorate that it is fully committed to constitutional means to achieve its objectives.

The lack of a widespread enthusiasm for political autonomy was evidenced in the 1997 referendum. With a turnout of just over 50 percent of the electorate, Welsh voters approved the creation of a Welsh Assembly by a very slight margin: 50.3 percent of those voting, or 25.2 percent of the total electorate, voted yes. In fact, only half of the eight local authority areas voted positively by majority vote (see Table 6.9). Those areas included regions where Plaid Cymru's support is strongest but were not limited to them. Majorities in the areas with the highest levels of unemployment also voted in the affirmative, but unemployment is not a reliable predictor of greater support. Nevertheless, a report published just eight days prior to the referendum argued that a Welsh Assembly would benefit the region's economy.

Despite a well-defined separate Welsh identity, Welsh ethnopolitics has not managed to convince the people of the region that separate political institutions are in their best interest. As the referendum result has shown, there is much ambivalence about a political assertion of Welsh identity. In comparison to Scottish ethnopolitics, the Welsh movement has focused more strongly on cultural and language issues. In part, it was in a better position to do so. Although the number of Welsh speakers has declined throughout most of the twentieth century, the language was a viable part of the Welsh social fabric to a much greater degree than was Gaelic in Scotland. Ironically, the inability to focus on linguistic aspects of a Scottish identity made it possible for pragmatists to rise to prominence in the SNP much earlier than they did in Plaid Cymru. Whereas the SNP from the beginning had strong moderate elements that prevailed in the party after 1945, Plaid Cymru's leadership in the 1960s was hard-pressed to maintain its focus on a constitutional strategy rather than direct action. As recently

Table 6.9 The 1997 Welsh Referendum Vote

Region	% Yes	% No
Clwyd	41.3	58.7
Dyfed	57.2	42.8
Powys	42.7	57.3
Gwynedd	53.0	47.0
Gwent	42.8	57.2
Mid Glamorgan	56.4	43.6
South Glamorgan	42.0	58.0
West Glamorgan	57.8	42.2
Wales	50.3	49.7

Source: British Election Pages.

as 1962, Saunders Lewis argued in a British Broadcasting Corporation radio lecture that the preservation of the Welsh language was more important than self-government. In fact, the preservation of Welsh was important enough to engage in direct action, such as painting over road signs in English.[78] The legacy of extraconstitutional action and Plaid Cymru's perceived association with such tactics has impeded its progress toward widespread acceptance as a viable alternative. The relatively stable proportion of the vote it has received across the years indicates that the party has a core of loyal supporters but has not effectively managed to attract votes beyond this core. The SNP, on the other hand, has seen marked fluctuations in its proportion of the Scottish vote, which has been explained as a "protest vote"; voters dissatisfied with politcs as usual apparently viewed the SNP as an acceptable alternative but did not necessarily continue to vote for it across elections.[79]

DISCUSSION AND CONCLUSION

The ethnopolitical parties in Scotland and Wales were founded around the same time, but they followed very different trajectories. The histories of the SNP and Plaid Cymru are in part a function of the differences in the environments within which they emerged. However, the differences in their leaderships and the priorities these set for their respective parties are significant as well.

The Scottish National Party has represented different forms of ethnopolitics at different times in its history. The moderate ethnopolitical course charted by the SNP is partly due to a power struggle during the early years of the party; as a result, the SNP lost its attachment to romantic notions of nationalism and the nation and took a more pragmatic and moderate stance. After the 1979 debacle, a new generation of leaders gained prominence and began to argue for independence. Under Alex Salmond's leadership, the party was (and is) at once more militant in its rhetoric and more savvy in its politics. Its main political rival, the Scottish Constitutional Convention, argued instead for Scottish autonomy within Britain.

Plaid Cymru's emphasis on socialist values and bilingualism is the result of a transformation to pragmatism that emerged within the party in the 1960s but only fully took hold in the 1980s. Romantic notions of an all-Welsh-speaking nation and extraconstitutional action to advance the ethnopolitical cause long appealed to the party and its members. After the 1979 referendum, Plaid Cymru metamorphosed definitively into a political party committed to constitutional means to advance its cause. Despite having contested all Welsh seats since the 1970 general election, the party has not yet effectively broadened its appeal. In addition to seats won, it came in second in just two districts in 1992 and four in 1997—perhaps an indication that the party has begun to broaden its appeal.

Despite its militant history, Plaid Cymru today is a party thoroughly committed to constitutional means. Indeed, its rhetoric has consistently emphasized self-government over independence. The SNP's rhetoric is somewhat more militant in that it explicitly demands independence. However, the two parties are similar in that they both envision their regions as autonomous units within an integrated Europe. Despite their subtle differences, both Plaid Cymru and the SNP have more in common with the Flemish Volksunie than with the Vlaams Blok in Belgian ethnopolitics. All three have adopted left-of-center politics and the idea of "independence in Europe."[80]

The political institutions, economic conditions, and strategic choices made by both the SNP and Plaid Cymru have made it difficult for the parties to gain the kind of political presence necessary to force the London government to seriously consider their ethnopolitical demands, albeit for different reasons. Although both Scotland and Wales depend on British subsidies, the former's unemployment rate has deviated more from the national average. This might lead to the expectation that ethnopolitics in Scotland would take more extreme forms than in Wales, but the reverse was true prior to the 1980s. More recently, the two parties differ in their rhetoric, but their basic aim is similar. Both regions have depended heavily on economic subsidies from the central government. If British subsidies are understood as a conscious effort by the government to lessen the gap between Scotland or Wales and the rest of Britain, this is consistent with Expectation 2a in Chapter 1. The British government thus appears to have been able to contain the ethnopolitical challenge from the Celtic fringe, while in Belgium, a gap between the economic performances of Flanders and Wallonia has contributed to the increasing strength of Flemish ethnopolitics.

The expectation that economic downturn would lead to greater extremism (Expectation 2b) is not supported by either the Scottish or the Welsh case, since the level of unemployment in these regions does not predict the level of support for the SNP and Plaid Cymru. In other words, in neither Scotland nor Wales does there appear to be an association between unemployment and ethnopolitics, while in Flanders there is some correlation between the two. The association between economic downturn and ethnopolitical demands is therefore, at best, mixed for the Western European cases.

The Scottish case shows the benefits of including ethnic groups in decisionmaking: From the time of the Act of Union of 1707, the Scots acquired representation in the British Parliament. Although the Scots at times found the London government less than responsive, they did have representation and were able to voice their demands (Expectation 5). This strategy of inclusion was expected to lead to a moderate form of ethnopolitics. The relations between Scotland and England certainly support that expectation. The Welsh case is somewhat different: Wales was incorporated into Britain earlier and was more thoroughly absorbed into the English government structure. Its elite became thoroughly anglicized, and although Wales had representation in Parliament, its representatives were not necessarily friendly to the ethnopolitical cause. In essence, Welsh representatives often functioned as English nationalists, which would explain the frustration and extraconstitutional tactics that were long a part of Welsh ethnopolitics. However, it does little to explain the more recent moderate stance of Plaid Cymru. This more moderate stance is perhaps better explained as an artifact of the incentives presented by the well-entrenched nature of the political institutions in Britain: In order to appeal successfully to a larger constituency, the party must play by the rules of the democratic game. The party cannot give in to frustration and extremist rhetoric if it wants to position itself as a credible alternative.

Of the two Western European cases, Belgium is more integrated into Europe than is Britain. It may therefore be expected that the former's ethnopolitical parties are less extreme than the latter's (Expectation 3); however, the case studies have shown the reverse to be the case. Although the Volksunie, the SNP, and Plaid Cymru have taken similar positions regarding the role of their respective regions in Europe, the electoral systems of Belgium and Britain provide different incentives. Whereas the British single-member district system makes it difficult for ethnopolitical parties to gain representation, thus forcing the ethnic movement to rely largely on existing parties to have their demands heard, the Belgian PR system facilitates the representation of ethnopolitical parties in government, thus legitimizing them. Not only does the Belgian system make it easy for new parties to gain representation, it also makes it easy for differences of opinion within the ethnopolitical party to lead to the formation of new parties. This, in turn, easily leads to the radicalization of ethnopolitics: There is little incentive to bridge ideological differences when breakaway groups can easily gain representation. In that case, the willingness of the voters to support a particular brand of ethnopolitics provides the only constraint. In Britain, on the other hand, the SNP's difficulty in gaining representation forced the party to settle its differences and remain unified. Plaid Cymru's internal struggles in part explain its failure to gain wider support (supporting Expectation 6).

The Western European cases do not support Expectation 4a: In the Belgian case, the scope of representation is broader than in Britain, yet Flemish ethnopolitics is also more radical. However, the expectation that representation based on individual, rather than group, competition will lead to less extremist ethnopolitical demands (Expectation 4b) is borne out: The Belgian PR system is based on party lists, whereas the British single-member district system favors individual competition within each district. The Labour Party has remained the strongest party in both Scotland and Wales, despite a mixed record regarding devolution, because individual Labour MPs have acquired the support of their districts.

In sum, the Belgian and British cases show that gaps in economic performance among ethnic groups can create the sort of grievances that lead to ethnopolitical movements. However, the electoral system plays a significant role in structuring both the potential for success and the quality of ethnopolitics: First, it determines the likelihood that an ethnopolitical party gains representation; and, second, it determines whether the party remains broad based and moderate or fragments and radicalizes. In fact, the Welsh case supports the notion that, if political institutions are well entrenched, they can become a convincing argument for moderation. Although moderate policies took longer to prevail within Plaid Cymru, the lack of them explains why the party's appeal has remained localized. In sum, within the established democracies of Western Europe, a single-member district system serves to constrain ethnopolitical parties, whereas a proportional representation system encourages their radicalization.

Notes

1. Hanham, *Scottish Nationalism*, 64–66.
2. Esman, "Scottish Nationalism," 252; Hanham, *Scottish Nationalism*, 66–68; Donaldson et al., "Scottish Devolution," 4–5.
3. Norton, *The British Polity*, 40; Moore, *Social Origins*, 33; Smout, *A Century of the Scottish People*, 233; Hanham, *Scottish Nationalism*, 71–72; Donaldson et al., "Scottish Devolution," 6.
4. Hanham, *Scottish Nationalism*, 71–73; Esman, "Scottish Nationalism," 26.
5. Donaldson et al., "Scottish Devolution," 6.
6. Esman, "Scottish Nationalism," 255.
7. Ibid.; Hanham, *Scottish Nationalism*, 158.
8. Donaldson et al., "Scottish Devolution," 7; Hanham, *Scottish Nationalism*, 75, 77.
9. Hanham, *Scottish Nationalism*, 82, 88, 92; Donaldson et al., "Scottish Devolution," 8–9; Smout, *A Century of the Scottish People*, 241, 252.
10. Donaldson et al., "Scottish Devolution," 9–11; Hanham, *Scottish Nationalism*, 106–108, 113–114, 116.
11. Hanham, *Scottish Nationalism*, 95–96, 118.
12. Ibid., 108, 117–118, 143, 150; Smout, *A Century of the Scottish People*, 273; Donaldson et al., "Scottish Devolution," 12.
13. Hanham, *Scottish Nationalism*, 155–159.
14. Donaldson et al., "Scottish Devolution," 12; Hanham, *Scottish Nationalism*, 157, 159–160, 169, 171; Harvie, *Scotland and Nationalism*, 155–156; Gallagher, "The SNP Faces the 1990s," 9.

15. Adamson, *Class, Ideology, and the Nation*, 84–85; Combs, "The Party of Wales," 37–39; D. Williams, *A History of Modern Wales*, 12–17, 39.

16. Combs, "The Party of Wales," 40–41; D. Williams, *A History of Modern Wales*, 33–36, 38; Davies, *Welsh Nationalism*, 10.

17. Combs, "The Party of Wales," 38, 47, 49; D. Williams, *A History of Modern Wales*, 273.

18. Adamson, *Class, Ideology, and the Nation*, 91, 95; D. Williams, *A History of Modern Wales*, 206–211, 213– 214; Combs, "The Party of Wales," 51.

19. Combs, "The Party of Wales," 50, 72–73, 80; D. Williams, *A History of Modern Wales*, 246–249; Jones, *Modern Wales*, 251; Davies, *Welsh Nationalism*, 12.

20. Jones, *Modern Wales*, 226.

21. Ibid., 226, 238–245; Combs, "The Party of Wales," 63.

22. Jones, *Modern Wales*, 245, 247, 256; Davies, *Welsh Nationalism*, 12–13; Adamson, *Class, Ideology, and the Nation*, 103, 121–123; Combs, "The Party of Wales," 79; D. Williams, *A History of Modern Wales*, 282.

23. Jones, *Modern Wales*, 254; Combs, "The Party of Wales," 81, 89; Davies, *Welsh Nationalism*, 14; Adamson, *Class, Ideology, and the Nation*, 123.

24. D. Williams, *A History of Modern Wales*, 292; Combs, "The Party of Wales," 97–99, 205–206, 216.

25. Donaldson et al., "Scottish Devolution," 12–13; Hanham, *Scottish Nationalism*, 169, 171–172.

26. Gallagher, "The SNP Faces the 1990s," 9; Hanham, *Scottish Nationalism*, 173, 176; Esman, "Scottish Nationalism," 262.

27. Hanham, *Scottish Nationalism*, 175.

28. Ibid., 177, 179–180.

29. Esman, "Scottish Nationalism," 272; Harvie, *Scotland and Nationalism*, 240, 254; Hanham, *Scottish Nationalism*, 177.

30. Hanham, *Scottish Nationalism*, 157, 184.

31. Donaldson et al., "Scottish Devolution," 15; Esman, "Scottish Nationalism," 264; Gallagher, "The SNP Faces the 1990s," 9; Harvie, *Scotland and Nationalism*, 247; Hanham, *Scottish Nationalism*, 185–186.

32. Scottish National Party, *A Short History*, 9.

33. Bayne, "The Impact of 1979," 46; Esman, "Scottish Nationalism," 265.

34. Kellas, *Modern Scotland*, 147; MacIver, "The Paradox of Nationalism," 141.

35. Bayne, "The Impact of 1979," 46, 57–60.

36. Gallagher, "The SNP Faces the 1990s," 12.

37. Ibid., 14.

38. Ibid., 9.

39. Combs, "The Party of Wales," 97–98, 158, 206; Jones, *A History of Modern Wales*, 214, 260; Christiansen, "Plaid Cymru in the 1990s," 21.

40. Adamson, *Class, Ideology, and the Nation*, 127; Christiansen, "Plaid Cymru in the 1990s," 21; Jones, *Modern Wales*, 266.

41. Philip, *The Welsh Question*, 73–74; Combs, "The Party of Wales," 173, 215.

42. Philip, *The Welsh Question*, 81–84; Combs, "The Party of Wales," 221; Christiansen, "Plaid Cymru in the 1990s," 22.

43. Philip, *The Welsh Question*, 87, 91; Combs, "The Party of Wales," 227–228.

44. Cited in Philip, *The Welsh Question*, 94.

45. Adamson, *Class, Ideology, and the Nation*, 132; Philip, *The Welsh Question*, 97–100, 102–103.

46. Combs, "The Party of Wales," 243; Philip, *The Welsh Question*, 105.

47. Combs, "The Party of Wales," 261–262; Adamson, *Class, Ideology, and the Nation*, 133.

48. Sharpe, "Devolution," 88.

49. Adamson, *Class, Ideology, and the Nation*, 137. See also Christiansen, "Plaid Cymru in the 1990s," 22.

50. Gallagher, "The SNP and the Scottish Working Class," 105, 119; Esman, "Scottish Nationalism," 254.

51. Esman, "Scottish Nationalism," 256; Saville, "The Industrial Background," 5, 17–18.

52. Esman, "Scottish Nationalism," 256–257; Gallagher, "The SNP and the Scottish Working Class," 106, 120; Harvie, *Scotland and Nationalism*, 165.

53. Gallagher, "The SNP and the Scottish Working Class," 106. See also Harvie, *Scotland and Nationalism*, 167.

54. McCreadie, "Scottish Identity," 43; Gallagher, "The SNP and the Scottish Working Class," 105; Harvie, *Scotland and Nationalism*, 169–171, 174–175; Esman, "Scottish Nationalism," 258–259, 267.

55. McDowall, "Coal, Gas, and Oil," 296–297, 301, 309. See also Brand, Mitchell, and Surridge, "Social Constituency," 621.

56. Esman, "Scottish Nationalism," 268.

57. Combs, "The Party of Wales," 116; Eurostat, *Portrait of the Regions*, vol. 2, 266.

58. Eurostat, *Portrait of the Regions*, vol. 2, 267.

59. Ibid., 264, 268; Davies, *Welsh Nationalism*, 64–65; Adamson, *Class, Ideology, and the Nation*, 164.

60. Leonard, *Elections in Britain Today*, 3; Lutz, "Diffusion of Nationalist Voting," 263.

61. Esman, "Scottish Nationalism," 261.

62. Harvie, *Scotland and Nationalism*, 243.

63. Davidson, "The Fall and Rise of the SNP."

64. Brand et al., "Social Constituency," 629.

65. Davies, *Welsh Nationalism*, 93; Jones and Wilford, "Further Considerations," 18.

66. Balsom, Madgwick, and van Mechelen, "The Political Consequences," 178.

67. McCreadie, "Scottish Identity," 46, 50; Gallagher, "The SNP Faces the 1990s," 13; Gallagher, "The SNP and the Scottish Working Class," 121.

68. Scottish Constitutional Convention, *Scotland's Parliament*.

69. Gallagher, "The SNP Faces the 1990s," 15; Gallagher, "The SNP and the Scottish Working Class," 124; "The Thirty-nine Steps to Home Rule," *Economist*, February 1, 1992, 66; Scottish Constitutional Convention, *Scotland's Parliament*, 9; McCreadie, "Scottish Identity," 50.

70. This proposed system closely corresponds to the German double ballot system, with the exception that the Constitutional Convention's proposals do not mention a threshold.

71. McCreadie, "Scottish Identity," 47. See also Gallagher, "The SNP Faces the 1990s," 25.

72. *Economist*, "The Thirty-nine Steps," 66.

73. "For Auld Lang's Syne," *Economist*, March 6, 1993, 59; "John Major's Hogmanay Madness," *Economist*, January 7, 1995, 46. See also Gallagher, "The SNP and the Scottish Working Class," 121.

74. "Labour's Devolution Plans: Toil and Trouble," *Economist*, February 18, 1995, 59; "Scottish Nationalism: Salmond Leaping," *Economist*, October 2, 1993, 63; Shirley English, "Margin of Victory for Double 'Yes' Campaign Is Emphatic," *Times* (London), September 13, 1997; Paul Routledge, "Yes, Yes to a New World: Labour Played Good Old-Fashioned Politics to Bring in the Scottish Devolution, but They Are Proud of What They Have Done," *Independent* (London), September 14, 1997; Robert McNeil, "SNP and Lib Dems Cosy Up as Salmond Urges 'New Politics,'" *Scotsman*; British Election Pages.

75. Plaid Cymru's home page. See also Christiansen, "Plaid Cymru in the 1990s," 27.

76. Christiansen, "Plaid Cymru in the 1990s," 25–26; Adamson, *Class, Ideology, and the Nation*, 137; Davies, *Welsh Nationalism,* 54–56.

77. Christiansen, "Plaid Cymru in the 1990s," 32–37.

78. Jones, *Modern Wales,* 268.

79. Brand et al., "Social Constituency," 620–622; McLean, "The Rise and Fall of the Scottish National Party," 357–372; Bochel and Denver, "The Decline of the SNP," 311–316.

80. This type of ethnopolitical aim is akin to what John Hall has termed "nationalism by trade" ("Nationalisms," 19).

7

Conclusion

The previous chapters surveyed the development and behavior of the principal ethnopolitical parties in Bulgaria, Slovakia, Estonia, Latvia, Belgium, and Great Britain in order to compile the necessary information to assess the six expectations that were presented in Chapter 1. The cases were selected on the basis of several reasons: All of them represent ethnically divided states where there are a few large ethnic groups in competition with one another, all of which are geographically concentrated (thus controlling for sociocultural structure); all represent parliamentary systems (thus controlling for the effects of presidentialism); and, finally, all have ethnic kin states across the border.

To assess the six expectations in Chapter 1, Table 7.1 outlines the results for the "dependent" variable of ethnopolitical party behavior, primarily conceptualized as the degree to which the party demanded the rearrangement of the existing political order. This behavior can range from demands for more equitable treatment without altering the basic features of the state to outright demands for a separate state altogether. For the purposes of comparison, each party surveyed in this study was coded using Joseph Rudolph and Robert Thompson's criteria: zero (0) for output oriented parties; one (1) for antiauthority parties; two (2) for antiregime parties; and three (3) for anticommunity parties.

As indicated in Table 7.1, the Eastern European ethnopolitical parties that are least inclined to demand a fundamental restructuring of the state are the MRF in Bulgaria and the Russian Citizens of Latvia Party. In both cases, the ethnopolitical parties have been satisfied with criticizing the existing political authorities for not doing enough for the community that they purport to represent, focusing largely on government outputs (such as guarantees for language and educational rights), as opposed to reordering the political structure. In addition, the HCDM and the HCP in Slovakia

Table 7.1 Ethnopolitical Party Behavior

Country	Party/Coalition	Orientation Regarding Arrangement of State[a]
Bulgaria	MRF	0
Slovakia	Coexistence	2
	HCDM	1
	HCP	1
Estonia	Russian Party of Estonia	1
	Russian People's Party of Estonia	1
Latvia	Russian Citizens of Latvia Party	0
Belgium	Volksunie	2
	Vlaams Blok	3
United Kingdom	SNP	2
	Plaid Cymru	2

Note: a. 0 = output-oriented parties;
1 = antiauthority parties;
2 = antiregime parties;
3 = anticommunity parties.

and the largest Russophone parties in Estonia have opposed the existing authorities, but these appeals have generally fallen short of demands for political autonomy. The most radical parties, at least in terms of their demands for political autonomy, are Coexistence in Slovakia and the more radical Russophone parties in Estonia, although the latter are relatively weak and unrepresented at the national level. For the West European cases of Belgium and Britain, the Volksunie represents a party that has demanded autonomy for the Flemish population, as have the SNP and Plaid Cymru, although Plaid Cymru has only recently abandoned the consideration of extraconstitutional means to gain political ends. These three parties are similar in their demands to the most radical parties in Slovakia and Estonia. Moreover, the single most radical party of all is the Vlaams Blok, which has demanded the outright independence of Flanders from Belgium.

At first glance, when comparing all of the cases, the most striking observation is that the Western European ethnopolitical parties are generally more radical in their political demands than their Eastern European counterparts. In other words, controlling for the presence of ethnic kin states across the border, parliamentary systems, and territorially concentrated ethnic communities, the ethnopolitical parties in the consolidated democracies are more likely to be radical than those in transitional systems (contrary to Expectation 1 in Chapter 1). This is a somewhat surprising finding, for we originally expected that, because of the frustrations accumulated under a previous authoritarian regime, the ethnopolitical parties in countries in transition would be more extremist than parties in consolidated democracies. However, this is not an entirely inexplicable finding. Indeed, as illustrated in the preceding chapters, many of the leaders of ethnopolit-ical parties in transitional systems, such as Ahmed Dogan of the MRF, are concerned that if the house catches fire, then the entire political system will burn down. This attitude has also been exemplified by the Hungarian parties in Slovakia (especially the HCDM and the HCP), which have been quite hesitant to press forward demands for political autonomy despite the anti-Hungarian measures adopted by the Meciar government, lest this pro-vide fodder for Slovak nationalists. For the Russophone parties as well, es-pecially in Estonia, where the perception that there is nowhere else to go is most apparent, there is a reluctance to pressure the government for fur-ther concessions, particularly on the part of the Russophone parties now represented in the Riigikogu.

Such reluctance is not so apparent, though, in ethnopolitical parties in consolidated democracies, such as Belgium and Britain. Indeed, these par-ties can press their demands for autonomy and/or independence without fear of igniting a conflagration. Thus, for instance, for the Vlaams Blok, peaceful separation along the Czechoslovak model is held out for emula-tion. Unlike transitional systems where demands for autonomy are per-ceived as "extreme" and "threatening" by even the ethnopolitical parties, such demands in Western Europe are viewed as "democratic." Hence it is more likely that Western European ethnopolitical parties are encouraged by the strength of the existing system to make even more extreme de-mands. Table 7.2 summarizes these findings for Expectation 1, as well as for the remaining expectations listed in Chapter 1.

Expectations 2a and 2b held that the larger the gap in the economic performance among ethnic groups and the greater the overall shrinkage in the economic pie, the more likely it would be that the ethnopolitical party representing the minority group would engage in extremist behavior. How-ever, the evidence from the Eastern European cases does not generally

Table 7.2   Were Expectations[a] Supported?

Expectations	Bulgaria and Slovakia	Estonia and Latvia	Belgium and Britain
Expectation 1	No	No	No
Expectation 2a	No	No	Yes
Expectation 2b	No	No	Mixed
Expectation 3	No	No	No
Expectation 4a	Yes	Yes	No
Expectation 4b	Yes	Yes	Yes
Expectation 5	Yes	Yes	Yes
Expectation 6	Yes	n.a.	Yes

Note: a. See Expectations 1–6 in Chapter 1, pp. 15–16, for a precise rendering of initial hypotheses.

support these contentions. For instance, although unemployment has been generally high for both the Turks in Bulgaria and the Hungarians in Slovakia in comparison to ethnic Bulgarians and ethnic Slovaks, following the end of Communist rule, the Hungarian parties in Slovakia have been much more radical in their demands for autonomy than has the MRF in Bulgaria, which contradicts Expectation 2a. Moreover, the level of overall economic contraction in both countries is similarly high, caused in part by the shock of the demise of the CMEA and the disappearance of markets for tobacco and other consumer products in Bulgaria and arms in Slovakia (counter to both Expectations 2b and 3).

Where the Bulgarian and Slovakian cases differ is in the form of political representation and the structure of competition (Expectations 4a, 4b, and 5). In the Bulgarian case, the fact that the MRF was able not only to gain a significant amount of representation in Parliament in the initial parliamentary election, but also to play a pivotal role as the political broker between the Bulgarian socialists and the democratic opposition afforded the party's leadership much greater influence on policy than the Hungarian parties have in Slovakia. Moreover, the MRF faced little competition for the allegiance of the Turkish population (largely due to the law that forbade the participation of ethnic parties, which the MRF had cleverly circumvented), and the anti-Turkish Bulgarian nationalists were only weakly represented in government (in support of Expectation 5). Taken together, this meant that the MRF leadership could afford to pursue a moderate, accommodationist approach to the BSP and the UDF (both of which needed the MRF in order to govern) from 1990 to 1994 and had little to fear from either anti-Turkish parties or potential competitors for Turkish votes.

For the Hungarian parties, there were different conditions. In the initial elections in Slovakia, although the Hungarian parties (i.e., Coexistence and the HCDM) had gained representation in the Slovak National Council, they played only a marginal role and did not have the political clout to block important legislation. Indeed, unlike in Bulgaria, where the MRF was actively courted as a coalition partner, the Hungarian parties in Slovakia were treated as pariahs with whom even the more moderate Slovak parties were reluctant to cooperate. Hence, although in Bulgaria there has existed a continual incentive for the MRF to rely on parliamentary means to advance its cause, in Slovakia, the strategy adopted by the Slovak Hungarian parties is similar to that adopted by outsider groups—namely, mass protest. Further, contrary to the situation in Bulgaria, Slovak Nationalists dominate the current political process. Coupled with the Hungarian socialist government's seeming disinterest in promoting the interests of Hungarians outside of Hungary, the Slovak Hungarian parties are isolated and marginalized and face the threat of renewed intolerant Slovak nationalism alone. Thus, it is little wonder that the Slovak Hungarian parties, even the most moderate ones, have pressed their demands for some form of regional political autonomy.

Another explanation for the relatively moderate strategy adopted by the MRF as compared to the Hungarian parties in Slovakia is that it is more internally diverse, a product of the pretransition developments (which supports Expectation 6). Represented within the MRF leadership are not only ethnic Turks, but Pomaks and Bulgarians as well. Further, especially until 1994, the MRF represented a broad coalition of Bulgarian Turkish politicians, ranging from those who favored some form of national-cultural autonomy to those who wished to maintain the commitment to multiethnic principles. This has meant that the MRF leadership must chart a middle course, making relatively forceful demands on the cultural front (particularly over language issues) while categorically rejecting any demands for cultural or political autonomy. Conversely, in Slovakia, the various subethnic political cleavages are represented by separate parties. Hence, within the parties (particularly Coexistence), there is less in the way of internal diversity, as well as a weaker internal "brake" on the actions of party leaders.

Turning to the next pair of cases, Estonia and Latvia, there are a number of observable similarities. First, ethnopolitics in both is greatly affected by external relations with the Russian Federation, especially since that ethnic kin state has taken an active interest in the welfare of the Russophone population. Second, in both Estonia and Latvia, Russophones constitute a very large proportion of the population (a fact that has led Baltic nationalists to view them as a threat to the cultural integrity of the titular nationality) that consists of relatively recent arrivals in the Baltics. Indeed, whereas the multiethnic Ottoman and Austro-Hungarian rulerships had ended in Bulgaria and Slovakia long before the democratic transition, the demise of the Soviet system coincided with democratic transition in the Baltic states. This has meant that, unlike the Turkish population in Bulgaria and the Hungarian minority in Slovakia, the Russophones in the Baltics lack a clear and fully developed identity as a community, beyond some lingering attachment to symbols of the Soviet past. Moreover, like other post-Communist states, both Estonia and Latvia have suffered economic difficulties associated with the transition (although the recovery has occurred sooner in Estonia than in Latvia), and Russophone populations in both states have suffered economic hardships following independence (although this is more pronounced in Estonia than in Latvia). Despite these general similarities, the development of the Russophone ethnopolitical parties of Estonia has been quite different from the experience in Latvia (counter to Expectations 2a, 2b, and 3).

In Estonia, the level of ethnopolitical party development has been far higher than in Latvia, despite similarly high levels of Russophone discontent with the activities of their respective governments regarding language and citizenship issues. To a large extent, this differential level of development was due to different experiences regarding the evolution of transitional politics prior to independence, marked by the emergence of a partially articulated party system prior to independence in Estonia, and the lack of one in Latvia.

Moreover, the Russophone political parties have generally been more aggressive in Estonia than in Latvia in terms of making demands for political autonomy for regions where Russophones comprise a majority of the population (particularly around Narva and Sillimae), the high point occurring with the local government-sponsored referendum on political autonomy in 1993. In Latvia, on the other hand, Russophones have thus far been content with focusing on the defense of language, educational, and cultural rights without seeking the fundamental restructuring of the post-independence political system.

However, the potential for more radical demands on the part of Russophones is probably far greater in Latvia than in Estonia. This is because Russophones in Estonia have not only gained representation in post-Soviet Estonian politics, especially after the local elections of 1993 and the parliamentary election of 1995, but the parties that represent the most moderate elements have emerged to become the political voice of the Russophone population. In Latvia, in contrast, Russophones remain essentially excluded from the political process: They have neither an independent voice nor moderate political parties that can channel demands into constructive directions (supporting Expectations 4a and 4b). Further, whereas the Estonian nationalists who had dominated the political process from 1991 to 1995 and had pushed for the most onerous legislation on language and citizenship (at least from the perspective of the Russophone population) suffered a political setback in the parliamentary election in 1995, the Latvian nationalists made significant gains just a year earlier. Thus the Russophone parties in Latvia have little recourse other than to continue to rely on other organizations to defend the interests of their community or, more ominously, to increasingly depend on the intervention of Moscow to promote their interests in postindependence Latvian politics (supporting Expectation 5). Although the current leadership of the Russophone population in Latvia does not appear to be inclined toward making demands for the fundamental restructuring of the Latvian state, this seems due to the fact that the Russophone population has yet to develop both a consciousness as a distinct group and the organizations necessary to articulate growing dissatisfaction with the present regime.

The Western European cases of Belgium and Great Britain exhibit both similarities to and notable differences from the Eastern European and Baltic cases. Importantly, gaps in economic performance between the

Flemish and Walloon regions appear to have fueled ethnopolitical demands. However, rather than economic downturn prompting greater extremism, the Volksunie emerged as Flanders was in the process of catching
up with, and eventually surpassing, Wallonia. The Vlaams Blok emerged
in the late 1970s, when Western European economies were experiencing
difficulties, but its emergence is less associated with economic dynamics
than with the fact that the Belgian electoral system provides easy access
for new parties. In short, there was little to no incentive for the Flemish
nationalists to settle their differences and stick together as one party. In
Britain, the economic differential between Scotland and Wales, on the one
hand, and the rest of United Kingdom, on the other, has always been me-
diated by investment and subsidies. Despite remaining differences between
Scotland and Wales and the rest of Britain, such efforts have lessened the
possibilities of utilizing economic differentials for ethnopolitical ends
(supporting Expectation 2a, but not Expectation 2b).

Regional integration has not led the Western European states to more
moderate ethnopolitics: Belgium was a founding member of the EU, while
Britain joined only in 1973. The former is more economically tied into the
EU and Europe as a whole. Yet it is in Belgium where we find the more
extremist ethnopolitical party (thus contradicting Expectation 3).

In addition, the scope of representation appears to have radicalized
Flemish ethnopolitics as compared to its Scottish and Welsh counterparts.
The Belgian political system makes it relatively easy for new political parties to gain representation in Parliament, thus providing little incentive for
disgruntled members of any party, say the Volksunie, to remain within that
party, as opposed to breaking another away to form another group, such
as the more radical Vlaams Blok. The SNP and Plaid Cymru, on the other
hand, have struggled to gain representation in Britain's single-member district system. Differences have at times led to difficulties within the party,
but the SNP's main competitor today is not an ethnopolitical party, but the
Scottish Constitutional Convention, a coalition of a wide array of organizations. The parliamentary seats the SNP has been able to hold have often
been the result of by-elections and have generally been quickly lost in subsequent elections. It has only occasionally been able to hold on to seats
across multiple general elections. The British electoral system is based on
individual competition, rather than on party program; and an ethnic party,
almost by definition, campaigns on a program—specifically, its ethnopolitical demands.

Similarly, the moderation of the Welsh nationalist movement is also the
product of electoral competition. Although Welsh romantic nationalists in
the twentieth century have often showed a willingness to employ extraconstitutional tactics to attain political ends, the incentives presented by the
well-entrenched nature of the political institutions in Britain contributed

over time to the recent moderation of Plaid Cymru. In order to appeal successfully to a larger constituency, the party must play by the rules of the democratic game. The party cannot give in to frustration and extremist rhetoric if it wants to position itself as a credible alternative.

Belgium's proportional representation, in contrast, promotes group competition through its party list system (contradicting Expectation 4a and supporting Expectations 4b and 6). Lastly, the Flemish perception that the government is dominated by Walloon interests endures, despite real changes that have taken place within the Belgian political system. The British political system appears more moderate and pragmatic in comparison: From the early days of the union, there was Scottish political representation and attention for Scottish economic interests. Although Scots have not always been convinced that the London government reacted promptly to the problems their regions faced, it would be difficult for them to argue that the government ignored their interests in favor of those of the English (supporting Expectation 5).

In searching for the common denominator that appears to explain the development and behavior of the ethnopolitical parties in both the Eastern and Western European cases, the most compelling set of factors relates to the form of representation. In particular, both the scope and the quality of representation appear to have played important roles in affecting the development and behavior of the ethnopolitical parties and, hence, the tenor of ethnopolitics. However, in the new democracies of Eastern Europe, the crucial variable appears to be the scope of representation. Thus, the primary difference between the MRF and the Hungarian parties in Slovakia is that the former was not only able to gain entrance into the political system, but that it was able to play a politically effective role as the balancer between two diametrically opposed poles. In Slovakia, on the other hand, although the Hungarian parties were able to gain representation, they were not afforded a pivotal role in post-Communist and postindependence politics. In sum, effective inclusion has served to provide the MRF with some stake in preserving the existing political system, hence leading to relatively moderate behavior; whereas in Slovakia, inclusion without influence has led to demands for the ethnic restructuring of the post-Communist political order.

In the Baltic states, the fact that the Russophone parties in Estonia gained representation in the political system and that in Latvia they did not appears to explain, at least in part, the differential paths followed by the Russophone parties. In the former, inclusion in the local elections of 1993 set the stage for the victory of moderate Russophone parties grouped in the Our Home Is Estonia coalition in 1995. In the latter case, exclusion in 1994 led to the greater potential for more extreme demands to be made by Latvian Russophones.

It should be noted that representation alone does not provide a sufficient explanation for ethnopolitical party behavior. The degree to which a relatively more inclusive scope of representation mitigates more extreme ethnopolitical demands depends on other variables, most notably, whether a single party or multiple parties that purport to represent the ethnic group exist and whether nationalists from the titular nationality hold a considerable degree of political influence. When the scope of representation is inclusive, when only one party represents the ethnic group, and when nationalists from the other side are weak (as in Bulgaria), it is likely that the ethnopolitical party will make only very moderate demands. When the scope of representation is inclusive, when several parties represent the ethnic group, and when nationalists from the other side are strong (as in Slovakia), the ethnopolitical party will likely demand some form of political and cultural autonomy (as in Slovakia and Estonia). Finally, when the scope of representation is exclusive, when numerous weak parties represent the ethnic group, and when titular nationalists are strong (as in Latvia), the ethnopolitical parties will likely demand something more than autonomy and are apt to turn to external support to push forward their agenda.

In the Western European cases, the form of representation affected the evolution and behavior of the ethnopolitical parties as well. In Belgium, the existence of a list proportional representation law, based as it is on a broad scope of representation and an emphasis on representing groups rather than individuals, has had two effects: First, the inclusive scope of representation has led to the effective split in the Flemish ethnopolitical movement into two distinctive parties, the Volksunie and the Vlaams Blok, each of which appeals to different segments of the Flemish population. Indeed, although the Scottish, Welsh, and Flemish movements have historically had their share of romantic nationalists and pragmatic politicians, in Belgium the romantic nationalists have fared much better politically than their counterparts in Scotland and Wales. In Scotland, the existence of a single-member district system also means that to compete, the SNP and Plaid Cymru have had to moderate their demands in order to secure representation. Second, the single-member district system has meant an emphasis on personality and the individual appeal of candidates, rather than on a program of independence for Scotland or Wales.

Overall, then, the political institutions and, more specifically, the electoral laws, have had a significant impact on the course taken by the ethnopolitical parties in all of the cases surveyed. Interestingly, in the Eastern European and Baltic cases, a broader scope of representation has been helpful in moderating the ethnopolitical demands, whereas in Western Europe, it has served to embolden the Flemish ethnopolitical parties. This suggests that the impact of the scope of representation may be different in transitional versus consolidated democracies. In other words, neither a proportional representation nor a single-member district system is a panacea for plural societies in general. Whereas a broader scope of representation appears important in containing ethnopolitical demands in transitional democracies, it does not appear to function in a similar fashion in the consolidated democracies of Western Europe. There, the greater hurdles presented by Britain's single-member district system, coupled with the relatively accommodative policies the London government has pursued across time, appear to have resulted in a persistent but moderate Scottish ethnopolitics. Had the London government been less accommodative, however, the appeal of the SNP to the Scottish voter might have been stronger, but the incentive for the party to maintain a united front would not have increased. Put differently, the stronger economic grievances of the Flemish as compared to the Scots cannot fully explain why the former's ethnopolitical demands radicalized while the latter's did not. Rather, the opportunities provided by their respective electoral systems provide the more compelling explanation. Thus, the absence in consolidated democracies of the fear that the entire system might collapse if ethnopolitical demands are presented in too radical terms explains why the Flemish see no reason to moderate their demands. Conversely, for the ethnopolitical parties in the transitional democracies of Eastern Europe, political representation is a hard-won good that must be approached with care. In addition to the interests of the ethnic group, another interest is paramount: the survival of the political system itself.

Ethnically plural states present those governing them with challenges that more homogeneous societies do not face. However, like other parties, ethnopolitical parties respond to incentives. The ethnopolitical parties surveyed herein, therefore, appear to navigate their respective political landscapes with an acute awareness of the circumstances they face. Although the specific subset of cases that have been the subject of this work—ethnically bipolar countries in Europe—limits the generalizability of the conclusions, it is readily apparent that in both consolidated and transitional democracies, ethnopolitical parties are, in the first instance, committed to the legislative dance. The challenge for the future will be to keep them on the dance floor, because they are likely to be impatient wallflowers.

Acronyms and
Abbreviations

AP	Agrarian Party
BAPU	Bulgarian Agrarian Peoples' Union
BBB	Bulgarian Business Bloc
BNS	Baltic News Service
BSP	Bulgarian Socialist Party
BTA	Bulgarian Telegraphic Agency
CC	Common Choice
CDM	Christian Democratic Movement (Slovak)
CDNI	Committee for the Defense of National Interests
CMEA	Council of Mutual Economic Assistance
CPCS	Communist Party of Czechoslovakia
CPE	Communist Party of Estonia
CPL	Communist Party of Latvia
CPSU	Communist Party of the Soviet Union
CSA	Campaign for a Scottish Assembly
CVP	Catholieke Volkspartij (Christian People's Party)
DU	Democratic Union
EC	European Community
ENIP	Estonian National Independence Party
EU	European Union
FBIS-EEU	Foreign Broadcast Information Service–Eastern Europe
FBIS-SOV	Foreign Broadcast Information Service–Soviet Union
FDF	Front Démocratique des Francophones Bruxellois
FPL	Fatherland Party of Labor
GDP	gross domestic product
HC	Hungarian Coalition (Madyardska Koalicio)
HCDM	Hungarian Christian Democratic Movement
HCP	Hungarian Civic Party (previously called Hungarian Independent Initiative)

HPP	Hungarian Peoples Party
LNCP	Latvian National Conservative Party
LNIM	Latvian National Independence Movement
MDS	Movement for a Democratic Slovakia
MP	Member of Parliament
MRF	Movement for Rights and Freedoms (Bulgarian party)
NATO	North Atlantic Treaty Organization
NPS	National Party of Scotland
OECD	Organization for Economic Cooperation and Development
OSM	Orkney and Shetland Movement
OSTK	Ob'edinennyi sovet trudovykh kollektivov (United Council of Labor Collectives)
PAV	Public Against Violence
PDL	Party of the Democratic Left
PFE	Popular Front of Estonia
PR	proportional representation
PRF	Party for Rights and Freedoms
PRL	Parti Réformateur Libéral (Liberal Reform Party)
PSC	Parti Social Chrétien (Christian Social Party)
PU	Peoples Union
PVV	Partij voor Vrijheid en Vooruitgang (Party for Freedom and Progress)
RAD/UDRT	Respect voor Arbeid en Democratie/Union pour la Démocratie et la Respect du Travail
RW	Rassemblement Wallon
SNP	Scottish National Party
SP	Scottish Party
SSDP	Slovak Social Democratic Party
SWA	Slovak Workers Association
SZDMS	Socialny a Demokraticky Zvaz Mad'arov na Slovensku (Social and Democratic Union of Hungarians in Slovakia)
TDP	Turkish Democratic Party
UDF	Union of Democratic Forces
USSR	Union of Soviet Socialist Republics
VLD	Vlaamse Liberalen en Democraten (Flemish Liberals and Democrats)
VNV	Vlaamsch Nationaal Verbond (Flemish National Union) (formerly Verbond van Dietsche Nationaal-Solidaristen Verdinaso; League of Dutch-Speaking National Solidarists)

Bibliography

Aasland, Aadne. "The Russian Population in Latvia: An Integrated Minority?" *Journal of Communist Studies and Transition Politics* 10 (1994): 233–260.

Abraham, Samuel. "Early Elections in Slovakia: A State of Deadlock." *Government and Opposition* 30, no. 1 (1995): 86–100.

Adamson, David L. *Class, Ideology, and the Nation: A Theory of Welsh Nationalism.* Cardiff: University of Wales Press, 1991.

Anderson, Benedict. *Imagined Communities.* London: Verso, 1983.

Annuaire Statistique de la Belgique (Statistical Yearbook of Belgium). Brussels: Institut National de Statistique, Ministère des Affaires Economiques, 1991.

Ashley, Stephen. "Ethnic Unrest During January." *Report on Eastern Europe* 1, no. 6 (1990): 4–11.

Balsom, Denis, Peter Madgwick, and Denis van Mechelen. "The Political Consequences of Welsh Identity." *Ethnic and Racial Studies* 7 (1984): 160–181.

Baltic News Service (BNS). Various years, various issues.

Barry, Brian. "Review Article: Political Accommodation and Consociational Democracy." *British Journal of Political Science* 5 (1975): 57–67.

Bayne, Ian O. "The Impact of 1979 on the SNP." In *Nationalism in the 1990s,* edited by Tom Gallagher. Edinburgh: Polygon, 1991.

Belgium, Ministerie van Binnenlandse Zaken, Directie Verkiezingen en Bevolking. *Parlementsverkiezingen: Uitslagen der Verkiezingen van 21 Mei 1995, Officiële Uitslagen* (Parliamentary elections: Results of the elections of May 21, 1995, official results). Brussels: Ministerie van Binnenlandse Zaken, 1995.

Bell, John. *The Bulgarian Communist Party from Blagoev to Zhivkov.* Stanford, CA: Hoover Institution Press, 1986.

Benčiková, Ivona. "The Internal 'Enemies' of National Independence." In *New Xenophobia in Europe,* edited by Bernd Baumgartl and Adrian Favell. London: Kluwer International, 1995.

Blejer, Mario I., and Guillermo Calvo, eds. *Eastern Europe in Transition: From Recession to Growth?* Washington, DC: The World Bank, 1993.

Bochel, J. M., and D. T. Denver. "The Decline of the SNP—An Alternative View." *Political Studies* 20 (1972): 311–316.

Brada, Josef C. "The Slovak Economy After One Year of Independence." In Hardt and Kaufman, eds., 1995, 518–530.

Brand, Jack, James Mitchell, and Paula Surridge. "Social Constituency and Ideological Profile: Scottish Nationalism in the 1990s." *Political Studies* 42 (1994): 616–629.

Brass, Paul R. *Ethnicity and Nationalism: Theory and Comparison.* Newbury Park, CA: Sage, 1991.

———, ed. *Ethnic Groups and the State.* Totowa, NJ: Barnes and Noble Books, 1985.

Breuning, Marijke, and John T. Ishiyama. "The Rhetoric of Nationalism: Rhetorical Strategies of the Volksunie and Vlaams Blok in Belgium, 1991–1995." *Political Communication.* In press.

Boothroyd, David. British Election Pages. Internet address: http://ny10.cs.edu:8001/~dboothro/home.html

British Election Pages. Internet address: http://www.club.demon.co.uk/Politics/Election

Bugajski, Janusz. *Ethnic Politics in Eastern Europe.* New York: M. E. Sharpe, 1994.

———. "The Fate of Minorities in Eastern Europe." In *Nationalism, Ethnic Conflict, and Democracy*, edited by Larry Diamond and Marc F. Plattner. Baltimore: Johns Hopkins University Press, 1994.

Bulgarian Telegraphic Agency (BTA). Various years, various issues.

Bungs, Dzintra. "A Further Step Towards Latvian Independence." *Report on the USSR*, March 2, 1990, 25–27.

———. "Latvian Communist Party Splits." *Report on the USSR*, April 27, 1990, 17–20.

———. "People's Front of Latvia: The First Year." *Report on the USSR*, April 27, 1989, 25–27.

Butler, David, and Anne Sloman. *British Political Facts, 1900–1975.* 4th ed. New York: St. Martin's, 1975.

Christiansen, Thomas. "Plaid Cymru in the 1990s: Dilemmas and Ambiguities of Welsh Regional Nationalism." Badia Fiesolana, Italy: European University Institute Working Paper SPS No. 95/3, 1995.

Clough, Shepard B. *A History of the Flemish Movement in Belgium: A Study in Nationalism.* New York: Octagon Books, 1968 [1930].

Combs, Thomas Dewitt, Jr. "The Party of Wales, Plaid Cymru: Populist Nationalism in Contemporary British Politics." Ph.D. diss., University of Connecticut, 1977.

Covell, Maureen. "Ethnic Conflict, Representation, and the State in Belgium." In Brass, ed., 1985.

Cox, Gary W. "Electoral Equilibrium Under Alternative Voting Institutions." *American Journal of Political Science* 31 (1987): 82–108.

Craig, F. W. S. *British Electoral Facts, 1832–1987.* Darmouth, England: Parliamentary Research Services, 1989.

Crampton, R. J. *A Short History of Modern Bulgaria.* Cambridge, England: Cambridge University Press, 1987.

Daalder, Hans. "The Consociational Democracy Theme." *World Politics* 26 (1974): 604–621.

Davidson, Fiona. "The Fall and Rise of the SNP Since 1983: Analysis of a Regional Party." University of Arkansas, n.d. Mimeo.

Davies, Charlotte Aull. *Welsh Nationalism in the Twentieh Century: The Ethnic Option and the Modern State.* New York: Praeger, 1989.

Demokratsiya. Various years, various issues.

Deschouwer, Kris. "The Decline of Consociationalism." In *How Parties Organize: Change and Adaptation in Party Organization in Western Democracies*, edited by Richard S. Katz and Peter Mair. London: Sage, 1994.

———. "De Politieke Partijen" (The political parties). In *Wegwijs Politiek* (Political guidebook), edited by Mark Deweerdt, Clem de Ridder, and Roger Dillemans. Louvain, Belgium: Davidsfonds, 1994.

———. "Small Parties in a Small Country: The Belgian Case." In *Small Parties in Western Europe: Comparative and National Perspectives,* edited by Ferdinand Müller-Rommel and Geoffrey Pridham. London: Sage, 1991.

Desolre, Guy. "The Far Right in Belgium: The Double Track." In *The Far Right in Western Europe,* edited by Luciano Cheles, Ronnie Ferguson, and Michalina Vaughan. 2nd ed. London: Longman, 1995.

De Standaard. Various years, various issues.

Deutsch, Karl W. *Nationalism and Social Communication.* New York: Wiley, 1953.

———. "Social Mobilization and Political Development." *American Political Science Review* 55 (1961): 493–514.

Dewachter, Wilfried. *De Wetgevende Verkiezingen als Proces van Machtsverwerving in het Belgisch Politiek Bestel* (The legislative elections as a path to power in the Belgian political system). Antwerp, Belgium: Standaard, 1967.

———. "Elite Circulatie en Maatschappelijke Ontvoogding: De Belgische Elite Tegenover de Vlaamse Beweging" (Elite circulation and social emancipation: The Belgian elite versus the Flemish Movement). *Tijdschrift voor Sociologie* (Journal for Sociology) 2 (1981): 199–258.

Deweerdt, Mark. "Verkiezingen" (Elections). In *Wegwijs Politiek* (Political guidebook), edited by Mark Deweerdt, Clem de Ridder, and Roger Dillemans. Louvain, Belgium: Davidsfonds, 1994.

de Winter, Noël. *Elections et Gouvernements: Eléments de l'histoire politique de la Belgique* (Elections and governments: Elements of the political history of Belgium). Brussels: Creadif, 1991.

Donaldson, Gordon, W. Ferguson, J. M. Simpson, J. W. M. Bannerman, and E. J. Cowan. "Scottish Devolution: The Historical Background." In *Government and Nationalism in Scotland*, edited by J. N. Wolfe. Edinburgh: Edinburgh University Press, 1969.

Downs, Anthony. *An Economic Theory of Democracy.* New York: Harper and Row, 1957.

Dreifelds, Juris. *Latvia in Transition.* New York: Cambridge University Press, 1996.

———. "Latvian National Rebirth." *Problems of Communism* 38 (1992): 77–94.

Druckman, Daniel. "Nationalism, Patriotism, and Group Loyalty: A Social Psychological Perspective." *Mershon International Studies Review* 38 (1994): 43–68.

Duchacek, Ivo. "Antagonistic Cooperation: Territorial and Ethnic Communities." *Publius* 7 (1977): 3–29.

Duma. Various years, various issues.

Dunn, James A. "The Revision of the Constitution in Belgium: A Study in the Institutionalization of Ethnic Conflict." *Western Political Quarterly* 27 (1974): 143–163.

Economic Development of Latvia, Report. Riga: Ministry of Economy of Latvia, 1996.

Economist. Various years, various issues.

Eesti Pank Bulletin. Various years, various issues.

Engelbrekt, Kjell. "The Movement for Rights and Freedoms." *Report on Eastern Europe* 2, no. 48 (1991): 5–10.

———. "Movement for Rights and Freedoms to Compete in Elections." *Report on Eastern Europe* 2, no. 46 (1991): 1–5.

———. "Nationalism Reviving." *Report on Eastern Europe* 2, no. 48 (1991): 1–6.

———. "Political Turmoil, Economic Recovery." *Transition* 1, no. 1 (1995): 19–22.

Enloe, Cynthia. *Ethnic Conflict and Political Development.* New York: Little Brown, 1973.

Epstein, Leon. *Political Parties in Western Democracies.* New York: Praeger, 1967.

Esman, Milton J. "Scottish Nationalism, North Sea Oil, and the British Response." In *Ethnic Conflict in the Western World,* edited by Milton J. Esman. Ithaca, NY: Cornell University Press, 1977.

Estonia Today. Various years, various issues.

Eurostat. *Portrait of the Regions.* 2 vols. Luxembourg, Belgium: Eurostat Commission of the European Communities, 1993.

Fearon, James D., and David D. Laitin. "Explaining Interethnic Cooperation." *American Political Science Review* 90 (1996): 715–735.

Fisher, Sharon. "Ethnic Hungarians Back Themselves into a Corner." *Transition* 1, no. 24 (1995): 58–63.

———. "Meeting of Slovakia's Hungarians Causes Stir." *RFE/RL Research Report* 2, no. 4 (1994): 42–47.

———. "Tottering in the Aftermath of Elections." *Transition* 1, no. 4 (1995): 20–25.

———. "Treaty Fails to End Squabbles of Hungarian Relations." *Transition* 1, no. 9 (1995): 2–7.

Fishman, J. S. *Diplomacy and Revolution: The London Conference of 1830 and the Belgian Revolt.* Amsterdam: CHEV, 1988.

Foreign Broadcast Information Service–Eastern Europe (FBIS-EEU). Various years, various issues.

Foreign Broadcast Information Service–Soviet Union (FBIS-SOV). Various years, various issues.

Frognier, André P., Michel Quevit, and Marie Stenbock. "Regional Imbalances and Centre-Periphery Relationships in Belgium." In *The Politics of Territorial Identity: Studies in European Regionalism,* edited by Stein Rokkan and Derek W. Urwin. London: Sage, 1982.

Frohlich, Norman, and Joe A. Oppenheimer. *Modern Political Economy.* Englewood Cliffs, NJ: Prentice Hall, 1978.

Gallagher, Tom. "The SNP and the Scottish Working Class." In *Nationalism in the 1990s,* edited by Tom Gallagher. Edinburgh: Polygon, 1991.

———. "The SNP Faces the 1990s." In *Nationalism in the 1990s,* edited by Tom Gallagher. Edinburgh: Polygon, 1991.

Gellner, Ernst. *Nations and Nationalism.* Ithaca, NY: Cornell University Press, 1983.

Geyl, Pieter. *Noord en Zuid: Eenheid en Tweeheid in de Lage Landen* (North and south: Unity and disunity in the Low Countries). Utrecht, Netherlands: Spectrum, 1960.

Gijsels, Hugo. *Het Vlaams Blok* (The Flemish Bloc). Louvain, Belgium: Kritak, 1992.

Girnius, Saulius. "The Baltic States." *RFE/RL Research Report* 2, no. 16 (1994): 5–8.

Gradev, Vladimir. "Bulgaria: Rediscovering the Balkans and Its Discontents." In *New Xenophobia in Europe*, edited by Bernd Baumgartl and Adrian Favell. London: Kluwer Law International, 1995.

Haas, Ernst B. *Beyond the Nation-State*. Stanford, CA: Stanford University Press, 1964.

———. *The Uniting of Europe: Political, Social, and Economic Forces, 1950–1957*. Stanford, CA: Stanford University Press, 1958.

———. "What Is Nationalism and Why Should We Study It?" *International Organization* 40 (1986): 707–744.

Hall, John A. "Nationalisms: Classified and Explained." *Daedalus* 12 (1993): 1–28.

Haltzel, Michael H. "The Baltic Germans." In *Russification in the Baltic Provinces and Finland,* edited by Edward C. Thaden. Princeton, NJ: Princeton University Press, 1981, 111–204.

Hanham, H. J. *Scottish Nationalism*. Cambridge, MA: Harvard University Press, 1969.

Hardt, Hon P., and Richard Kaufman, eds. *East Central European Economies in Transition*. Armonk, NY: M. E. Sharpe, 1995.

Harvie, Christopher. *Scotland and Nationalism: Scottish Society and Politics, 1707–1977*. London: Allen and Unwin, 1977.

Horowitz, Donald L. *Ethnic Groups in Conflict*. Berkeley: University of California Press, 1985.

———. "Three Dimensions of Ethnic Politics." *World Politics* 23 (1971): 232–236.

Hroch, Miroslav. *Social Preconditions of National Revival in Europe: A Comparative Analysis of the Social Composition of Patriotic Groups Among the Smaller European Nations*. Cambridge, England: Cambridge University Press, 1985.

Huntington, Samuel. *Political Order in Changing Societies*. New Haven, CT: Yale University Press, 1968.

Huyse, Luc. "Amerikaanse, Canadese, en Engelse Politiek-Wetenschappelijke Publikaties over België, 1976–1986" (American, Canadian, and English political scientific publications about Belgium, 1976–1986). *Res Publica* 29 (1987): 193–206.

Inbel. *Belgium: Basic Statistics*. 4th ed. Brussels: Inbel, Belgian Information and Documentation Institute, 1991.

Independent (London). Various years, various issues.

The International Yearbook and Statesman's Who's Who, 1944–95. 42nd ed. East Grinsted, United Kingdom: Reed Information Systems, 1995.

Ishiyama, John T. "Founding Elections and the Development of Transitional Parties: The Cases of Estonia and Latvia, 1990–1992." *Communist and Post-Communist Studies* 26 (1993): 277–299.

———. "Representational Mechanisms and Ethnic Partisan Conflict: The Evidence from New Democracies in Eastern Europe." *East European Quarterly*. In press.

Izvestiya. Various years, various issues.

Jackson, Robert H., and Alan James. "The Character of Independent Statehood." In *States in a Changing World: A Contemporary Analysis*, edited by Robert H. Jackson and Alan James. Oxford, England: Oxford University Press, 1993.

Jalali, Rita, and Seymour Martin Lipset. "Racial and Ethnic Conflicts: A Global Perspective." *Political Science Quarterly* 107 (1992–1993): 585–606.

Janda, Kenneth. *Political Parties: A Cross-National Survey*. New York: Free Press, 1980.

Janssens, Peter, Stefaan Fiers, and Mieck Vos. "Morfologie van de Vlaamse Politieke Partijen in 1991 en 1992" (Morphology of the Flemish political parties in 1991 and 1992). *Res Publica* 35 (1993): 503–559.

Jones, Barry, and Rick Wilford. "Further Considerations on the Referendum: The Evidence of the Welsh Vote on Devolution." *Political Studies* 30 (1982): 16–27.

Jones, Gareth Elwyn. *Modern Wales: A Concise History, 1485–1979.* Cambridge, England: Cambridge University Press, 1984.

Kalvoda, Joseph. "National Minorities in Czechoslovakia, 1919–1980." In *Eastern European National Minorities: A Handbook, 1919–1980*, edited by Stephen M. Horak. Littleton, CO: Libraries Unlimited, 1985.

Karklins, Rasma. *Ethnopolitics and the Transition to Democracy: The Collapse of the USSR and Latvia.* Baltimore: Johns Hopkins University Press, 1994.

Katzenstein, Peter J. *Small States in World Markets: Industrial Policy in Europe.* Ithaca, NY: Cornell University Press, 1985.

Kellas, James G. *Modern Scotland.* 2nd ed. London: Allen and Unwin, 1980.

———. *The Politics of Nationalism and Ethnicity.* New York: St Martin's, 1991.

King, Gundar J. J., Thad Barnowe, and Svetlana Bankovskaya. "Complementary and Conflicting Personal Values of Russophone Managers in Latvia." *Journal of Baltic Studies* 25 (1994): 249–272.

Kionka, Riina. "'Alternative' Plebiscite in Estonia." *Report on the USSR,* March 15, 1991, 26–28.

———. 1991. "Identity Crisis in Estonian Popular Front." *Report on the USSR,* May 10, 1991, 6–10.

Kirch, Aksel, Marika Kirch, and Tarmo Tuisk. "Russians in the Baltic States: To Be or Not to Be?" *Journal of Baltic Studies* 24 (1993): 173–188.

Kirschbaum, Stanislav J. *A History of Slovakia: The Struggle for Survival.* New York: St Martin's, 1995.

Kohn, Hans. *The Idea of Nationalism.* New York: Macmillan, 1960.

———. *Nationalism: Its Meaning and History.* New York: D. Van Nostrand, 1965.

Koi Kak've b Isborite '91 (Who's who in election '91). Sofia: Bulgarian Electoral Commission, 1991.

Konstantinov, Yordano. "Gift for Mr. Dogan." *Kontinent,* December 14, 1992, 6.

Kossmann, E. H. *The Low Countries, 1780–1940.* Oxford, England: Oxford University Press, 1978.

Kostya, Sandor A. *Northern Hungary: A Historical Study of the Czechoslovak Republic.* Toronto: Associated Hungarian Teachers, 1992.

Krause, Stephen. "Elections Reveal Blue Cities amid Red Provinces." *Transition* 1, no. 29 (1995): 52–55.

Lakeman, Enid. *How Democracies Vote: A Study of Majority and Proportional Electoral Systems.* London: Faber and Faber, 1974.

Lamberts, Emiel. "Staatsvorming via Conflictbeheersing" (State formation through conflict management). In *Wegwijs Politiek* (Political guidebook), edited by Mark Deweerdt, Clem de Ridder, and Roger Dillemans. Louvain, Belgium: Davidsfonds, 1994.

Lampe, John R. *The Bulgarian Economy in the Twentieth Century.* New York: St. Martin's, 1986.

Landis, Dan, and Jerry Boucher. "Themes and Models of Conflict." In *Ethnic Conflict: International Perspectives*, edited by Jerry Boucher, Dan Landis, and Karen Arnold Clark. Newbury Park, CA: Sage, 1987.

Latvia Human Development Report. Riga: United Nations, 1996.

Latvijas Statistikas Gadagramata, 1993 (Statistical yearbook of Latvia, 1993). Riga: Latviajas Republikas Valsts Statistikas Komiteja, 1994.

Leonard, Dick. *Elections in Britain Today: A Guide for Voters and Students.* 2nd ed. New York: St. Martin's, 1991.

Lieven, Anatol. *The Baltic Revolution: Estonia, Latvia, Lithuania, and the Path to Independence.* 2nd ed. New Haven, CT: Yale University Press, 1994.

Lijphart, Arend. "Democracies: Forms, Performance, and Constitutional Engineering." *European Journal of Political Research* 25 (1994): 1–17.

————. *Democracy in Plural Societies: A Comparative Exploration.* New Haven, CT: Yale University Press, 1977.

————. *The Politics of Accommodation: Pluralism and Democracy in the Netherlands.* 2nd ed. Berkeley: University of California Press, 1974.

————. *Power-Sharing in South Africa.* Berkeley: Institute of International Studies, University of California, 1985.

————. "Proportionality by Non-PR Methods: Ethnic Representation in Belgium, Cyprus, Lebanon, New Zealand, West Germany, and Zimbabwe." In *Choosing an Electoral System: Issues and Alternatives*, edited by Bernard Grofman and Arend Lijphart. New York: Praeger, 1984.

————, ed. *Electoral Laws and Their Political Consequences.* New York: Agathon, 1986.

Lindberg, Leon N. *The Political Dynamics of European Economic Integration.* Stanford, CA: Stanford University Press, 1963.

Linz, Juan. "The Perils of Presidentialism." *Journal of Democracy* 1 (1990): 51–69.

Lipset, Seymour Martin, and Stein Rokkan. "Cleavage Structures, Party Systems, and Voter Alignments: An Introduction." In *Party Systems and Voter Alignments: Cross-National Perspectives*, edited by Seymour Martin Lipset and Stein Rokkan. New York: Free Press, 1967.

London Financial Times. Various years, various issues.

Lorwin, Val R. "Segmented Pluralism." *Comparative Politics* 3 (1971): 141–175.

Lutz, James M. "Diffusion of Nationalist Voting in Scotland and Wales: Emulation, Contagion, and Retrenchment." *Political Geography Quarterly* 9 (1990): 455–463.

Luykx, Theo, and Marc Platel. *Politieke Geschiedenis van België, van 1789 tot 1985* (Political history of Belgium, from 1789 to 1985). 5th rev. ed. 2 vols. Antwerp, Belgium: Kluwer International, 1985.

Macartney, C. A. *Hungary: A Short History.* Edinburgh: Edinburgh University Press, 1962.

MacIver, D. N. "The Paradox of Nationalism in Scotland." In C. Williams, ed., 1982.

Mainwaring, Scott. "Presidentialism, Multi-partyism, and Democracy: The Difficult Combination." *Comparative Political Studies* 26 (1993): 198–228.

Mair, Peter. "The Electoral Universe of Small Parties in Postwar Western Europe." In *Small Parties in Western Europe: Comparative and National Perspectives*, edited by Ferdinand Müller-Rommel and Geoffrey Pridham. London: Sage, 1991.

Matthijs, Koen. "Bevolking." In *Wegwijs Politiek* (Political guidebook), edited by Mark Deweerdt, Clem de Ridder, and Roger Dillemans. Louvain, Belgium: Davidsfond, 1994.

McCreadie, Robert. "Scottish Identity and the Constitution." In *National Identities: The Constitution of the United Kingdom*, edited by Bernard Crick. Oxford, England: Blackwell, 1991.

McDowall, Stuart. "Coal, Gas, and Oil: The Changing Energy Scene in Scotland, 1950–1980." In *The Economic Development of Modern Scotland, 1950–1980*, edited by Richard Saville. Edinburgh: John Donald, 1985.

McIntyre, Robert. *Bulgaria: Politics, Economics, and Society.* London: Pintner, 1988.

McLean, Ian. "The Rise and Fall of the Scottish National Party." *Political Studies* 18 (1970): 357–372.

McRae, Kenneth D. *Consociational Democracy: Political Accommodation in Segmented Societies.* Toronto: McClelland and Stewart, 1974.

Metcalf, Lee Kendall. "Outbidding to Radical Nationalists: Minority Policy in Estonia, 1988–1993." *Nations and Nationalism* 2 (1996): 213–234.

Michnik, Adam. "Dignity and Fear: A Letter to a Friend." In *Europe's New Nationalism: States and Minorities in Conflict*, edited by Richard Caplan and John Feffer. New York: Oxford University Press, 1996.

Milne, R. S. *Politics in Ethnically Bi-polar States.* Vancouver: University of British Columbia Press, 1981.

Ministry of Foreign Affairs, Republic of Estonia. Final Election Results (March 9, 1995). Internet address: http://www.vm.ee

Misiunas, Romuald, and Rein Taagepera. *The Baltic States, 1940–1980: Years of Dependence.* Berkeley: University of California Press, 1983.

Moore, Barrington, Jr. *Social Origins of Dictatorship and Democracy.* Boston: Beacon, 1966.

Moscow News. Various years, various issues.

Nikolaev, Rada. "The New Noncommunist Government." *Report on Eastern Europe* 2, no. 47 (1991): 1–5.

———. "Property of Bulgarian Turks to Be Returned." *OMRI Daily Digest,* March 3, 1992.

Nordlinger, Eric A. *Conflict Regulation in Divided Societies.* Cambridge, MA: Center for International Affairs, Harvard University, 1972.

———. "Representation, Governmental Stability, and Decisional Effectiveness." In *Representation*, edited by J. Roland Pennock and John W. Chapman. New York: Atherton, 1968.

Norgaard, Ole, Dan Hinsgaul, Lars Johannsen, and Helle Willumsen. *The Baltic States After Independence.* Cheltenham, United Kingdom: Edward Elgar, 1996.

Norton, Philip. *The British Polity.* 3rd ed. New York: Longman, 1994.

NRC Handelsblad. Various years, various issues.

October 13, 1991, Legislative and Municipal Elections in Bulgaria. Washington, DC: National Democratic Institute for International Affairs, 1991.

Olson, David. "Political Parties and the 1992 Election in Czechoslovakia." *Communist and Post-Communist Studies* 26 (1993): 301–314.

Olson, Mancur, Jr. *The Logic of Collective Action.* Cambridge, MA: Harvard University Press, 1965.

Oltay, Edith. "Hungarian Minority in Slovakia Sets Up Independent Organizations." *Report on Eastern Europe* 2, no. 11 (1991): 13–15.

———. "Hungarians in Slovakia Organize to Press for Ethnic Rights." *Report on Eastern Europe* 1, no. 22 (1990): 6–10.

Open Media Research Institute (OMRI) Daily Digest. Various years, various issues.

Organization for Economic Cooperation and Development (OECD). *Bulgaria: An Economic Assessment.* Paris: OECD, 1992.

Panebianco, Angelo. *Political Parties: Organization and Power.* Cambridge, England: Cambridge University Press, 1988.

Parkinson, Fred. "Ethnicity and Independent Statehood." In *States in a Changing World: A Contemporary Analysis,* edited by Robert H. Jackson and Alan James. Oxford, England: Oxford University Press. 1993.

Pederson, M. N. "Towards a New Typology of Party Lifespans and Minor Parties." *Scandinavian Political Studies* 5 (1982): 1–16.

Pehe, Jiri. "Political Conflict in Slovakia." *Report on Eastern Europe* 2, no. 18 (1991): 1–6.

Perry, Duncan M. "The New Prime Minister and the Moslems." *Report on Eastern Europe* 2, no. 2 (1991): 9–10.

Philip, Alan Butt. *The Welsh Question: Nationalism in Welsh Politics, 1945–1970.* Cardiff: University of Wales Press, 1975.

Plaid Cymru home page: Internet address:
http://www.wales.com/political-party/plaid-cymru/englishindex.html

Powell, G. Bingham. *Contemporary Democracies: Participation, Stability, and Violence.* Cambridge, MA: Harvard University Press, 1982.

Prava I Svobodi. Various years, various issues.

Pravda (Bratislava). Various years, various issues.

Pravda (Moscow). Various years, various issues.

Ra'anan, Uri. "The Nation-State Fallacy." In *Conflict and Peacemaking in Multiethnic Societies,* edited by Joseph V. Montville. Lexington, MA: Lexington Books, 1990.

Rabie, Mohammed. *Conflict Resolution and Ethnicity.* Westport, CT: Praeger, 1994.

Raun, Toivo. *Estonia and the Estonians.* Stanford, CA: Hoover Institution Press, 1987.

———. "Post-Soviet Estonia, 1991–1993." *Journal of Baltic Studies* 25 (1994): 73–85.

Reisch, Alfred. "Hungarian Parties Prepare for Czechoslovak Elections." *RFE/RL Reseach Report* 1, no. 8 (1992): 26–32.

———. "Slovakia's Minority Policy Under International Scrutiny." *RFE/RL Research Report* 2, no. 49 (1993): 35–42.

Radio Free Europe/Radio Liberty (RFE/RL) Daily Report. Various years, various issues.

RFE/RL Newsline. Various years, various issues.

Reuters News Service. Various years, various issues.

Rochon, Thomas R. "Mobilizers and Challengers: Toward a Theory of New Party Success." *International Political Science Review* 6 (1985): 419–439.

Rose, Richard, and Christian Haerpfer. *New Democracies Barometer II: Adapting to Transformation in Eastern Europe.* Glasgow, Scotland: University of Strathyclyde Studies in Public Policy No. 212, 1993.

———. *New Democracies Barometer III: Learning from What Is Happening.* Glasgow, Scotland: University of Strathclyde Studies in Public Policy No. 230, 1994.

Rose, Richard, and William Maley. *Nationalities in the Baltic States: A Survey Study.* Glasgow, Scotland: University of Strathclyde Studies in Public Policy No. 222, 1994.

Rosimannus, Rain. "Political Parties and Identification." *Nationalities Papers* 23, no. 1 (1995): 29–42.

Rothschild, Joseph. *East Central Europe Between the Two World Wars.* Seattle: University of Washington Press, 1974.

———. *Ethnopolitics: A Conceptual Framework.* New York: Columbia University Press, 1981.

Rudolph Joseph R., Jr., and Robert J. Thompson. "Ethnoterritorial Movements and the Policy Process: Accommodating Nationalist Demands in the Developed World." *Comparative Politics* 15 (1985): 291–311.

Rustow, Dankwart A. *A World of Nations.* Washington, DC: Brookings Institution, 1967.

Said, Abdul A., and Luiz R. Simmons, eds. *Ethnicity in an International Context.* New Brunswick, NJ: Transaction Books, 1976.

Sartori, Giovanni. "Political Development and Political Engineering." *Public Policy* 17 (1968): 261–298.

Saville, Richard. "The Industrial Background to the Post-War Scottish Economy." In *The Economic Development of Modern Scotland, 1950–1980,* edited by Richard Saville. Edinburgh: John Donald, 1985.

Schlesinger, Joseph A. "On the Theory of Party Organization." *Journal of Politics* 46 (1984): 369–400.

Scotsman. Various years, various issues.

Scott, Roger. "The Politics of New States: General Review." In *The Politics of New States,* edited by Roger Scott. London: Allen and Unwin, 1970.

Scottish Constitutional Convention. *Scotland's Parliament: Scotland's Right.* Edinburgh: Scottish Constitutional Convention, 1995.

Scottish National Party. *A Short History of the Scottish National Party.* Edinburgh: SNP, 1994.

Semenov, Aleksei. "The Formation of a Legal State and the Russophone Community in the Estonian Republic." *Nationalities Papers* 23 (1995): 235–242.

Seton-Watson, Robert W. *History of Czechs and Slovaks.* Hamde, CT: Archon Books, 1965.

Shafir, Gershon. *Immigrants and Nationalists: Ethnic Conflict and Accommodation in Catalonia, the Basque Country, Latvia, and Estonia.* Albany: State University of New York Press, 1995.

Sharpe, L. J. "Devolution and Celtic Nationalism in the UK." *West European Politics* 8 (1985): 82–100.

Shugart, Matthew, and John Carey. *Presidents and Assemblies.* New York: Cambridge University Press, 1992.

Simsir, Bilai N. *The Turks of Bulgaria, 1878–1985.* London: Rustem and Brothers, 1988.

Sixth Saeima of the Republic of Latvia. History of the Legislature of the Republic of Latvia. Internet address: http://www.saeima.lanet.lv

Smith, Anthony D. *The Ethnic Revival.* Cambridge, England: Cambridge University Press, 1981.

———. "Nationalism, Ethnic Separatism, and the Intelligentsia." In C. Williams, ed., 1982.

———. *Theories of Nationalism.* New York: Harper and Row, 1971.

Smith, Gordon. "In Search of Small Parties: Problems of Definition, Classification, and Significance." In *Small Parties in Western Europe: Comparative and National Perspectives,* edited by Ferdinand Müller-Rommel and Geoffrey Pridham. London: Sage, 1991.

Smith, Graham, Aadne Aasland, and Richard Mole. "Statehood, Ethnic Relations, and Citizenship." In *The Baltic States: The National Self-Determination of Estonia, Latvia, and Lithuania,* edited by Graham Smith. New York: St. Martin's, 1994.

Smith, M. G. *The Plural Society in the British West Indies.* Berkeley and Los Angeles: University of California Press, 1965.

Smout, T. C. *A Century of the Scottish People, 1830–1950*. New Haven, CT: Yale University Press, 1986.

Snyder, Louis. *The New Nationalism*. Ithaca, NY: Cornell University Press, 1968.

Sovetskaya Estoniya. Various years, various issues.

Standart News. Various years, various issues.

Statesman's Yearbook. New York: St. Martin's, various years.

Statisticka Rocenka Slovenskej republiky, 1994 (Statistical yearbook of the Slovak Republic, 1994). Bratislava: Statistical Office of the Slovak Republic, 1995.

Statisticka Rocenka Slovenskej republiky, 1995 (Statistical yearbook of the Slovak Republic, 1995). Bratislava: Statistical Office of the Slovak Republic, 1996.

Stepan, Alfred, and Cindy Skach. "Constitutional Frameworks and Democratic Consolidation: Parliamentarianism Versus Presidentialism." *World Politics* 46 (1993): 1–22.

Szayna, Thomas S. "Defense Conversion in East Europe." In Hardt and Kaufman, eds., 1995, 133–146.

Szlovakiai jelentes. A magyar kisebbseg allapotarol (Slovak Dispatch, *The plight of the Hungarian minority*). Paris: Magyar Fuzetek, 1982.

Taagepera, Rein. "Size and Ethnicity of Estonian Towns and Rural Districts." *Journal of Baltic Studies* 13 (1982): 105–127.

Times (London). Various years, various issues.

Tiryakian, Edward A., and Ronald Rogowski, eds. *New Nationalisms of the Developed West*. Boston: Allen and Unwin, 1985.

Urwin, Derek. "Social Cleavages and Political Parties in Belgium: Problems of Institutionalization." *Political Studies* 18 (1970): 320–340.

Vabariigi Presidendi ja Riigikogu Valimised 1992: Dokument ja materjale (Election of the president and parliamentary elections 1992: Documents and materials). Tallinn: Eesti Vabariigi Valimiskomisjon, 1992.

Van Nieuwenhove, Jeroen. "De Bevoegdheidsverdeling Tussen de Federale Overheid, de Gemeenschappen, en de Gewesten" (The division of powers among the federal, community, and regional authorities). In *Wegwijs Politiek* (Political guidebook), edited by Mark Deweerdt, Clem de Ridder, and Roger Dillemans. Louvain, Belgium: Davidsfond, 1994.

Vermeersch, Arthur J. *Vereniging en Revolutie: De Nederlanden, 1814–1830* (Union and revolution: The Netherlands, 1814–1830). Bussum, Netherlands: Fibula-Van Dishoeck, 1970.

Vlaams Blok. *Nu Afrekenen! Verkiezingsprogramma 1995* (Settle up now! Electoral program 1995). Brussels: Vlaams Blok, 1995.

———. *Uit Zelfverdediging:Verkiezingsprogramma 1991* (In self-defense: Electoral program 1991). Brussels: Vlaams Blok, 1991.

VM Info: Ministry of Foreign Affairs of Estonia Bulletin. Various years, various issues.

Volksunie. *Iemand Moet z'n Nek Uitsteken: Verkiezingsplatform, 24 November 1991* (Someone must stick out his neck: Electoral platform, November 21, 1991). Brussels: Volksunie, 1991.

———. *Met Hart en Ziel voor Vlaanderen: Verkiezingsprogramma, 21 Mei 1995* (With heart and soul for Flanders: Electoral program, May 21, 1995). Brussels: Volksunie/Vlaams Nationaal Studiecentrum, 1995.

von Rauch, George. *The Baltic States: Year of Independence, Estonia, Latvia, Lithuania, 1917–1940*, translated by Gerald Onn. London: C. Hurst, 1974.

Whitaker, C. S., Jr. *The Politics of Tradition: Continuity and Change in Northern Nigeria, 1946–1966*. Princeton, NJ: Princeton University Press, 1970.

Wightman, Gordon. "Czechoslovakia." *Electoral Studies* 9 (1990): 319–326.

Williams, Colin H., ed. *National Separatism*. Vancouver: University of British Columbia Press, 1982.

Williams, David. *A History of Modern Wales*. London: John Murray, 1965.

Wils, Lode. "Introduction: A Brief History of the Flemish Movement." In *The Flemish Movement: A Documentary History, 1780–1990*, edited by Theo Hermans. London: Athlone Press, 1992.

Witte, Els, Jan Craeybeckx, and Alan Meynen. *Politieke Geschiedenis van België, van 1830 tot Heden* (Political history of Belgium, from 1830 to present). 5th rev. ed. Antwerp, Belgium: Standaard, 1990.

Wolchik, Sharon. *Czechoslovakia in Transition*. London: Pinter, 1991.

Wyzan, Michael. "Bulgaria: A Country Study." In Hardt and Kaufman, eds., 1995.

Zariski, Raphael. "Ethnic Extremism Among Ethnoterritorial Minorities in Western Europe: Dimensions, Causes, and Institutional Responses." *Comparative Politics* 19 (1989): 253–273.

Zvidrins, Peteris. "Changes in the Ethnic Composition in Latvia." *Journal of Baltic Studies* 23 (1992): 359–368.

Index

Antall, Jozef, 65
Autonomy demands, transitional versus consolidated systems, 15, 171–173. *See also specific parties*

Baltic Russophone population: history of, 80–82; immigrant status of, 82; lack of community identity, 82–83, 104; postindependence economy and, 88–89. *See also* Estonian Russophone parties; Latvian Russophone parties
Bauer, Gyozo, 58
Belgium: communitarian conflict in, 118–120, 124–125; creation of, 109–110; economy of, 118–121; elite structure in, 125, 129; federal structure of, 121–122, 130n15; foreign residents in, 120; party system in, 122–123; segmentation and allocation of resources in, 118. *See also* Flemish ethnopolitical movement
Borschova, Katya, 102–103
Bugár, Béla, 57, 64, 66, 67, 68, 71, 72–73
Bulgaria: assilimilation campaigns in, 22–25, 38, 41; Communist rule in, 23–24; Ottoman rule in, 22; post-Communist politics and economic transition in, 24, 27–28, 174; resurgence of Bulgarian nationalism in, 22–23, 25, 33; termination of CMEA and, 27, 28, 46; Turkish property redress and language rights demands in, 25, 33, 40–41. *See also* Movement for Rights and Freedoms (MRF)
Bulgarian Socialist Party (BSP), 26–27, 33–34, 36, 37, 38–40; anti-Turkish rhetoric, 24; Kardzhahi campaign and, 42–44; 1994 parliamentary elections and, 41, 46–47

Caubergs, Jan, 128
Chuikin, Vladimir, 99–100
Coexistence (Hungarian Slovak political party), 55, 175; constituency of, 51, 56–57, 64; marginality of, 174; radicalism of, 172
Communist Party of Latvia (CPL), 104; proindependence-loyalist split in, 86–87; as pro-Russian, 88; successors to, 92
Council of Mutual Economic Assistance (CMEA), 27, 28, 46, 58
Cultural revivalism, defined, 5–6
Cymru Fydd (Wales to Be) movement, 139

Democratization, ethnopolitical party behavior and, 7–8, 15, 171–173
Denys, André, 127
Dillen, Karel, 113, 114, 116, 117
Dimitrov, Fillip, 36–37, 38
Dimitrov, Ilcho, 41

195

About the Book

What makes some multiethnic states integrate and others descend into civil war? Ishiyama and Breuning extend traditional explanations centered on socioeconomic, cultural, and historical factors to argue that the actions of leaders of ethnic segments—too often ignored—are also critical determinants of policy outcomes.

Applying a framework derived from comparative politics and IR theory, the authors explore two sets of empirical cases: the emergence of new nationalisms in old European democracies (the United Kingdom and Belgium) and the reemergence of old nationalisms in several new democracies (Bulgaria, Slovakia, Estonia, and Latvia). Their work sheds crucially important light on an issue that is one of the most prominent in world politics today.

John T. Ishiyama is an associate professor of political science and **Marijke Breuning** is an assistant professor of political science, Truman State University.

DATE DUE

Demco, Inc. 38-293